Heather for Your Luck, My Dear

By

RAY WILLS
(THE GYPSY POET)

Copyright © 2024 Ray Wills

A GYPSY POET PUBLICATION

All rights reserved, including the right to reproduce this book, or portions thereof in any form. No part of this text may be reproduced, transmitted, downloaded, decompiled, reverse engineered, or stored, in any form or introduced into any information storage and retrieval system, in any form or by any means, whether electronic or mechanical without the express written permission of the author.

Cover image courtesy of Barrie Law Yorks

ISBN: 9798308050964

Farming days

When gypsies trod upon the downs
when heather sweet was scattered round
when vardos were true caravans
when kyers rode upon these lands

Where rabbits ran the meadows sweet
where fox gave chase and lords did meet
where grouse and pheasants were dismissed
amongst the hills where Gypsy's kissed

Where forests walks and grassy mounds
hid all the wealth of gentry found
where springs did burst throughout the land
where Gypsy songs were loud and grand

Where zunners ran most every day
amongst the gorse they hid and played
where bees did buzz and warblers song
caressed the mornings and days so long

Where bare knacked fights were all in rage
upon the booth where folks did stage
where youth and charms were on display
where farmers worked amongst the hay

Where church bells chimed
where wheels did roll
upon the tracks where folks did go

where factory hand and market stalls
were rich in life for one and all

Ray Wills

A right to roam

When once we had a right to roam
to settle down in our own home
to graze our horses, donkeys, cows and mares
to chase the rabbits, boars and hares

To cut the turf on turbary common
and to rest a while in this our land
afore they enclosed our freedom rights
the right to roam was our delight

When once we grazed on Aychen tans
afore they robbed it underhand
when gentlemen bartered free
when handshakes were deals upon the leas
for now, we lost our right to roam
stolen by laws no more atoned

Ray Wills

Country life and Gypsy lore

In country life and Gypsy lore
when skies were blue and trees were tall
when farmers locked their pens at night
with young men's bodies full of sprite

On heather-ed down and village green
where artists bold would paint the scene
where baccy pipes and fire lights glow
would lighten our world in times of snow

When country lass and laddies danced
upon the green to true romance
where bells did ring each Sunday morn
where birds did sing and love was born

Where orchards branches hung with fruit
where daisy chains and lilies roots
where tractors rolled across the downs
where vardos spread their ways around

The Gypsy Queen smoked her clay pipe for free
whilst one could hear the buzz of bees
with scent of heather gorse and fern
where sheep did wean their lambs just born

The old town clock struck each hour
within streets of ancient histories towers
whilst school kids ran to greet each day
whether back at school or holiday

In country life and Gypsy lore
the artist poet went to war
with easel's brush oil and plan
whilst the poet etched the world of man

When life was rich in time and space
where each young man did know his place
where rivers flowed through country scene
from springtime joys to Halloween

Ray Wills

Life in an English Village

With a neat or handsome parsonage and grey church set in the midst; there was the pleasant tinkle of the blacksmiths anvil, the patient carthorses waiting at his door; the basket-makers peeling his willow wands in the sunshine; the wheelwright putting the last touch to a blue cart with red wheels; here and there cottages with bright transparent windows showing pots of blooming balsams or geraniums, and little gardens in front all double daisies or dark wallflowers; at the well clean comely women carrying yoked buckets and towards the free school small Britons dawdling on, and handling their marbles in thehave ir pockets of unpatched corduroys adorned with brass buttons."

GEORGE ELLIOTT

WHEN WE WERE BOYS

When last I met up with William and Tom
we were just boys all young full of sprite and strong
we climbed the hills and those big trees
we rarely fell or scraped our knees
We wrote with pen and ink with nib so free
the finest of our crafted Durzet poetry
then we talked and charmed the girls a few
sometimes we were lucky with kisses too
Oft times we talked that Durzet way
from Wareham Ridge, Arne
and down Bere Regis Kingsbere way
we climbed up high to that Woodbury fair
and met with many a travelling Roma Gypsy there
We took all of their Duckerreen tales and woes
their idle talk at the busy Autumn
yearly fair and shows
we chased the village gals and more
then fell in love with Rosa and Jane
sisters of Paul from up Butts Lane
Then we ambled down to poets green
there I had me a kiss
with a young buxom and pretty Gypsy Miss
Then when the sun was high oer Egdon moors
we sauntered over many of those heather miles just to explore
the woodland glades and plush green knapps
then we caught the red admiral butterflies
which all flew bye and landed there
upon our boyish laps

Ray Wills

How soon we forget

How soon we forget
the brickyards and clay
the pipes that they smoked
the light of the day

How soon we forget the wheels as they roll along
the Gypsy man and the Gypsy man song
how soon we forget who worked the land
the potteries and chimneys
the old Gypsy tan
who tended the land and worked on the clay
built all the bricks in those olden days

How soon we forget
the lavender fields where Gypsy gals gathered
the best of the crop
sold flowers in Bournemouth square
in baskets full tops

How soon we forget and cast them aside
turn out their trailers and waved them goodbye
how soon we install the ole trespass laws
the Lord of the manor dawns here once more
and the Gypsy Gals songs not heard no more

Ray Wills

CONTENTS

ABOUT THE AUTHOR

PREVIOUS PUBLICATIONS

ACKNOWLEDGEMENTS

INTRODUCTION

CHAPTER ONE
FREEDOM CALLS – THE EARLY HISTORY OF GYPSY TRAVELLERS

CHAPTER TWO
VARDO DAYS

CHAPTER THREE
CANFORD DAYS

CHAPTER FOUR
DAYS OF GYPSY LORE

CHAPTER FIVE
NEWTOWN

CHAPTER SIX
SIR GUSTAS

CHAPTER SEVEN
THE MANNINGS HEATH

CHAPTER EIGHT
THE ALDERNEY AND WALLISDOWN TRAVELLERS

CHAPTER NINE
POOLE HEATH

CHAPTER TEN
THE VILLAGE

CHAPTER ELEVEN
WEST HOWE

CHAPTER TWELVE
GYPSY TRAVELLERS AND THE FAIRGROUNDS

CHAPTER THIRTEEN
THE GYPSY CAMP

CHAPTER FOURTEEN
CORFE MULLEN CAMPS

CHAPTER FIFTEEN
GYPSY TRAILS

CHAPTER SIXTEEN
GYPSY TRAVELLERS ON THE PURBECK

CHAPTER SEVENTEEN
TRAVELLING TIMES

SOURCES

THE WAY OF LIFE

The Gypsy way of life is under threat
their taking away our stopping places
whilst the grounds still wet
the culprits of oriental origin
known as a Tory wet, I do not jest

Barnes the Dorset poet warned us
they'd be no blade of grass left
they are taking away our stopping places
so as we cannot see all our folks cousins
and meet up all our families

The Gypsy way of life is under threat
with nowhere to park our wagons
nowhere to reminisce
to cut our pegs
our flowers for to twist

Our heritage their taking
just like the colonials did
in the days of the Indian nation
and the aboriginal kids

The Gypsy way of life is under threat
save your stories tell your tales
the plans afoot
the grounds still wet.

Ray Wills

William John the Wessex Gypsy king said in 1930 that "Our race is dying out. In a few years' time there will be hardly an encampment left. life is too rapid for us. We cannot keep up with the speed ... Horses? ... Mules? ... The motorcar has come now. Even we poor Romanies travel the country in saloon cars! ... Oh! they were good old days when the world went slower. We Gipsies have a devil of a time nowadays, what with the police, the Customs officers, the tax collectors, and the rest."

The Gypsy Camp

The Gypsy's camp was not afraid.
I made his dwelling free.
Till vile enclosure came & made
A parish slave of me

CLARE

Gypsy Rides

Down some quiet country lane
where oak trees stood so proud
where chaffinch sang amongst the ferns
and poppies they all bowed

Where honeybees they blessed the thorns
where rose petals bloomed
the traveller's trotted down the lane
where sun did beat at noon

The crowds all gathered on the grass
and the tractor turned the soils
the geese did fly across the skies
and the lassies looked forlorn

Where cocks did crow at early morn
and the farmer kissed his wife
beneath the chimneys thatch with hope
and the labourer's retired

The Gypsy travellers used that lane
where the children sang their rhymes
alongside grass and heather downs
where country folk resides

Ray Wills

Gypsy Walk

The language it was rich in tome
the vardo tall and gay
whilst children danced upon the green
just a little way away

The Gypsy crowd that walked the road
alongside vardos decked
with good things crafted in their hands
and the windows with neat nets

The steps were hard and mighty there
and the Gypsy boy he sang
whilst gals did dream of long off days
a courting in the sun

The walks and rides to the village fairs
where ponies trade was free
whilst landed gentry smiled that smile
from hilltop o'er to sea

The gaffers talked of far-off days
when land was open fields
were Gypsy gal and Gypsy boy
was all one brotherhood

The lessons learned around the fires
and the dogs they barked it was true
whilst old ones told of olden days
and ate their mushes stew

The sailors sailed to far off lands
and the soldiers went to war
but the poor old Gypsy worked the land
and he never knew what for

The nights were dark, and the stars were rich
with jewels all set to see
from common lands where travellers roamed
too far off liberty
whilst story tellers told their tales
to poets like you and me.

Ray Wills

Dorset

I wandered o'er these heath lands
Where the sun comes up each dawn
Where the rabbits run to greet you
Each and early morn

Where the meadows and the pastures
Are blessed by Gods own hands
Where the farmer and the tourists
Savour this sweet land

From Lyme to Christchurch Priory
Through Wareham with its mill
The effigy of T.E Lawrence
In the St Martins church upon the hill

The rivers Frome and Stour
The swans that sail on by
The pastures and the meadows
The birds up in the skies

there's a view to send you crazy
a scene to blow your mind
with hills of Maiden Castle
Creche Burrow you will find

The quay of Poole that flourished
In times of pirates bold
Where Gulliver sailed the waters
Contraband and Spanish gold

Woodes Rogers sailed to Newfoundland
With its cods, Ropes, hopes and dreams
Poole pottery it is famous
Like Dorset's haunting scenes

I strolled the hills of Purbeck
Saw that Portland stone
Which Wren used for London
And all those grand celestral homes

Here Hardy wrote his novels
Barnes penned poetry
Stevenson lived at Westbourne
With views out to the sea

There's views like Corfe Castle
With Rivers running free
Where the books of Enid Blyton
Came to life for me

Ray Wills

Gypsy Show

He said he was a showman a fairground king by trade
but to my understanding he was a hawker to his grave
he said he was the king of trade with his trailer and his spin
but he was just a fairground boy accounting for his sins

He said he was not a Gypsy and he never told a lie
but only when the chips were down he ate that hedgehog pie
he said he was a Castle related to the Kings
they sat around the yog back then for they did that kinda thing

He said he was a rich man now and forever told the tale
until he spoke the Gypsy words he'd lost them for awhile
I asked him for a minute of his truly precious time
but he was on the Ferris wheel and i was on the vine

Ray Wills

ABOUT THE AUTHOR

I was born in one of my grandfather's Reginald Rogers properties on the Ringwood Road Newtown Poole. Shortly after the 1939-45 war had ended.

Iris Rogers, my late mother (right), with Peggy Gillingham and Irene Barnes in Websters factory uniforms

My early childhood was spent living on the Mannings house small holding farm, on the Mannings heath common next-door to the Mannings heath Gypsy traveller's site.

THE MANNINGS

My ancestors the Rogers and Fancy families had strong traveller ancestry. It was there at the Mannings heath at a young age I first encountered the travelling people of Canford heath and Augustus John the artist whilst he was painting the family rented home of Lady Wimborne's Heather view. I attended local schools at Sylvan Road, Branksome heath then later Kemp Welch, all of whom had many gypsy traveller pupils. Many of my cousins were from traveller families such as the Castles and Dominy's. In my leisure time as a small child,

RAY WILLS WITH RUSTY ON THE MANNINGS HEATH

I was fortunate as a child to have such freedom. Taken rabbiting on the Canford commons by my uncle's Bill and Tony Rogers. Along with travellers Johnny Warren and the Turners Billy and joey. I had my very own ferrets which I carried with me in my deep trousers' pockets in a cloth bag. I also spent some of my early years assisting my grandfather Reginald Rogers and my uncles at the Rogers two brickyards. Nearby at Mannings Heath and Broom Road. Working on the hot Firey kilns.

The Alderney Brickworks (Dorset Brick and Tile Co.), had a prominent chimney to their kiln. The works flourished between 1919 and 1957 on a heathland site in Broom Road at Mannings Heath and was later acquired by British Drug Houses (BDH) for their offices and chemical store.

The Rogers were skilled brick makers since my great grandfather William Charles Rogers and his brother Alfred had first established the family's numerous brickyards of Dorset brick company. With monies raised from my great gran Emily Fancy's pig sties smallholding in Fancy Road Newtown. In my later childhood I lived in the Purbeck market town of Wareham. Before returning to the Mannings. My first job on leaving school was at Bluebird caravans as a painter and chassis sprayer. After numerus employments through my teenage youth years, I became an Adventure playground leader establishing these in numerous towns throughout the UK over three decades. In recent years I have campaigned on behalf of the traveller community as a researcher with Kushti Bok the traveller's welfare organisation. Before retiring in recent years and concentrating on writing numerous books on Gypsies and children's play. For a few years I lived at a writer musicians' crafts community's at Bere Regis Dorset village. Whilst there I was commissioned by the Arts Council to take part in the Dorset festival held there in autumn 2023 as a performing poet. I continue to exhibit my work throughout the county in Museums history centres and libraries as well as giving talks and readings as well as my poetry.

Gypsy Song

The wind whistles over the heath,
The moonlight flits over the flood;
And the Gypsy lights up his fire,
In the darkness of the wood.
Hurrah!
In the darkness of the wood at night
free is the bird in the air in flight,
And the fish where the river flows;
Free is the deer in the forest,
And the Gypsy wherever he goes. Hurrah!

Ray Wills

LIVING ON THE EDGE OF YOUR TOWN

The books you read at school.
Do not mention me.
Because I am the invisible man
In this country's history
And I am living on the edge of your town.

Ted Atkinson and Paddy Hoolahoy.

GYPSY ROOTS

Baskets of lavender flowers
With Curtain of lace
The finest of pottery, cups, saucers and plates
Bright shining mirrors to show off your face
Nice, polished floors with a welcome for strangers
no locks on the doors

Dogs outside barking and cockerels in yard
Cobs in the fields and crows in their nests
Shiny fine jewellery all looks the best

Vardos and benders tents and fine trailer vans
Chavvies a playing sees their dark gypsy tans
Trips to the fairgrounds to work on the shies
Swish backs and boxers with daredevil rides

Journeys to Appleby and other fine fairs
Hop picking seasons down countryside lanes
Tell you your fortune's then we be on our way

Stopping place's handshakes whilst old tales be told
Gentlemen's agreement with Turbary gold
Courtships and cousins the finest of days
Baptisms funerals and marriage ablaze
Families united from Penzance to Poole
ships to the new world Newfoundland crews

Work on the brickyards and the inns finest brews
Prayers in the morning the church bell doth rings

Gypsies and travellers roaming eyes
The tales of the Queens and the king who was wise

Music a playing round the yog fire flames
Accordion Samsons with Emily n Jane
Dancing and merriment starlight at night
the wheels they keep turning its spokes red and white
Kushti bok family's memories so proud of their roots
Mushes and ladies so wise in them tooths

Ray Wills

ACKNOWLEDGEMENTS

I am indebted to the following people to include their material within this publication.

BILL HILL -ARTICLE FROM HOME NEWS

BOURNEMOUTH BOROUGH COUNCIL

MICHAEL JOHNSON- PHOTOS AND ARTICLE

NICOLE GREEN- PHOTO PHILLIPS YARD

BETTY SMITH BILLINGTON- PHOTOS HEAVEBLY BOTTOM ENCAMPMENT BOURNEMOUTH FLOWER GIRLS AND ARTICLE ON THE FLOWER GIRLS

THE LATE JEAN HOPE MATTHEWS- INTERVIEW MEMORIES OF PEMBERTON ROAD AND HEAVENLY BOTTOM

BRENDA CAVERLY- PHOTOS OF KINSON

PAUL BENNETT- PHOTOS WOODBURY FAIR BERE REGISU

BOB LOVELL FOR HIS WRITES ON THE EARLY DATES OF GYPSY LIFE

CHRISTOPHER SCOTT

JANET ROGERS

Front cover photo permission granted by Barrie Law Yorks

PREVIOUS PUBLICATIONS

AVAILABLE FROM AMAZON

THE FORGOTTEN PEOPLES- NON-FICTION

WHERE THE RIVER BENDS- NON-FICTION

THE GYPSY CAMP- NON-FICTION

GYPSY TALES- NON-FICTION

THE LAST STOPPING PLACE- FICTION

THE TIME TRAVELLER -FICTION

DORSET DAYS- POETRY ANTHOLOGY

FUTURE PAST TIMES IN A NEW WORLD ORDER- FICTION

ADVENTURES IN CHILDS PLAY Non-Fiction

STARLIGHT AFORE THE DEW Poetry Anthology

A COMMUNITY ACTIVIST AT PLAY Autobiography

A VILLAGE OF CROWS Novel

FUN DAYS IN POOLE Anthology of poetry

AVAILABLE FROM LULU.COM

ROMANCE IN THE EVERGLADES POETRY ANTHOLOGY PUBLISHED BY XpressPublications.com

WHERE THE RIVER BENDS -NON-FICTION HARDBACK - LULU

CONTACTS FOR ADVICE AND INFORMATION IN THE COMMUNITY Published by The National Playing Fields Association 1975.

THE GYPSY CAMP Hardback LULU PUBLICATION

Stopping Places

I recall our stopping places and many Aytchen tans
way out in the waste lands where the wind did chill our hands
winters they were lonesome we tended to stay free
hidden in the woodlands of this great forestry

I remember all the folki why they could tell a say
sitting round the yog at night the horses chewing hay
the chavvies tucked in their beds and the babes fast asleep
their mother's bedtime stories they sometimes took a peep

Way out in the country down some old Gypsy Lane
where the masons cut the stones by day
and the rabbits ran the lanes
where the blossoms shed their perfumes

Where the gorse did catch your toes
way out in the country lanes
there the places I loved most

All those stopping places
where the old ones tell their yarns
where the queen of Gypsies honoured us
with her tales and old dam songs

Where the gaffers were a sleeping
in their mansions and their farms

whilst we were out a roving the hillsides and the lanes
where songbirds were our music
and the fires shed their flames.

Ray Wills

INTRODUCTION

Most historians believe that the Gypsy Travellers first arrived in England around the 16th century. Though they may have been in the country much earlier. For Winstedt (1916) at Lambeth London wrote. Lambeth was then a growing suburb of the city with lawlessness, and now a densely built-up part of the city just south of the Thames. Gypsies had been recorded in the area as early as 1514 with references concerning the death of a 50 Gypsies and Travellers in housing 'gentleman' leading to enquiries being made of an 'Egyptian' woman who talked with Sir Thomas Moore who lodged at Lambeth and was said to have told fortunes in the area. She was said to investigate one's hand and tell Marvellous things. The presence and distinguishing apparel of Romany migrants were familiar enough to courtiers by 1517, that we are told by Vessel-Fitzgerald. That several memoirs and letters refer to court ladies dressed in finery and 'attired like to the Egyptians, very richly' by that date. Oral tradition even suggests that Gypsies were present in East Anglia as early as after the Black Death of 1348-1349.

When Gypsy folk first arrived on these shores the country was far different then today. Most of the country was covered in forests and woodlands or common lands. The roads were often just tracks and transport was by horse and carts. Most of our Gypsy ancestors lived within the forests such as Epping the new forests or on common heathlands. Or on the great estates such as at Canford.

By 1621 Ben Johnson was able to present a court masque entitled 'The Gypsies Metamorphosed' pertaining to stereotypes of subversive vagrants and the linkages between Romany wanderers and border-crossing migrants who change allegiances and appearances to suit their current need. Whilst on 11 August 1668 Samuel Pepys recorded his wife, her friend and their servant going to visit the Gypsies at Lambeth to have their fortunes told (Netzloff, 2001).

In earlier times young men including some Gypsies had been pr ganged. Press gangs were legalised from 1664 onwards, the press had been set up to help supply the Royal Navy with the large numbers of seamen it needed in time of war. Washed, cheaply clothed and given a knife, spoon, comb, and a piece of soap each they found themselves on board cod ships at Poole and Weymouth for the Newfoundland trade, where they could at least be sure of avoiding starvation. Due to the numerous vagrancy acts over the years many gypsies were transported and some as slaves to countries such as Trinadad, Jamaica and as prisons in Australia. Often for no more a crime than damaging the Lord's property or catching a rabbit or deer on the Lord's estate. Many were iron shackled and sold on blocks on the local quaysides. Some were slaves on the three great estates of the Drax family in Trinadad and Jamaica and other. Many Gypsies were hung for minor offences or just being a Gypsy. Portland boys of thirteen or fourteen are often found to look as if they were two years older to gain work. and taken onboard cod ships at Poole and Weymouth for the Newfoundland trade.

One of its merchant families the Whites were prominent in the cod industry with Newfoundland. They had built a fine grandiose mansion house in the high street.

Other Poole merchants such as the Jolliffe and the Barfoot families, had also additionally profited from the trans-Atlantic slave trade. Numerous slave ships sailed from Poole during this time including "The Molly" which was owned by William Jolliffe. Which at one time had 200 enslaved people below deck. Thirty of the enslaved died on one of its journeys, while the rest would have been auctioned on arrival. Henry Laurens, a Charleston slaver and merchant recorded numerous Poole slave ships entering the Charleston harbour, including "The Elizabeth" in 1755, bringing up to between 15 to 112 slaves a journey. Although many of the other Poole merchants did not actually carry slaves or directly involve themselves in the market they were still complicit in the trade. For many sold their cheapest grade of salt cod to all of the American and Caribbean plantation owners. This was in order to feed all of their slaves. The Poole merchants Barfoots and the

Jolliffe families bought grandiose mansions with their mercantile and slavery success. Their addresses No. 87 High Street was home to William Barfoot, while Jolliffe House was on West Street. There is a memorial to William and his father in St. James' Church.

Due to the changes in society from a mid-century rural agricultural environment to an industrial environment with the introduction of the railways and the factories. The Gypsy travelling community gradually changed their skills from basket making, chair making, peg making and farming labour. To the new demands for clay, for bricks, stone and pottery. The Gypsy traveling community were living on the common lands where the clay and stone where plentiful and they worked in harvesting these materials, for building the new railways viaducts and houses. Many Gypsies worked hard long hours often in terrible conditions in creating bricks in the kilns and in the quarries where clay and stone were plentiful. This was particularly so in Dorset and with its access to transport worldwide trade via the Poole harbour. Plus, the county had its Quarries in the Purbeck region and its sand and gravel, clay pits throughout the region. In this changing landscape environment, the region soon became literally full of clay pits, brick yards and potteries this was particularly so by the 18 and 19 centuries. Many Gypsy travelling families became proficient in these new industrious as brick makers, clay cutters and quarry men. There were metal waggons carts which were used to transport these materials which became known as monkey waggons. The whole region was full of Gypsy encampment whose members were a ready source of labour for these new industries, whilst others became involved in haulage of these material's such as sand and gravel and many new companies were created by local gypsy traveller families in scrap industries haulage along with brick making potter and stone quarry work.

Although it was not uncommon for a girl of thirteen years to marry during these years. In fact it was quite usual. Even a woman in her lifetime could well have given birth to up to a dozen children. So it was that a woman may well have been in a constant state of pregnancy throughout her child bearing years. Due to the poor living conditions and unhealthy life styles with poor nutrition or those babies who were breast fed from an unhealthy mother. As result of which many babies died at birth or shortly after and there were also many pregnant woman also who died giving birth during these times.

On Sundays at the church hat they had to stand throughout the service. For the common laborer could not afford to pay for the pleasure of sitting upon the pews. It was only the land owners, the aristocratic gentlemen only these men of fine estate and breeding who could afford to pay for the privilege of sitting in the Lords house on Sunday the Lords day. Besides that John knew it was still his Christian duty to attend each and every Sunday he was obliged to for it was expected of all good God fearing men. John felt that there was the peace of humanity here among the works of men, along with the Turberville aisle amid the works of God and the windows when lit up are a sight to behold. There on the south wall of the church the Turberville arms are displayed in the many panels of its window. Whilst the Turberville aisle has its decorated and other empty tombs. John admired the late Norman arches, the ancient tiles and the skillful woodwork of its proud beams. The roof was indeed the wonder of this place.

A good laboring man such men always deserved their wages. Though he knew once he had paid his Tithes rent to landlord such as Drax for their small wee cob dwelling along with the hearth tax there there was very little left over for essentials. Such as their grub, clothing and other bare essentials. Never the less, he was grateful for all that which the Lord God had provided. Along with all the blessings that he their Savior the lord God, had bestowed on him along with his beloved wife and their children. He knew that life expectancy was not very long among his fellow workers, most were lucky to make it to their fiftieth year and even of those who did many were crippled with ill health in their later years.

Initially those employed in brickyards and potteries in the early days had their wages paid inside of the public-houses. It was a terrible situation and should never have happened, but it did. For it was a known fact that if wages were paid over a bar-counter men would be encouraged to spend their wages there on alcohol and to treat their workmates to a round of drinks. The wages were very poor and the work often not regular. The brick workers received their wages within the premises often driven to do so for the good of the pub. And so consequently one drink led to another. So it was that often both health and wages were wasted. With little or none left. In these poor streets, wives were often seen waiting outside the to take their husbands home before all wages were spent. To ensure they had sufficient money to pay for rent and food. Some Brickworks also provided drinking houses, with Inns, public houses and Breweries in close vicinity to the brickyard or pottery. This was another means of extra income for the rich grand master owners from the workers wages. As a result the owner proprietors of these establishment saw this as an opportunity as another means of income for themselves. By creating nearby inns or public houses/boozers. The pubs were open all day long as brick making and burning was thirsty work. It was commonly asserted that the poor lower classes were paid poor wages because they were inclined to waste money. It was said they would most likely squander it on alcohol consumption. The contrast between these brick making areas and where the middle classes and wealthy landowners lived was tremendous. For the bricks made were used to build their fine houses, grandiose mansions and villas.

Whilst those who laboured and created the bricks lived in hovels. Brick makers usually rested on Mondays for time in their family homes and to recover from a hard weekends drinking after getting their pay at 12.30pm on a Saturday. Often they spent most of our little leisure time in these Inns and unfortunately most of our wages too. As a result there was a substantial numbers of alcoholics amongst the workers with many of them were found to be drunk and often disorderly. Many were often known for their drunkenness and gambling. Some gained a reputation and notoriety for riotous living. As a result many of the early brick fields were said to be lawless places. Those found to be involved in affrays or physical assaults were dealt with accordingly. With many appearing at the local police station or courts and were subsequently heavily fined, imprisoned or even deported to the new world, some even as slaves.

Gypsy travellers were initially in the early days called tent dwe. The early gypsy travellers built their bender homes in the n___. Then later came the Vardo wagons, before the caravans and today's trailers. Their families were often extremely large with up to 17 children. So many histories and stories of the travelling people give the entirely false impression and simplification that they were simply mainly hawkers and farm workers with skills in basket making and telling fortunes. Whilst in fact many were skilled in brick making, pottery, metal ironmongery, sportsmen and women herbalists and were fairground workers too. Brick Making was then a Seasonal occupation and one commonly undertaken by the Travelling population. The Baptisms of the children indicate a Seasonal pattern in terms of the presence of the tribe, since tasks such as Brick Making were carried out in the late Autumn, and then concluded in the Spring when the Winter Weather had helped break down the Clay. Sojourning (or staying somewhere temporarily) over the Winter months, when Travel was often difficult & sometimes impossible, meant that the Gypsies were available for the Seasonal Labour of Brick Making, so popular in the area, and could spend the Winter mending their material Goods, making Besoms & Clothes Pegs and, of course, Churching their children in the Villages close to the Common Land where they Camped.

Gypsies are a versatile people and yes, they once were makers of pegs and baskets along with the whittled wood they fashioned tin and were great breeders of horses. Their many occupations in history may well fill a book a large volume no doubt. A natural development from horse dealing was to be second hand cars dealers, scrap metal or haulage contractors. Same as in the logging businesses. They once could sell door to door their many skilful items, their baskets of flowers or tell fortunes. This changed with the sale of goods acts and trading laws with the requirements of licenses. They had to fill in documents and as most were uneducated and could not read and write this became this with their travelling life made it impossible.

So many Romanies & Travellers were involved in Brick Making because many of the Kilns were on the Commons, which was the Poorest Land in the locality. This meant that the Topsoil was thin and therefore easy to strip away to dig out the Clay necessary for making the Bricks; in addition, there was local Woodland, Gorse or Brush, for Firing the Kilns. This made the Sites where Gypsies often Camped perfectly suited to this, and the Travellers provided a ready Workforce. They were Sand carriers, as well as Brick Makers & Brick Burners. Articles in local Newspapers often focused on the Brick Works, which were considered such a significant part of life in the area. Reporting Accidents, Sale of a Yard, or appealing for Workers at Sites, became commonplace. Whilst the Workforce rarely made much money out of such seasonal activity, the Owners usually did very well financially.

During the winter months when work eased off the brick makers also worked in the local Breweries. Many of the brickworks had three tall chimney stacks these were landmarks which could be seen for miles. The clay here was originally dug out by hand, put on wagons and taken to the end of a wire rope way, which transported the clay buckets to the mixing pans and firing kilns nearly a mile away. It was an all-year job though in many brickyards' bricks were only made during the summer months because of the problem of drying the bricks during the winter. As a result, most of the men were laid off for the winter months. Whilst a fortunate crew were kept on digging clay which they called "Good diggin" and they would be seen piling it up to "weather", ready for the next summer's brick making. They dug out the clay, in seams some 20 to 50ft down then we put it into large lumps ready for the brick making process. The brick maker would dig a hole about 4ft square and about 3ft deep, the top of this hole would have a wooden board, 18inches wide, he would then stand in the hole and make the bricks. At the start of the day workers called "Clay Jammers" fed the brick maker. After first jamming the clay with their bare feet, these men went to and from their homes in bare feet. The brick making process was done at a very fast pace, and we often worked from dawn to dusk. Ridge tiles, finials, chimneys were also made along with utility items such as drainage pipes. These were all part of the terracotta range of the brick maker's art. Many products required expert modelling and an eye to the fashions of the day

Hand-made bricks were "made to measure". Anything but standard bricks must be matched up. Which took time and skill, and these 'fancy' bricks could only be made by hand. Such ornate carved bricks adorned many old buildings. Sometimes only one brick of a certain type is needed and so a special mould would be made. A hand-made brick was not compressed it was fired slowly for more than 48 hours. Till it was truly "cooked" and so would not chip or flake like an ordinary brick.

It was also quite common for some brick-makers to also be farmers and beer sellers. Whilst many of the brick and tile works, were a one-man business with small clamp kilns. The hillside was a highly industrialised scene, shrouded in smoke from the many types of kilns around where the ground churned into mud by clay extraction and the heavy cart tracks. Many Gypsies were also employed in specialist jobs of dropping chimneys of the obsolete Kilns and paid £25.00 each man. For this job they would put explosive at the base of the five legs of the kiln and often after several abortive attempts we finished the job. At one time Dorset boasted more than 200 hundred brickyards. Gypsy travellers such as my ancestors were proud to be a brick maker though these times were hard, they would not change it despite the harsh conditions for they knew no other life.

Small scale crimes offences committed by gypsy travellers were dealt with severely by the Local Courts, although it is worth pointing out that most of the poor were dealt with in a similar manner for their many & frequently Petty infringements of the Law. Often, these Crimes committed by the Gypsies & Travellers were specific to their way of life, but Gypsies and the locals alike found themselves in Court for Crimes such as stealing Hay or Poaching a Rabbit and given harsh sentences for these misdemeanours. When not working some Gypsies took part in cockfighting and bullbaiting. Many of their dogs were kept for dogfights and killing rats. There were within some Gypsy encampments lots of Pigs too, these providing a good supply of pork. I had heard that in some areas there were thousands. They built large kilns to fire up the tiles and bricks. Which were supplied to local merchants in their fine houses. When these shanty towns of shacks, sheds and outhouses began to develop they were often seen a cause for concern due to overcrowding and poor sanitation. Many lived under roofs, whilst others were living in vans hidden away.

A good many Gypsies young men paired off with the local non-Gypsy girls and marriages often took place though some still jumped the broom. While some Gypsy women kept their own surname after they married.

The Gypsy men tethered their horses away from the vans on long tethers to enable them to roam, but not move away too far. Many bands of workers were clustered together on the encampments.

The local population in the Villages adjoining the Commons also, like the Farmers, depended on the Traveller Community who mended pots & kettles, sharpened tools & knives & mended umbrellas. Little boys with their Pocket Knives & the Household Scissors would run after the Gypsy & his Grinding Machine, and watch the sparks fly from the Grindstone, perhaps also buying a Paper Windmill for a Penny. So, if the relationship with the Travelling fraternity was one of wariness, it was also one of inter-dependence.

Many Gypsy Travellers were also accomplished Musicians and played at the Village Feasts, Local Fairs, Morris Dancing & Dancing Booths. These were all Events that provided the Gypsy Fraternity with the opportunity to make money to supplement their income by playing for the local population. Such opportunities for gaining financial rewards bolstered their casual Labouring work, fruit picking, hop picking, pea picking and the summer harvest, as well as apple picking, hawking & Brick Making, all important occupations for the Traveller population. As well as providing much of the Music and running the Dancing Booths & Shooting Galleries, the Gypsies also Hawked Goods they had made, pegs, lace, shawls, wax flowers or real ones, the latter often gathered from the Woodland that abutted the Commons. In the Spring, in particular, the Travellers would gather the Flowers growing wild, primroses, bluebells, snowdrops, and later in the year broom & heather, to fashion them into Bouquets & Bunches to sell. Carpets of such wildflowers were nurtured by the tribes, and the results ca still be seen in the Woodland Copes, where the Gypsy Families would often return to the same Camping spot year after year, and made sure of this source of Income.

The Gypsy travellers contributed towards the wider community in so many constructive ways. With so many companies and traders who made a lasting impact on so many of our communities.

Travelling families worked for farmers which was seasonal work and as brick makers, worker s, potters and clay kiln workers. Before the Act of 1871 all members of the Gypsy families were used as labour many often working 12-hour shifts. It was very labour-intensive hot work in brick yards with poor lighting and over the years a number were killed from suffocation and fumes.

Mayall (1988) observes that 'The Gypsies pitched their tents and halted their vans in areas of transition, on brick fields and on waste ground, on sites of intended buildings and where old buildings such as brickyards and potteries had been pulled down.

They also had to find some where's to live and often in desperation encamped amid chaos and filth. Many of their camps were in such depressed areas that they were said to be satisfied to put up their tents. The Gypsy families often travelled hundreds of miles., though many kept to their own familiar family territories for most of the time particularly during winter months. Gypsy encampment and stopping places over the years have included those parked up on lay byes, roads, lanes, crescents, rows of houses. Often, these were situated on the edge of the town on any available wasteland or common land or one large dwelling in the forests itself. In earlier centuries these encampments were of all sizes and numbers. It included those set within woodlands, fields outside the towns, in forests, on common lands, quarries, brick works, potteries, shore lands and marshes. Their first homes were often built out of mud or clay with tents and sackings. Whilst other gypsies-built benders which were no more than shelters made from blankets, felt waterproof tarpaulin sheets draped over bent rods or ash, willow or hazel. Often their donkeys or ponies transported these sheets, and the rods were cut out at each of their many stopping places. The floors were covered with carpeting and mats all made from nearby bracken or straw at hand. Their benders were in many sizes to suit requirements size of family units. Their days were spent in occupations depending on their family occupations. Then they returned to their encampments in the evenings and gathered around the yog sharing food and entertainment. The elders told stories of their exploits and family successes or tragedies. With tales of the fairgrounds, fayres, brick yards and potteries, hop picking and fruit picking days and events. Often these included tales of persecution and stories of the great gatherings of Gypsy communities.

There were great Gypsy pugilist boxers who conquered the world so many became world professional boxing champions and Poole was one place where we had no shortage of these boxing kings. Many of these boxers came up through the local fairgrounds before going professional and becoming famous. These included local Gypsy Traveller boxers fought here at Poole such as Freddie Mills, Abe Stanley, Ted Sherwood, and Teddy Peckham. These local boxers were often seen standing outside the boxing booth in Poole's famous fairground. Freddie Mills ho at 17 was the "darling" of the British fight scene was born at Bournemouth in 1919 and was given a pair of boxing gloves for his 11th birthday. Becoming British Commonwealth European and World Light heavyweight Boxing Champion. In 1950 he retired and ran a highly successful nightclub and starred in films and on TV. He died of gunshot wounds to the head on July 25, 1965, under a cloud of mystery. The officially suicide, though many believed it was due to his involvement with the Kray brothers.

The popular song of the brick yards workers of that day was …

In the days we went a- gypsying
"When lads and lasses in their best
Were dressed from top to toe,
In the days we went a-gipsying
A long time ago;
In the days we went a-gipsyingA long time ago.

Every "brick-yard lad" and "brick-yard wench" who would not, in singing these lines was always looked upon as a "stupid donkey," and the consequence was that upon all occasions, when excitement was needed as a whip, they were "struck up;" especially would it be the case when the limbs of the little brick and clay carrier began to totter and were "fagging up." When the taskmaster perceived the "gang" had begun to "slinker" he would shout out at the top of his voice, "Now, lads and wenches, strike up with the: *"In the days we went a-gipsying, a long time ago."*'

And as a result, more work was ground out of the little English slave. I imagined that it related to fortune-telling, thieving and stealing in one form or other, especially as the lads used to sing it with "gusto" when they had been robbing the potato field to have "a potato fuddle," while they were "oven tenting" in the nighttime. Roasted potatoes and cold turnips were always looked upon as a treat for the "brickies." Many times, I have been like the horse that shies at them as they camp in the ditch bank, half frightened out of my wits and felt anxious to know either more or less of them.

From the days when carrying clay and loading canal-boats was my toil and "gipsying" my song, scarcely a week has passed without the words

"When lads and lasses in their best
Were dressed from top to toe,
In the days we went a-gypsying

A long time ago," ringing in my ears, and at times when busily engaged upon other things, "In the days we went a-gipsying" would be running through my mind.

"Old Elijah Cotton," a well-known character in the Potteries, who got his living by it, to ask him all sorts of questions. Sometimes he would look at my hands, at other times he would put my hand into his, and hold it while he was reading out of the Bible, and burning something like brimstone-looking powder—the forefinger of the other hand had to rest upon a particular passage or verse; at other times he would give me some of this yellow-looking stuff in a small paper to wear against my left breast, and some I had to burn exactly as the clock struck twelve at night, under the strictest secrecy. The stories this fortune-teller used to relate to me as to his wonderful power over the spirits of the other world were very amusing, aye, and over "the men and women of this generation." He was frequently telling that he had "fetched men from Manchester in the dead of the night flying through the air in the course of an hour;" and this kind of rubbish he used to relate to those who paid him their shillings and half-crowns to have their fortunes told. My visits lasted for a little time till he told me that he could do nothing more, as I was "not one of his sorts."

(From: Gipsy Life, by George Smith, 1880)

CHAPTER ONE

THE EARLY HISTORY OF GYPSY TRAVELLERS

Pedlar Days

There once was a pedlar who took him a wife.
she brought him nothing but troubles and strife all the days of his life.
oh, the cradle did rock there and the wheels they did roll
oh, they had troubles and trials wherever they'd go
the winds they did roar and the rain it did pour.
whilst the logs they did crack spit and the tales he did spin more
across all the country where the chaffinch did sing
first days of summer and last days of spring

Where the embers were red around the yog they did sit
all the best and the worst to market and sing
the gaffers and his humble servants did say.
that it was right to delight in their labour each day
the girls they were buxom and a sight to behold.
to warm you at night when the weather was cold.

For to honour the master's and give the young lads a thrill
oh, the gal she did sing like the birds in the tree
in their tumbledown trailers and their rich honesty
for she bit on the apple and the curse it was set free
in the neck of the woods neath the old shady tree

She had many lovers, but none could compare.
with the pedlar's young son was so devil may care
all debonaire with curls in his hair
though she kissed all the village, and the lads all gave chase.
she was blessed with the beauty and the smile of her face.

Where the young gals were pretty and the young lads so bold
with their hands in their pockets and their heads full of gold

The chaffinch did sing and the sky it was blue
where she laid down her beauty for the diddle lee doo
though her life knew no borders and her heart knew no dues
the fruit of her virtue was deemed to be true.

Where the pedlar he sheltered neath the full moon each night
and the gypsy told fortunes before each morning light.

Ray Wills

Rabbiting

I took my dogs a rabbiting along the beaten tracks.
there were ferns upon the hillsides there.
and a sack upon my back

I had ferrets in my pockets.
and some bread rolls for my tea
there were lots of stingers on the downs.
and none of them troubled me.

The tracks were sandy narrow walks.
and the lizards squirmed a few.
I heard a chaffinch sing across at Waterloo.

The walks to Lodge hill were so steep.
the dogs they did a play.
I called them over to my side.
as we walked the narrow ways

The Canford broom did smell.
and the furze bloom was perfume.
I heard a hawk screech in the air.
whilst a blackbird sang its tune

There were Gypsy vardos on the hills.
where Knotty never went
there was swampy ground beneath your feet
reeds were a growing oh so deep.

The sun was high into the sky.
which was painted saintly blue?
I saw some Gypsies playing chase.
then heard a cuss or two.

My catapult was in my belt.
my eyes were set to free.
the cast of dogs upon my back
delighted in this spree.

The tracks all led to higher ground.
where burrows were rich in grass
held treasures yet to be explored.
by dogs so proud and fast

The dogs sniffed around the holey grounds.
then we let the ferret's play
whilst nets were laid o'er holes of grass and soil

Whilst dogs did chase and bark
then rabbits ran and dogs had fun
before the setting sun
where below the ferrets did explore
where tunnels met below the soil
who could want for more?

Ray Wills

FOREST DAYS

In the forest of England they tethered their mare's
they worked on the land from craft to repair's
they lit of the fire's from bracken and log
where the wind it was brisk and the snow it was deep round the yog
they bedded in bender's where hog's once did sleep
their gown's they were long and their shawl's they were wool from the sheep
where the chaffinch did sing and the man sang the blue's

For year's they did roam from Boldre to Poole
where the vardo's did roll and the weather was cruel
though summer's were warm beneath the starry blue skies
where the birch grew so wild and the heather's and grasses were rye

Their father's were blessed with the call of the free
where the forest's were rich from the village to the sea
their children were many and their old un's were wise
they worked on the land with hope in their eye's

The wheel's they did roll and the ponies ran free
where Rufus stone stood there amidst the villager's plea's
the bracken was course and the berries were sweet
with lizard's and snake's squirmed just beneath of your feet

They gathered their families and took them to Poole
where the lodge hill's of Canford were rich in the dew
where the rabbit's and foxes ran free on the down's

where gaffer's and landlord's were rich by the crown

They settled so freely on the Wimborne's estate
where the Guest family resided and the turves's were to waste
they built them their home's there beneath the warbler's nest's
where the gravel was rich and the clay it was blessed

From Talbot to Magna and over the down's
they gathered their families and all bedded down
in Kinson's New England and Heavenly Bottom's abode
they ran with the wind in the summer's so warm and the winters
so cold

All through the war year's they traveled this land
from south to the north with their merry band's
they were branded and moved on like thieves in the night
with landlord's and mean men who took of their right's

They fought in the war's like true British grit
worked on the land and the factories shift's
they built the great wall's with viaduct's and brickyard's so tall
and mean
then they were herded like cattle and grounded in team's

Their stories are rich and their histories are keen
from the New Forest walk's to the home of the Queen
they talk with a richness and will give you the eye
like a true Romani trooper with a didykoy guise

Ray Wills

From as early as the 1500s many Gypsy travellers settled in the area known as Canford heath within the wide Kinson parish. which at one time covered some 83,000 acres. The landscape being very similar to the new forest of today. Many of these living in their encampments upon the common lands in later years this was courtesy of the landowners the Guests, Talbots, and George families. In past decades Gypsy travellers had once occupied a vast variety of these numerous campsites throughout Dorset.

Stretching the whole length of the old Wareham Road and Wallisdown and Branksome. As well as at Sea view which was there till 1939 with others going back to the mid1700s.

These folk were skilled artisans, horse traders, builders, flower sellers, craftsmen, tinkers, fortune, and story tellers, show people and farm labourers. They moved around on these encampment numerous encampment sites as stopping places. Sometimes staying on an encampment for a short period or often as not for a lifetime. Often this was depending on work opportunities and pairing up and marrying other gypsy travellers which was the norm. Though in time they also married into the local communities.

Many used their numerous skills over the centuries developing new industries in the locality. Local gypsies were involved in brick making because most of the kilns were on the commons which was not only the poorest land in the locality it was where gypsies had their encampments. Taking advantage of the demand for house building with sand and gravel pits, clay potteries and brick yards, Assisted no doubt largely by the nearby thriving shipping port of Poole for trading to its Newfoundland fishing and worldwide trade from the busy Poole harbour. From the late 16th century, a marked increase in the prosperity of the port was brought about by the opening of the Newfoundland trade: cargoes of cod, salmon, oil, seal skins and furs being brought back in return for fishing implements and household necessities. This trade flourished particularly in the 18th century and especially during the Napoleonic wars, but after 1815 it rapidly collapsed in the face of foreign competition, being replaced by a less lucrative general foreign and coastal trade.

Poole harbour was also known originally as Luxford Lake being 50 miles in circumference. It was at one time very rich with handsome buildings and was recognised as maybe the top port in Britain. It traded to the Baltic, Portugal, America, Greenland, and Newcastle. With it emphasise on its great cod trade with Newfoundland and its export of a great quantity of Portland stone.

Many of these Gypsy travelling communities lived in tents or benders in the early days. Then later, they lived in caravans or Vardos before present day trailers. Over time there were regular Gypsy traveller family's occupants living on a vast variety of numerous campsites scattered throughout the big parish of Kinson and on the turbary commons themselves. The vast Canford estate in those days covered thousands of acres.

Often these Gypsy traveller encampment sites had their own unique names such as Cuckoo Bottom, sugar knob mountain, monkeys Hump lanes, cinders town, frying pan, Wally Wack, high moor, Hemley bottom, bribery island, New England, top common and many more. Despite their earthy sometimes muddy surroundings some of these Gypsy encampments contained caravans that were spotlessly clean. With highly polished brass lamps and glass and trinkets inside. Often the Gypsy women were to be seen sitting on the vardo van step's outside smoking their clay pipe's. Many of these traditional stopping places and encampments nationally were eventually taken over by local councils or by settled individuals decades ago. These have subsequently changed hands on very many occasions however Gypsies have long historical connections to such places and do not always willingly give them up.

Brick making was a major industry in Dorset for well over 3 centuries it was at its peak in the 1800s with more than 200 brickyards in the county. These provided regular employment for the local population many of whom were Gypsy Traveller families. Many. gypsies left their tents to find a home in, the miserable garrets, damp cellars, dirty lanes, and wretched alleys of our villages, towns, and cities".

Many Gypsies were very proficient in their occupations. bricks being handmade, many of the kilns were found on the commons known as Turbary which was the poorest land in the locality and was where the Gypsies had their encampments. From the 1800s the gypsy travellers built thriving businesses locally in the haulage, sand and gravel, potteries, coal, brickworks, house building and scrap metal industries. These often emerged out of small successful local initiatives. From humble beginnings such as pony and cart or pig styes, small holdings initiatives. Over the years these thrived and grew both in size and demand to eventually become extremely wealthy local enterprises. Some of which are very familiar to us and are still with us here today. Many of these travelling Gypsy travelling families remain rooted in our communities today and their names are well known and respected. These became part of our local heritage.

In recent times due to various governments land Acts and reforms a great many of these families' descendants were ultimately to be housed locally. It is hard to ignore these ancestors' effects had such an impact on our local community and locality. Thes Gypsies were a versatile work force skilled in the process of brick making also as sand carriers and brick burners too.

The tradition of travelling with regular stopping places is very important to travelling folk. It has over the years allowed Gypsies and Travelers to move around the country. To meet up with their relatives to take up employment opportunities and to meet with family members regularly to attend special family occasions such as christenings, weddings, illnesses, and funerals historical Horse Fayres, thus these Stopping places have always been a necessary feature of the traveller's life and is essential for them to retain their ethnic identities and heritage.

Most gypsy travellers' families are identifiable by their traditional wintering base, where they will stop travelling for the winter, this place will be technically where a family is from.

Gypsies have been part of the background to British life for centuries, but by the early part of the 20th century, travelling families recognised that their children needed schooling and increasingly their children attended the local schools.

In Dorset many Gypsy children were christened in such places as Coombe Keynes, at Wool in 1803 and Yetminster in 1799 and later at Bere Regis and Iwerne Courtney. Gypsies were also involved locally in vital local successful craft industries such as Dorset button making. Charles, I went to his execution wearing a waistcoat with Dorset Buttons. In the 1800s with famine in the countryside, young men including gypsies flocked into Poole and were pressed in large numbers.

During the industrial revolution, in the 18th and 19th centuries, when Britain became the "workshop of the world", the pottery towns of the Midlands and Northern England took vast quantities of local clay shipped by barge from Poole Quay.

It is estimated that 30 million bricks were made in Poole where at one time there were over 50 brickyards. The potteries, brickyards and clay pits were the main employers the end of the Newfoundland trading days.

We need to get away from the recent hostility towards the travelling the few instances where travellers have left sites covered in litter. Were as it being a fact so much of the illegal fly tipping and littering of our communities is done by non-Gypsies. So many of our seaside resorts are left covered in litter by holiday makers and our town centre s are often a disgrace particularly at weekends, at a huge cost to the numerous city councils. None of these are because of traveller's involvement.

Another area is the issue banded about that the fairgrounds were operated only by show people needs also to be corrected. For so very many of the early fairground peoples and those who managed them were Gypsy traveller families.

CHAPTER TWO

VARDO DAYS

Vardo Days

I once had a vardo and its wheel thy did roll n spin
I rode it to Ringwood the great show in the spring
My father he boxed at the fairgrounds to the Lord Queensbury rules
Oh, the days they were long then when we lived down near Poole
I once had a wife she was dark n so wise
she sang with the birds and had sparkling green eyes
she would tell folks their fortunes
so gorgas beware
don't you dare go pick all the heather from Pooles baskets fair

We worked in the meadows picking the hops and down at Poole quay, for a many long hours our wages to see
We often drank beer outside the pubs by the sea
the lights they did shine there and the stars they were bright n twinkled at night
Where the streetlight did glow
when we danced there at night whilst the old ones did sew

Though those days have long gone, and the gaffers have too
Although I remember the days when we camped near sea view
there were cones on the hillsides and boats in the bay

Constitution hill was so steep, and our lives were so gay
Our homes in our wagons were so rich then
decked out with satins and lace
with our tattoos and fancy artwork all over the place
our lamps they were gold and our talk it was free
when we lived by our wits for, we were true Romani

Ray Wills

Travellers Lament

She took a reading whilst he worked the forge
She collected flowers and mixed the herbs
He bred the horses and mules a few
it was full of birdsong on the heaths of Poole

He worked the fairgrounds
whilst she flew the darts
He rode the cars it was starlight in the dark
She cooked the stew whilst he told the tales
the land was rich then with wagons ponies and tails

He shook the hands and bartered deals
She picked the fruit turn turn turn wagon wheels
they used the stopping places and atchen tans
He told the stories he was the man
wise old ways gypsy man

She stood for Munning's art pictured frames
Stanley's, Lees, Coopers, James the same
She dressed in skirts and wore gay bright rings
He wore the waistcoat and boxed the sports of kings
She fashioned flowers with paper crepe
He worked with clay gravel and bricks
She sang the songs of Caroline Hughes
He wrote the stories like Dominic Reeves
She modelled for Augustus John at Alderney
He built the cottages Lady Wimborne rented free

She danced at pubs in new forest glades
he collected iron scrap
She was Queen thousands were at her grave
He was a scholar poet bard
She was a countess whilst he played the cards
She was a sweetheart of Byron too
He was a wanderer traveller from Poole

She was a coal merchant whilst he was a Gypsy king
She was a Crutcher he was a White
where miners did sing.

She was a dreamer whilst he was a priest
She saved lives he saved souls to teach
She was a beauty, and he was a rogue
She was a prophet indisposed
He was a fool, and they rode their wagons
through the streets of Poole

Ray Wills

Ballad of the Baro Rai and Bari Rawni back in Victorian Days and Beyond.

Once there were these people all of the academic type who went out and studied the people travelling Britain's roads.

From Universities and The Gypsy Lore Society these Gentle man & Ladies would out there go

Searching for the Gypsies camped in the Lanes along the hedge rows

Or open fields also.

They were out to study the Gypsies who while were seen as simple folk exotic all the same.

It was Culture and language these searchers went after with Pen Paper & gifts in tow.

When they spied a Gypsy camp it was hey come let's go rushing in with no respect for the Gypsy way.

They offered up tobacco food and drink to get a Gypsy to speak in the chib they brought from India all those years ago.

The Rai would ask the Questions the Rawni wrote it all down while the Gypsy hid a smile while telling the Rai huge white lies.

After research was over it was back to university desks to write this strange language in Proper English text.

Some words wrong of course like Suv for going to sleep, Suv means something else which I dare not speak.

Many words were changed to suit the Gorga Academics mind even though Oral based a living language see; The Rai ignored that and did what he pleased.

Later Rai's and Rawni's in letters to each other did write using Romanus in a wicked sexual play.

They thought no one would understand if Romanus they used but since Romany have learned to read the hidden secrets are out.

2.

A blatant misuse of the Romany Language in the most disrespectful way -------by these Learned Ladies and Gentlemen of those Victorian Days.

So next time you read the GLS rag or a book by Rai or Rawni learn to read between the lines the truth you will find.

Don't be shocked by misuse of our Chib you are warned in advance of the wicked ways and practices by the Baro Rai's & Bari Rawni back in Victorian Times.

Bob Lovell/Kamulo.   C 2024.

Ballad of the Baro Rai and Bari Rawni. By Bob Lovell/Kamulo. C 2024.

Note! = For those that don't know of the Baro Rai's and Bari Rawni --------
- Here is a Brief Explanation.

In Victorian Times and after in England there was a number of Middle to Upper Class people who took great delight in the study of the People they came across who were clearly of other Races & Different cultures to them!

Many of these Rai's and Rawni were Academic and university People Such As John Sampson / Dora Yates / Eric Otto Winstedt/ and people like R A Scott Macfre/T W Thompson and Artists such as Augustus John to mention a few.

These People also were members of the Gypsy lore society (GLS) this society attracted many People from the Middle & upper English, Scottish Classes, it was a society formed as these people were becoming aware of the Gypsies seen throughout the British Isles, a colourful people who for these Victorians appeared Exotic / Romantic /Colourful and clearly coming from afar Also the Gypsies were very private people who kept to themselves.

So in late 1800s Early 1900s one of these Victorians a John Sampson a self-taught Linguist who first wrote a paper on a Dialect Shelta of the Tinker Travellers -------- which then became cant a part language used by Travellers throughout the British Isles.

Sampson then became Liberian at Liverpool University where he did more linguistic studies aided by two young Woman Students a Dora Yates and the other name I forget.

Sampson had studied a bit of the Chib = Language Spoken by Gypsies (Romany) in England but he found in his opinion that much of this language had been lost and was fast disappearing to be replaced with a broken tongue called Pogadi.

Sampson was then made aware of a certain Gypsy family in North Wales who it was said still spoke the old inflicted form of Romanus chib.

2. 3 of 3R rBR

He along with his two understudies made a bee line for North Wales where they were introduced to members of the Woods Romany family,

Who by this time were Settled Gypsies and had become well known for their fine playing of the Welsh harp.

Of course Sampson approached all Gypsies with gifts, often tobacco and Drink such as whisky and if the Gypsies accepted his gifts in return he would ask to hear the inflected Romanus spoken by these Gypsies.

He of course was helped by his two under studies Yates and the other young woman – NOTE this other young woman became Pregnant a bit later on and disappeared from the scene not to be heard of again?

Sampson and Yates collected much Language from the Woods and Roberts and would go back to Liverpool university to write it all up properly as Sampson planned to produce a book on the subject = The Dialect of The Gypsies Of Wales .

I would point out here that Sampson did NOT approach Other Main Romany families found in North & South Wales at the time who also spoke an Inflected Romanus chib -------- This lead to an attitude by many in the GLS that only two or so Romany Clans (tribes) in North Wales still spoke The Old Romany language. This is still a current belief today and also among some Romany people in G Britain.

Note! I did not know of books about Us Romany Gypsy folkie written by Non Romany and among members of the GLS , as there were a number of books written and published on Britain's Gypsies ----------- It was really only in 1999 I was in England and I visited a well-known Romany who had a Yard & Romany museum. He had on his book shelves every book and GLS journals ever written. Even John Sampson's book = Dialect of The Welsh Gypsies.

I must admit I was staggered as I was unaware of such books (later I was able to read a couple of these types of books but not the Dialect of the Welsh Gypsies.

I had by this time become aware that for some Older Romany such as my Father and his generation – they had Stories about the Rai's and Rawni but they mostly could not read or write well enough to have read

C 024

3. B of B R & E R.

any of Said books --------- Yet my Father spoke an inflected Romanus which I learned from him as we worked on a car engine or out haymaking using horses to build the hay stacks, just every day talk in the old Romany Chib.

Yet my Father did mention the Baro Rai's to me saying our family his father my Granddad never would talk to these Rai's or members of the GLS. When I asked my father why not? he said because these people the Baro Rai's and Bari Rawni wrote Hokanie = Lies about certain Romany Families and it had become known among some Romany at the time, so these Rai's and Rawni were to be avoided at all times.

Later I discovered more on this and have the evidence needed to say yes These Baro Rai's & Bari Rawni and members of the GLS were indeed not all good people and their interest in things Gypsy had a hidden dark side.

I will finish by saying, if your interest is up due to my words here I suggest YOU do some searching --------- all the Books written by these Rai's. And Rawni's are available I believe via Cottage Books UK and such book shops.

Abbreviations = GLS = Gypsy Lore Society. Baro Rai, Non Romany Gentleman/ Lord Etc., Rai's =plural. Bari Rawni. Non Romany Lady/a Lords wife etc.

Chib = Tongue as in Language Spoken by Romany Gypsies.

Hokanie.= Lies.

Pogadi – Broken.

46

The following is a fictional account of a possible gathering of Gypsy travellers on their encampment way back in time in Dorset..

Encampment Times

We lived here in the vast fertile common lands known as Canford Heath. Our encampment was in an area of fern heath land, known as New England. An area which had Turbary rights, dating ways back to the Doomsday book of 1000. Rights which included the grazing of cattle and the cutting and gathering of peat for fires such as at the Turbary common lands. Our encampment was situated within a village parish known then as Kinson. We lived here with our extended families of parents and offspring of chavvies, Grandparents, Elders, cousins and friends amongst the silver birch, yellow furze, and heather. A horde of Gypsy Travellers encampments evolved from around the early 1800s throughout these Canford Parish common lands. With close to forty or more by the early 20th century. These all were very different in size and numbers with extremely unusual names. Names which included the following list-Cuckoo bottom, Frying pan, heavenly bottom etc. Our small strip of land now known as "New England" was just one of many similar encampments on the heathlands of Kinson village in greater Canford. It was given its name by our own Gypsy travelling folk from the New Forest who favoured it amongst all the scores of Canford encampments. Many of our forefathers had their origins in the new forest and other areas of the land which was then mainly forests. For it reminded them of the Forests itself.

Some of our fore bearers such as the Stanley's had left for a new life as horse breeders and farmers in the new worlds of America and Australia of their own choosing. Though history shows that so many of our folk were exploited as slaves or sent to prisons in the new world often deported for very petty crimes such as catching rabbits or trespassing on the Lord's estate. They having little monies were often unable to pay fines to the magistrate's courts often he himself was the landowner. As a result, they were sent to work on plantations or on convict ships to Australia imprisoned for numerous crimes from simple poaching of rabbits, horse theft to assault.

Our community of Travellers despite our in-built wanderlust had been loyal to our country with many being active in the armed services through numerous wars and campaigns. We were particularly loyal to the farmers who depended upon our labour each season of crops and fruit picking. Then Britannia one of the young women present spoke up. She said "Hey Sam any news on the Hughes family at Corfe Mullen, do they still live on the "Downy" encampment on Colonel Georges land by the woods there and is Caroline still there and does she still sing all those old songs". I quickly responded, "Yes Britannia, Aaron and I visited them just recently they are still there, and we saw Colonel George and had a pleasant chat with him". "He told us he is keen to employ workers in brick to build a new town on the large heathlands by the Bourne river estuary which we know as Poole heath. He said that he plans to start work there sometime in the future". "He will need good brick makers, craftsman and labourers for the brickyards he owns". I investigated the burning red glint of the fire and told them "You know years ago the gentry at Corfe Mullen had plantations and labouring slaves working there. Many of these were young Gypsy lads and in later years lots of these fellows were shipped to Newfoundland as apprentices to the slave masters and the cod industries. This sort of thing went on in many areas in Dorset over the years such as at Bere Regis under the rich Drax estate as well as the nearby Frampton's, Lees, Welds, and others". The babes and chavvies were tucked up in their beds tonight. It had been a long day and tonight the folk were enjoying the comradeship of the occasion. Along with the evening, the fire, and the starlit night sky. Talk was also of the morrow the illnesses of the clan and the deals done in town, with the bartering of pony sales and at the marketplace. The evening continued likewise but interrupted only occasionally by the occasional sounds of a concertina small piano accordion played by the nimble fingers of one of its members. A local Clapcott lad and the dancing of the Smith Gypsy Gal's. We worked on their farms each year for which they allowed us to park in their farmlands, to camp our tents, wagons, and benders. Some of us bought the land or came to mutual arrangement with the farmer/landowner as a trade for services. Much of these transactions were by a Gentleman agreement, often consisting of no more than a customary handshake between the gentleman farmer and the gentleman Gypsy. So often these strips of land were passed on from one generation of traveller to the next over many decades or even centuries.

The Dorset Canford area boasted not only a strong history with famed smugglers. Such as the likes of Gulliver the landlord living in his Brook Road lodge in Kinson, East Howe just a stone's throw away. Whilst the grand Pelhams house in Millhams Lane in the village itself stood majestically nearby with its spacious gardens and majestic trees and close to the nearby village school and chapel. Along with the 11th century St Andrews church at the end of church lane later to be known as Millham Lane. Where it was oft-times said that smugglers hid their contraband in the church grounds and where a tea smuggler is buried. Alongside so many of our people. Of course, there were others in the Parish where our folk were baptised, wed, and buried including at St Marks in Talbot Wallisdown and in Newtown's St Clements cemetery.

The rich owners of the brickyards throughout the county even got around their common rights by allowing all brick makers workers to employ their own children with the children own father paying their wages. The children would carry heavy wet clay on their heads and were to be seen busy working on every strip of land and worked the same long hours as their fathers. A pusher-out, carry up to two hundred- and seventy-pounds weight of bricks on a one-wheeled spring barrow. Pushing it fifty yards or more. These poor pug-boys frequently suffered from having to carry the lumps of cold wet clay against their chests in damp weather. By the time they reached their teens, they carried or lifted a far heavier load than many of the strongest men during their lives. The young girls who worked with the clay were poorly paid working 12 hours daily. One of their main jobs were to keep the fires fed with coal and often their dresses caught fire which often resulted in their limbs and their hair catching fire. The clay was originally dug out by hand, put on monkey wagons and taken to the end of a wire rope way, which transported the clay buckets to the mixing pans and firing kilns.

It was an all-year job, though in many brickyards in the county bricks were only made during the summer months. As a result of which in these times most of the men were laid off or worked in the local Breweries or a fortunate crew were kept on digging clay which they called "Good diggin" and they would be seen piling it up to "weather" ready for the next summer's brick making. In claiming that the work was healthy. Many of the brick and tile works, where a one-man business with small clamp kilns hillsides were a highly industrialised scene.

These areas were shrouded in smoke from the many types of kilns around where the ground churned into mud by clay extraction and the heavy cart tracks. Most men were proud to be brick makers despite the harsh working conditions for many of them had never known any other life. Often ait was family occupation for generations and they took pride in their craft and would press their thumb print into the brick as evidence that it was handmade.

Initially those employed in brickyards and potteries in the early days had their wages paid inside of the public-houses over a bar-counter. Men would be encouraged to spend their wages there on alcohol and to treat their workmates to a round of drinks. And so consequently one drink led to another. So it was that often both health and wages were wasted. With little or none left it was often in these poor streets, that wives were often seen waiting outside the inns to take their husbands home before all their wages were all spent and to ensure they had sufficient money to pay for rent and food. Some Brickworks provided drinking houses, Inns, public houses and Breweries in close vicinity to the brickyard or pottery. This was also extra income for the rich property-owning class. Pubs were open all day long as brick making and burning was thirsty work. The contrast between these brick making areas and where the middle classes and wealthy landowners lived was evident. With the bricks made used to build their fine houses, grandiose mansions and villas. While those who laboured and created the bricks often +lived in hovels. Often, they spent most of our little leisure time in these Inns. most of our wages too.

Many of the early brick fields were said to be lawless places. Those found to be involved in affrays or physical assaults were dealt with accordingly. With many appearing at the local police station or courts and were subsequently heavily fined, imprisoned or even deported to the new world, some even as slaves. Groups of men were crouched down moulding the clay bricks with their bare hands. There were great movements of people, men women and children using barrows, known as monkey wagons some heaped up high with clay and others with bricks. They were all busy pushing and wheeling the wooden wheelbarrows all to and from backwards and forwards over planking, around the hot burning kins. One could barely breath in such hot humid environment.

Throughout their lifetime many of the Gypsy travellers lived on numerous encampments having moved for many reasons including local employment in the brickyards clay pits or community or finding a partner and settling down. In more recent years a good many Gypsies young men paired off with the local non-Gypsy girls and marriages often took place though some still jumped the traditional broom. Some Gypsy women kept their own surname after they married.

The Gypsy men tethered their horses away from the vans on long tethers to enable them to roam, but not move away too far. Many bands of workers were clustered together on these encampments. Within some Gypsy encampments there were lots of Pigs too, providing a good supply of pork. The workers built large kilns to fire up the tiles and bricks. Which were supplied to local merchants in their fine houses Many Gypsies having little monies to pay fines to the magistrates for their minor offence the Magistrate was the landowner.

Gypsy Travellers despite their wanderlust had been loyal to the country with many actively serving in the armed services through numerous wars and campaigns Gypsies who worked on the farms each year were often allowed to park in their farmlands, to camp their tents, wagons and benders. Some Gypsy travellers bought the land or came to mutual arrangement with the farmer/landowner as a trade for services. Much of these transactions were by a

Gentleman agreement often consisting of no more than a customary handshake between the gentleman farmer and the gentleman Gypsy. So often these strips of land were passed on from one generation of traveller to the next over many decades or even centuries.

Many worked the viaducts, brickyards and claypits using their families' numerous skills in these developing industries with the demand for house building.

Thomas Hardy character in The Return of the Native was called Diggory Venn, the Reddleman. This Victorian travelling salesman made his living by selling reddle or raddle, a red powder widely used by shepherds. Hardy described Venn as 'completely red' with dye covering 'his clothes, the cap upon his head, his boots, his face and his hands'. Long before Hardy's death in 1928, Dorset's Reddleman had been succeeded by the Reddle woman. Mary Ann Bull.

Dorset writer Olive Knott remembered the Reddle woman's visits to Sturminster Newton before the First World War. 'Year after year this woman pitched her tent on the same spot in the grassy lane,' Olive wrote. 'To the children of the neighbourhood, she was wrapt in mystery.

'A fire of sticks usually burned outside her tent. Nearby was her dark brown pony tethered to a four-wheeled open van. Even the van was bright red in colour.' At sheep-dipping time she would peddle her wares, also selling brick dust for cleaning harness.

'Se was said to have a weather-beaten countenance and wore layers of petticoats, which made a good hiding place for her money. 'She trusted her monies to various publicans and collected on the return journey 'Mary Ann smoked a pipe and had a bad temper, like the lurcher that was tied to her cart.

'She knew the value of herbs and prescribed cures for many ailments. 'The Reddle woman was a regular at events such as Shroton Fair and Woodbury Hill Fair, Bere Regis.

She slept under bags and canvas beneath the cart, guarded by the lurcher. The dog took its duties so seriously that when its mistress fell ill at Stourpaine chalk pit, it had to be put down before she could be helped. Mary Ann was taken to Cerne Abbas Union and died on waste ground at Cerne.

CHAPTER THREE

CANFORD DAYS

On Canford Magna road

We drove to Canford Magna road with rhododendrons on the way
the lane was steep and pastures wide
hadn't been there for don't know when
we passed the school where zunner kids did play
and cuckoos chirped each day

Out by the Merley waste about where the houses spread their way
on village life it was quiet then in days of Lady Wimborne's time
where zunners knew their place where toffs were mean and lads were lean
where farmers worked the land whilst bees did buzz
amongst the fuzz

Whilst children played their games down such country lanes
the cottages were declared with thorns of roses red and white
the bricks were red where poets led their dreams into the night

The cottage thatched and tall green grass with narrow lanes to walk
the talk was proud where willows bowed and chestnuts fell to ground
whilst Gypsy crew from here to Poole made flowers fit for shrouds

the meadows sweet with berries to eat and daisies at your feet
where folks did pray and some did say that church is where you'll meet
the school still stands within those grounds and the village sleeps for sure
Saved by the plans of wisdom's man though rabbits run for cover true
far from the shores of Bournemouth core just a journey up from Poole

The birds do sing there from winters to spring and summers play the tune
where the Canford Lady did live and heart did give to bless the peoples core
the likes of her we'll see no more

Yet the village speaks its all
the Dorset bricks and common tricks of poets steeped in grace
cannot explain the heritage fame of Guests that once did preach
the rights of man to understand the beauty of this place

Ray Wills

Gypsy days and night

Working at the forge with Reuben and George
sitting around the yog got my handle and my cards
telling tales of long ago says and wonders drinking slo
chavvies and babe's tales of olden time slaves
kingdom and little Egypt home
royal blood horses cobs n Shetland prime
forest days shows and fairs

The carousel turns and the jukey plays
blue skies and starry nights
wind of change fortunes told, and fine wreaths made
flower girls and cousin Mary's dance
lots of mushes and evil eyes

New England, Heather lands and old gals wise
Kings and Queens, tins and pans
sing us another song Gypsy man

Ray Wills

The Gypsy Encampments of the Comments

In the woodlands and forest of England, they tethered their mare's
they worked on the land from craft to repair's
they lit of the fires from bracken and log
where the wind it was brisk and the snow it was deep round the yog

They bedded in bender's where hogs once did sleep
their gown's they were long and their shawl's they were wool from the sheep
where the chaffinch did sing, and the man sang the blue's

For year's they did roam from Boldre to Poole
where the vardo's did roll and the weather was cruel
though summers were warm beneath the starry blue skies
where the birch grew so wild, and the heathers and grasses were rye
Their fathers were blessed with the call of the free
where the forests were rich from the village to the sea
their children were many and their old un's were wise
they worked on the land with hope in their eye's

The wheel's they did roll, and the ponies ran free
where Rufus stone stood there amidst the villager's plea's
the bracken was course and the berries were sweet
with lizard's and snake's squirmed just beneath of your feet

They gathered their families and took them to Poole
where the lodge hills of Canford were rich in the dew
where the rabbit's and foxes ran free on the down's

where gaffer's and landlords were rich by the crown

They settled so freely on the Wimborne's estate
where the Guest family resided and the turfs were to waste
they built them their home's there beneath the warbler's nest's
where the gravel was rich and the clay it was blessed

From Talbot to Magna and over the down's
they gathered their families, and all bedded down
in Kinson's New England and Heavenly Bottom's abode
they ran with the wind in the summer's so warm and the winters so cold
All through the war year's they travelled this land
from south to the north with their merry band's
they were branded and moved on like thieves in the night
with landlord's and mean men who took of their right's

They fought in the wars like true British grit
worked on the land and the factories shift's
they built the great walls with viaduct's and brickyard's so tall and mean
then they were herded like cattle and grounded in team's

Their stories are rich, and their histories are keen
from the New Forest walks to the home of the Queen
they talk with a richness and will give you the eye
like a true Romani trooper with a didykoy guise.

Ray Wills

In Kinson at the rear of the St Andrews church was a small estuary of the river Stour which sported a wooden bridge used by the many visitors to the Canford Magna's, the lodge home of the aristocratic Lord and lady Cornelia of Wimborne's Guest family.

In 1846, Sir John Josiah and Lady Charlotte bought the Canford manor estate near Poole where they entertained leading members of society, politicians, aristocrats and royalty in house parties, shooting parties, political fetes and horticultural shows. Lady Cornelia Churchill Married Ivor Bertie Guest, Ist baron Wimborne of Canford Magna. When Cornelia died in 1927 the Poole and Dorset Herald wrote "She was considered one of the most beautiful women of her day and her charming manner impressed all who came into contact with her." The Guest family had strong links to the royal family and the Churchill dynasty.

Canford in the very early days covered some 83,0000 acres of common land which covered much of southern England. They were themselves members of the upper-class aristocracy with strong links to the royal family and the Churchill dynasty. Lady Cornelia Henrietta Maria Spencer-Churchill was born on 17th September 1847. She was the daughter of John Winston Spencer-Churchill, 7th Duke of Marlborough and Lady Frances Anne Emily Vane. She married Ivor Bertie Guest, Ist baron Wimborne of Canford Magna, son of Sir Josiah John Guest, and lady Charlotte Elizabeth Bertie. Lady Cornelia was invested as an Officer, order of the British Empire. She was a leading evangelical in the country being a great Philanthropist and champion of education. She advocated charitable social improvements and continued all the many projects started by her mother-in-law besides initiating many of her own. Lady Charlotte had decided to improve the living conditions of Canford tenants the working poor These were spread out throughout the Kinson parish of Poole and Bournemouth. by building 111 cottages in a rustic gothic design to the very latest standards. These 'Lady Wimborne cottages' were eventually built, mainly during Lady Cornelia's regime, and many of them can still be seen today all over the former Canford estate. Lady Wimborne continued the philanthropic project until 1904. The Guests also sponsored the building of schools at Hampreston, Hamworthy and

Broadstone in the same distinctive gothic style as the cottages and gave generously towards the founding of churches in Parkstone and Broadstone and offered land for sale at low prices. Lord and Lady Wimborne's donated acres of land on the shores of Parkstone Bay for the creation of Poole Park. Lady Wimborne will perhaps be best remembered for her creation of the Ladies walking fields at Poole as a gift to the Poole people. Along with her philanthropist ideals particularly her support of the local Gypsy community who had their many encampments on her land. The Canford Manor was sold in 1923 and became Canford School.

For many years Gypsies had Lady Wimborne's permission to live on the heath of Canford. Until it all came to an end when Poole council bought some of the land in 1954 and sold it to developers with the proviso that the housing plots would have restricted prices for private sale to resolve the problem of a shortage of housing in the borough.

My grandfather Reg Rogers knew Lady Wimborne well and bought land from her to build his property on the Mannings heathlands after renting from her the delightful Heather view cottage on the Mannings heath road at Alderney.

Within this vast parish of Kinson itself it covered a wide land area mass including the Kinson village itself. As well as many miles covering the districts of Parkstone, Newtown, Branksome, Oakdale and Poole.

At earlier times Poole ships had embarked nearly as many migrants to Newfoundland as its own total population. As a result, it is said that there is a community in north American in Michigan where the common dialect is still the Dorset dialect so well aired by the likes of Dorset poet and Dorchester Mayor William Barnes.

The merchants of Poole founded whole dynasties, which through inter marriage and alliance, formed an elite group, and became known as the "merchant princes" of Poole. Olive Knott described this very well: *"Recruits for the [Newfoundland] fishing trade were drawn from many villages and small towns in the area. Agricultural work was badly paid and scarce, so that there was no lack of volunteers for this arduous but more highly profitable occupation". "They went usually for one winter and two summers to Newfoundland where they fished extensively for cod and other fish, salted and packed it".*

THE LADY WIMBORNE BRIDGE RINGWOOD ROAD
ALDERNEY

Another major employer was Warboys in Parkstone which operated from 1884.

CHAPTER FOUR

DAYS OF GYPSY LORE

The days of Gypsy lore

Those were the days of Gypsy lore no idle hands to feed the poor
there were stopping places here n there making bricks mending rocking chairs
days and nights November there were ole Poole fair lots of chavvies nippers all went there
were folks who knew you with quirky names the Kings n Castles, Lees and James
quirky places uncle toms on the commons we got along
up on hill on Wally Wack in the benders, vardos, tents n sacks
cuckoo bottom and Corfe Mullen ridge, heavenly bottom, Rogers Sid's.
crooks and tally's deals and more, Wally Cave, Johnny Turner, Ronnie Moore,

Freddie Mills the boxing ring.
Ted Sherwood and Charlie King
up at Sea view and down the Poole Lane
to the pub shoulder of mutton
with the family James.

Reg Rogers, he did make the bricks
with Brixey's and Mabey's and the dam little midge
Lady Wimborne and her cottages and bridge

run and roll of the dice and flower gals in the square
Augustus John, Grace Clapcott too,
Emily Fancy and ladies bare
those were the days of long time past
when dreams were made, and curse was cast

When Gypsy travellers roamed the lanes
of old lodge hills and the Stours pane
where Longham bridge did mighty roar
and the saw pits Rossmoor
and the brickyard chimneys soared high
where once rabbits ran free and foxes too
from all Canford Magna and across to Waterloo

Ray Wills

BRICK MAKERS OF OLD POOLE TOWN

There were scores of Inns in old Poole town
where brIcks ere made for king and crown
with yards and breweries and potteries too
they made a fortune for the lords of Poole

The brick makers and potters worked from dawn to dusk
to gain a living earn a crust
they worked the kilns and brickyards hot
fathers mothers the children the lot
their wages paid in inn retreats and lodge
they drank the liquor and the laws did dodge
for the clay was hot the heavy loads
the kilns were many and the sweat they groaned

There were scores of inns in old Poole town
fancy dames in fancy gowns
coppers caught the drunken slobs
they put them in the clinks and money robbed
gypsy brick makers and local yobs
the brick they made the Bournemouth town
the landed gentry estates and their London city homes
the gypsies slept upon the common lands and downs
some in the brickyards out of town

In the autumn they worked the fairground booths and stalls
pugilist fighters strong men daredevil riders and pretty girls
the old gal went dunkerrin fortune telling skills
from fairground frolics to canfords lodge hills

lavender and heather flowers and herbs to save
the health of the nation
home of the brave

Ray Wills

When I was a small boy on the Mannings. We visited another smallholding, across the extensive Canford estate at Waterloo to buy the giant big and ugly pig a boar that we named, 'Waterloo George'. George was very big fat and ferocious with big buck teeth. My uncle Bill refused to go into his pig sty to muck him out. But I went in with a stiff hard broom to show this "Waterloo George" who was the boss. At another time we walked over the common with the dogs and brought home a new nanny goat which grandad had bought from one of his many lady friends. The nanny goat wore a collar and was on a long heavy metal chain. When we all reached the Old Wareham Road bus stop on our way home, we all caught a double-decker bus home with our three dogs and the goat. We all clambered up to the top floor of the bus with the goat on her long heavy metal chain and our dogs. Much to the amusement of the passengers and the bus conductor. Something that one could not so easily do in our present society.

As I grew up, I once again rediscovered my Gypsy ancestral heritage. For my earliest memories of childhood, brought back to me that I was fortunate to have lived and grown up within a community setting of Gypsy encampments. Newtown then was such a setting a unique community in many ways unlike any other. For here were hordes of Gypsy families who had lived on their many encampments on the commons for centuries. All of these encampments had quirky names. In my early childhood there were many Gypsy families roaming the commons with their Vardos wagon's, horses and dog pack's. Their encampments were scattered everywhere throughout the terrain right up to to Canford Magna where Lady Wimborne had her Manor. I spent much time amongst them all and watched as they caught hedgehogs which they called hotchi. They took the hedgehogs from out amongst the dead leaves or dry grasses in the bushes. Then they killed them by uncurling them and smashing their nose with a stick. Then their sharp prickles were burnt off, before they were covered with wet clay. Before being placed in the hot ashes of the yog fire then cooked. I loved eating them, to me they tasted like pork sort of similar to chicken.

I watched as the Gypsy travellers created their bender homes. They always chose the best young branches of hazel. Some of these benders were so high you could stand in them. The doors were of sacking, and they sometimes used old army blankets as coverings or else tarpaulin as they were waterproof. These benders were always very warm and comfortable inside. Gypsy travellers created benders so high you could stand in them. The doors were of sacking, they sometimes used old army blankets as coverings as they were waterproof or else they used tarpaulin. These benders were always very warm and comfortable inside. The Old Wareham Road was just a track then in 1950s just before they built a Council estate at nearby Tower Park and West Howe.

Arne Avenue

Arne Avenue seems to have been an area where Gypsy Travellers lived in these familiar while terrace houses. Yet many still preferred to live in their vardos in their front gardens. It gained the unfortunate slang name of Cackers Canyon.

Papa Benedetto organ grinder of Arne Avenue was an Italian Immigrant who had emigrated to the UK in 1952 and had fought for the U.K in the First World War. In the warm summer months of the year, he would often be seen strolling down Arne Avenue, Parkstone, Poole. Carrying on his shoulder his hand operated Barrow Organ. As soon as all the local kids saw him come down the road, they would all sit on the path with their feet in the road to listen to him play. With his Dancing Monkey perched on his shoulder and who would dance to whatever Papa played. After around 10 minutes Papa would stop playing and the children would drop pennies into his tin. He was probably the Gypsy whose favourite spot was on Ashley Road Parkstone Poole Dorset. Which may account for where in later years outside the building there the conservative club which was called the monkey house.

The Monkeys hump encampment also may have got its name from these Italians who lived in Arne Avenue/Herbert Avenue prisoner of war house. Or from the carts which carried the bricks and clay were called monkey's cart. All the Many of these local accordion and organ grinders musicians usually were Italian immigrants, who played what was known as a barrel or street organ. It was a lot like a player piano, in that a paper cylinder with punches inserted into the box told the organ pipes what notes to play. The musician simply turned the crank on the side, which also operated a bellows that pumped air through the organ's pipes. Bigger street organs needed a cart, but there were also smaller wearable versions. Street organs started out as the musical accompaniment for puppet theatres in Italy. But eventually, itinerant Italian street musicians took them to other parts of Europe and to England. They eventually started using monkeys who would scamper around and collect change from the audience. The organ grinder would set up on a street corner, wearing his instrument on a strap over his shoulder, and then support its weight with a stick while he played. Meanwhile, the monkey, tethered to a leash, would scamper around with a tin cup, collecting change. Audiences were dependable, and "the organ man always knew what the monkey would bring back," Organ grinders and their animals provided entertainment to people who were too poor to afford to go to music halls or purchase phonographs. It was true, though, that the monkeys and their owners got into scrapes. Organ grinders spread their news in songs Singing popular songs of the times in later more recent years the 50s they sang the current pop songs like Mack the knife, Frankie and Johnnie or singing the blues. Children loved to see them.

Sugar knob Mountain

At Sugar Knob Mountain
by monkey's hump lane
The Gypsies kept goats on long iron chains
In Cinders Town near Frying pan
the chavvies danced where rabbits ran

Gypsies came to Wally Wack above High Moor
local folks had never seen their likes before.
Their caravans vardos n wagons were decked with the finest of lace
With polished glass n lamps for to show your face

There were so many Gypsies camps
folks did say they travelled from over France.
Hemley bottom was the home of the fairground Kings.
There were Sherwood's and Whites remembering.

At Bribery Island folks did vote for Lady's boy
for to keep their homes n keep their quotes
For Lady Guest did free rent them out
to local lads to pay for their digger shag and baccy snout

They say there were upper class Gypsies
that lived in Wolsey Road.
Yet the chavvies spinning tops were busy
that side of the road.

The rag n bone Man Horace Cooper came
with wagon and heavy loads.
At least there the stories he to me told.

Ray Wills

Sugar Knob Mountain encampment

The camp was on a hill north of Gwyne Road by Wharfdale road. Goats were kept here on long chains, and it was a favourite playground for local kids who built ingenious camps and tunnels underground in its sandy soil.

The new migration work force came to upper parkstone. These included the large influx of Irish navies who built major road works and the railways and viaducks at Branksome. Which added to the already growth of brickyards, potteries, kilns and estates. They looked so different from the locals. With their familiar thick coats and corduroy trousers tied with thongs beneath the knees and cloth caps slanting over one ear. They would integrate and marry into the local community such as at Newtown and Ashley Road Parkstone Branksome which was known by locals as "up on hill".

Heather lands encampment

Major White 1869-1958 dealer March 15th, 1897, at Heather lands Kinson was the Son of James White and Selvy White 1881 Of Heather land Village. He was Married aged 28 to Venus Ayres - Born 1871 at Kinson. His death 25thn 1958 Burial Place: Heather lands Parkstone. Elderion White, Samuel White 10 yrs, Elizabeth White 8 yrs. 1911 They lived there, and Daisy White was christened. Major White was for many years a popular quarryman in the Purbeck region.

The Gypsy Travellers were permitted to live on the Canford heath with the full consent of Lady Wimborne. Over the years hundreds of families lived here within the Kinson parish.

Principle Gypsy Travelling families in the early Kinson parish including Newtown included the following … Arnold's, Ayres, Allen's, Baileys, Bungay's, Burtons, Barnes, Barneys, Bartletts, Benham's, Bennett's, Bests, Biddle's, Bonds, Bonsais, Brixey's, Brewers, Budden, Buttons, Castles, Coft, Chapmans, Chaton's, Cherretts, Clarks, Coles, Coopers, Copes, Crutchers, Crockers, Does, Darts, Domoney's, Everetts, Farms, Fancy, Fairplay, Fishers,

Frankham, Fudge, Gales, Gentleys, Gibbs, Goulds, Green, Gladwinfields, Gillingham's, Hoare, Hobgood's, Hankins. Hughes, Hurdles, Halls, Hanford's, Hayler's, Hibbard's, Hillman, Hills, Hopes, Hodges, James, Jeff's, Johnston's, Kerls, Kutchers, Kings, Keets, Lamb, Lees, Loveridge, Lovells, Lights, Mabey's, Macartney's, White Manley's, Mills, Millers, Mitchell's, Munden's, Moorcroft's, Novell's, Nippard's, Orchards, Penfolds, Phillips, Pidgley, Proudly, Raggett, Rabbits, Randell's, Ridgeley's, Rogers, Rose, Rowneys, Scott's, Saunders, Scarrots, Sellers, Sherwood's, Skinners. Smalls, Scott's, Smiths, Sheen, Squires, Thomas, Stacey's, Stanley's, Squires, Tocks, Trent's, Turners, Tuckers, Waltons, Walls, Wells, Wallburton, Whallers, Whites, Willetts, Williams, Woods, Warrens, Whalley's, Whites.

Brick making was a major industry in Dorset for well over 2 centuries and was at its peak in the 1800s, with well more than 200 brickyards in the county at one time. These provided regular employment for the local population many of whom were Gypsy Traveller families. The 1841 census of Canford shows these were many brick makers mainly Lees, Francis, Henry, James and Thomas, John Cherrett, William henry Fancy, Lockyer, Masterman and Shoreland's who were mainly women.

In 1830 one third of the pottery in England was made in Poole clay. Gypsy brick makers families included Hibberds, Leggs, Buddens, Cherretts, Wares, James and Lees. There were stone masons such as Drapers at sea view and also blacksmiths. China clay was transported by horse and carts, mined by miners underground and weighed on a weighbridge. The clay wagons were put on the railways and it went to Stoke.In 1854 the Kinson clay fields and Fired pottery Company was established. Orders were dispatched by horse and cart from the potteries to Poole Quay by barge to London. Or Southampton, across the Atlantic to Quebec or Montreal, by raft or barge up the St. Lawrence river to York(present day Toronto), by railway to Collingwood harbour, by raft along the southern shores to Nottawasaga Bay to the beach nearest the site and by hand the rest of the way. George Jennings owned a 70 acre plot at Ashley Cross and supplied the sanitation at the Great Exhibition at Crystal Palace in London where 800,000 people paid a penny to use his 'monkey closets' (hence the first use of the phrase 'to spend a penny').

In the vast wide Kinson Parish area, its brickyards and potteries were thriving throughout that time on Canford in the 1800s. The Kings and Castles were basket makers and knife grinders and were often seen at Epsom Downs. The Castles forebearers were originally fairground swing boat people too from Hitchen in Hertfordshire and in Surrey. They specialised in the swing boats rides at many fairgrounds before settling down in Poole and they are also related.

There was a total of over 2,400 of known kiln sites in S. E Dorset before the establishment of the current joint conurbations of Poole, Bournemouth, Wimborne, Christchurch etc. It expanded into much larger industrial Quarries and Brickworks. Coinciding with the gradual rebuffing of the Travelling Brick makers who had established the campsites in the area. Who unfortunately soon discovered that in the face of this competition - they were no longer welcome in the area.

Sites of Clay Workings Prior to 1939

Site	Owners/Makers	Date
Cuckoo Road	Not Known	C18-194
Fancy Road	H C Brixey	1905-27
Fancy Road	S G Ward	1927-62
Wool Road	C Rogers	c1927
Mannings Heath Road	(Old) Alderney Brickworks S D Ballam	1903-35
Mannings Heath Road	Rogers Bros, Omnium Mfrs Ltd	1927-55
Mannings Heath/Broom Rd	Alderney Brickworks (Rogers Bros) Dorset Brick & Tile Co	1919-57
Old Wareham Road	Perfumed Pottery & Tile Works, Brixey & Champion	1927-37
Foxholes/Haymoor Road	Not Known	C18-19(
Foxholes/Hythe Road	J Maidment	1923-27
Foxholes/Hamble Road	W L Ballam	1907-62
Foxholes/Dunstans Lane	Victoria Brickworks, D Ballam	1907-62
		c1887

The working of clay pits in the region was immense.

Christopher Scott wrote the following on a facebook page:

Way back in the early 70s when I was honing my skills as a photographer, I went to Cuckoo Bottom to do some various shots of the moorland, I was very close to the gypsy encampment and very soon became aware that I was being watched by some of the gypsies, some of which became quite hostile to my presence, not wanting to make waves I struck up a conversation with them and it appeared that they thought that I was from the Council, when I explained that I was nothing to do with the Council, just an ordinary guy looking to better my skills they quickly became very friendly and invited me to join them for a cup of tea and a chat which I happily accepted. Being gypsies I was a bit uneasy about their hygiene, I really didn't need to worry, whilst we all sat around a camp fire I was served the best cup of tea that I have ever had in the most beautiful and immaculately clean China cup and saucer, to say I was shocked would be an understatement, you hear so many things about gypsies, yes they were poorly dressed, yes they looked like they could all do with a good bath, but oh my goodness, I enjoyed a wonderful couple of hours with these very hospitable people, when I left I thanked them sincerely for their hospitality and no I didn't get any photos of any of them, they are very private people and I respect that. Incidentally I was born and raised very close to Heavenly Bottom. I became a full time self employed professional photographer eventually, and enjoyed many years in the profession before retiring.

Bribery island encampment

This was a gathering of smallholdings situated by the gas works and owned by Lady Wimborne. Tenants lived there on the understanding only if they voted for Lady Wimborne's son in the local elections. The earliest brick works in the area were here around 1755. The first pit was established later in 1852 and the Bourne Valley Potteries 1853. There was a great demand for bricks in those days for the building of the massive viaducts at Branksome along with new roads and bridges for the new southern railways. Nearby Bournemouth was also rapidly growing, and many houses and trades people were in high demand hence the growth of such heavy labour industries in the area. Clay pits, brickyards and quarries were springing up everyone, in an area so rich in sand, lime, gravel, stone and peat. Many of these new industries were self-financed and developed by local families like my great grandmother Emily Elizabeth (Fancy)Rogers financed and developed the family brickyards the Albion Brick Company and Alderney Brickworks which her sons managed from her humble beginning with one pig!! Many local families had their own smallholding farm in those days.

The Seaview Donkey encampment

This encampment was close to the sea view wooded area.

The Cinders Town encampment

It was so named due to its group of breeze block bungalows. it was situated close to Southall and Churchill roads and the top of hill up to Rossmore Road.

The Witteys wood yard encampment

This site was situated opposite the football ground on Ashley Road and to the left of the old police station.

The Frying pan encampment

This encampment was situated in a dip south of Herbert Avenue by Rossmore sawmills near to Bourne valley centre. Wheatley road.

The Veldt encampment

The encampment was situated next to Wroxham Road and Cromer Road north of Sharp Jones.

Monkeys hump encampment

Monkeys Hump ran from Stafield road/Southill roads to the Rossmore sawmills. It was on the site of the present New Inn. It was at one time home to a large group of Italians. Many of whom assisted with the demand for house building after the war years. They also lived at Arne Avenue others were housed in the Italian prisoner of war camp by Herbert Avenue. Some were street musicians barrel organ grinders with miniature monkeys often perched on their shoulder. They were known to be lovers of miniature monkeys, and many were organ grinders with monkeys and played music with the monkeys often perched on their shoulder. Many of these were Italian immigrants. The wagons which carried the clay and bricks at the brick works and clay pits were called monkey wagons. This and the monkeys in the area may account for the name of the encampment.

Alder hills commons encampment

This encampment was close to where Sainsburys is now.

Wheelers Lane Encampment

This encampment was situated to the left of Bere cross. Families living here included the Sherwood's, Bonsais and Coopers. Jack & Jill Sherwood later ran a garage in Rosemary Rd Newtown. Many local families worked in the factories in the area at Wallisdown and in the many brickyards and clay pits which had been around for very many years.

Sandy lane encampment

There was a popular encampment in the late 1950s at Sandy Lane Red hill common it was based in a gravel pit and managed by a Mr Luther. There were many horses within this camp.

Gypsy women gathered outside Woolworths in Poole high street on a regular basis. Often the women were to be seen sitting on the van step's smoking their clay pipe's.

Alton Milstead, Binstead and Horton heath encampments

Many Travellers who made Kinson their home, still returned every year to these popular stopping places and the West Moors Common for the hopping and strawberry and pea-picking.

On Saturday nights local Gypsies visited Poole pubs The Jolly Sailor, Lord Nelson and the Crown. Often challenging the dockers from the pub to join them outside in a fight to see who the best man was. Usually, a great crowd gathered watching these unofficial bare-knuckle fights. Often the fighters had drunk a great deal of alcohol at the time, so the fights did not last very long with both men usually too drunk and dazed to finish with no serious injuries.

CHAPTER FIVE

NEWTOWN

Newtown days

I remember New Town when I was just a kid
sherbet dabs after breakfast with liquorice on the lid
I remember the old school bell the playground where we played
the days seemed cold and long then in my childhood days

I remember the sea view that walk upon the hill
with coney's falling to the ground and squirrels a running still
I recall the little church with bell that rang each morn
the number 8 school bus and picnics on the lawn

I recall those simple days with dobbin on the heath
the walks across to Waterloo and the wide commons where we cut
our teeth
old Sankey ward the clay pits man and old Buller Archer too
where Bill knotty built his caravans next to Trent's cars too

Those rides up to the regal we called up on hill
the old brown Rossmore flyer bus I hear its running still
the old shoulder of mutton pub where only few could stand
the Albion where they played shove halfpenny when life was
simply grand

The kids all played at conkers then and most were diddy kye
I ran around upon the heaths or at the fairgrounds shies
where the Gypsies roamed the heaths so free and spun a tale or
two
I chased the gals around a lot and tied my laces too

Some kids went to salvation hall to see Nativity's
I spent nights with granfer Reg inside Hamworthy engineering
sites
we ate bread n cheese and chased with dogs
a ferriting on the run
with strings of rabbits all in line up afore the sun

The school truant man was Waterman he rode a bike with bell
you could see him coming down the lane like a dam foul smell
the roads were quieter those days and there was no TV
the gals picked flowers on the heath and we had bread n jelly for
our tea

Some kids played flick cards every day or marbles on the mac
you could buy sweets for just half pence or take a high rise slide
the trees were tall and fine those days and we could climb them
true
there was no silly strangers then and no foolish health and safety
rules

Ray Wills

BEFORE THE HOUSES

From Bourne Valley bottom and along the dirt track
the caravans rumbled to Lodge hills and back
though thick hedges laden full of bramble and gorse
with lovely chestnuts to nibble by our little horse
there at Coy meadows we drank from the stream
little fresh springs and wonders to dream

There were Gypsies at Beales in Bournemouth today
so, we tell you your fortune then be on our way
the village kids saw us, and they gave us the eye
in our caravans' homes which smoked right up to the sky

With rabbits to ferret and hedgehogs to eat
With songs around the campfire and family to greet
the wheels rolled their daily whilst the stars shone at night
there were folks in their glory with clothes to delight

There was food on the table and rugs on the floor
the candles n lamps lit with designs on the doors
Whilst the music was played with accordion Joe
whilst the songs that we sung were older than dough

There were times which were hard then and folks they did stray
But we were far wiser than many today
the grass grew so course and the daisies were spread
like creation was labelled for the good and the dead

The Queen of the Gypsies was dark and so rare
she had braided long hair and spent nights at Poole fair

the wagons were rich and the lamps they were gold
whilst the little chavs all danced naked upon their tip toes
the chaffinches sung at the break of the day
as we ambled along our stories to say

Now there's just tarmac on Tower Park ridge
where there was once magic with our uncle Sid
For we lived on the heaths then when the land it was free
Before Lord Wimborne sold it to Poole for houses for thee

Ray Wills

WITHIN THE GYPSY'S ARMS

Her dress it was of scarlet red
and her eyes were so sea blue
she lived upon the heather lands
not far from ole sea view

Her sisters were of the meadow lands
and her brothers were raised upon the fells
her voice was like the birds at dawn
though her heart was so forlorn

She loved him like no other then
he took her breath away
she lost him to her heart and soul
and then he rode away

She met him on the Ferris wheel
for fairgrounds were their life
the swish backs and the bumper cars
the swing boats and the rides

The shooting galleries with their little ducks
all the stars that lit the skies
but she lost him to the pretty girls
and the fortune telling kind

He took her in his arms that day
he promised her the world
then loved her in the deepest woods
he said he was so misunderstood

it was then he rode away

She wore the look of love that day
she wore the look of pain
the sky was dark and fearsome
and the clouds were full of rain

The crows were in their nests that night
she took herself to mourning then
put way her bright red dress

She lost her soul and lover then
within the Gypsys arms
as he rode away to freedom
with all his Gypsy charms

Ray Wills

There were many Gypsies involved locally in brick making. George Lees had gravel pits in Newtown, George Hibberd was a brick maker of Newtown, Charles Rogers at Newtown. Gypsy brick makers. included the Fancy and Rogers, Hibberds, Leggs, Budden's Cherretts, Wares, James, and Lees. ST Clements church Newtown.

The local Gorja people of the Newtown Parkstone area were very tolerant, friendly, and approachable people. There was no racial prejudice then and no interference. Their neighbours were the Arnold's, Dunnings, Martins, Clapcotts and Becks. Also living here was John Henry Walton known as Jack who was a circus bareback rider.

The Heavenly Bottom encampment

The Heavenly Bottom encampment was probably the best-known Gypsy encampment of all those in the area. It was situated in the dip the natural valley at bottom of Albert Rd across Churchill and up to Victoria, roughly. Beresford Road. The following folks lived here. This was a Beresford Road Gypsy encampment which operated from the late 1800s.

G Webb a local man recalled when he first saw Gypsies, as a small boy living on the west side of Bournemouth just at the end of the first World War 1914-1918 discovered the spot in Parkstone where they lived. Where they pitched their tents and wagons. He was out walking on the heath with his mother. There were at least 5 or perhaps seven caravans. To him they seemed enormous of vast proportions. Each one led by a man and a big horse, whilst horses were not rare during those years. The man who leads the caravans had a startling effect on him. The man was very dark with jet black hair He wore a felt hat and his clothes jacket and trousers were all black, He was much different from those men he often saw on the Poole Quay. For he wore a bright yellow neckerchief. All the men in the group of Gypsies were dressed similarly. Whilst one of the older women amongst the group wore what looked like a big, coloured handkerchief on her head. Her hair was white, and her face lined and wrinkled. Stranger was the short clay pipe clamped firmly within her jaws. He was told by his mother that these were Gypsies who lived in those houses on wheels. Rows of bungalows now engulf the area, but then it was just a barren spot on the edge of the heath. By a rutted gravel road. Then it was spoken of with bated breath as being "Heavenly Bottom" the place where the Gypsies live. There were usually several caravans there some of them were very fine indeed. They were painted out in all kinds of bright colours, reds, blues, greens, and yellows. All were embellished with a wealth of fine carvings. A little stream, tributary of Bournemouth Bourne ran past the site which supplied the camp with water.

Families and their prominent members living at Heavenly bottom encampment included Emma Saunders, the James family, Benny Colemans and the Hopes family. Some of them were immaculately dressed the men wearing diamond rings, diamond tie pins and gold watch chains hanging from their waistcoats. Some the women wore gold sovereigns on chains about their necks along with five-pound coins as brooches and bag.

Among families living here over the years included Arnolds, Ayres, Barneys, Bartletts, Benham's, Blick's, Bungay's, Burtons, Budden's, Bradley's, Carters, Chapman's, Cherretts, Crouchers, Coles, Coopers, Corbin's, Fancy's, Farms, Frankham's, Fudges, Gales, Gibbs Gales, Gentle's, Hurdles, Hillmans, Hopes, Hurdles,

Hughes, Janes, James, Kings, Macartney's, Manley's, Matthews, Munden's, Nippards, Randell's, Saunders, Sweetapple's, Stanleys, Smiths, Turners, Wall's, Warburtons, Whallers, Whalley's, Whites and Williams.

There was Samuel and Elizabeth Stanley and family, William and Mary Ann Stanley, William and Mary Saunders and family, Caroline Saunders and family, Edward and Emily Hughes and family, William and Selby James and family, James and Sarah James and family, Sampson and Phobe Stanley and family, Sampson and Kate James and family. William and Passions Frankham and family, William Manley and family, Ben and Annie Benham and family, Thomas and Pavie Frankham and family, Brittania James and Family.

In the 1908 census around 50 Gypsy families were living there. Families were much larger in those days with up to 15 children, parents and grandparents. This site could well have over 400 members present there at any one time.

Joe Fudge was born at Heavenly Bottom before he moved to Monkey's Hump. In later years he was an Estate Agent and preacher.

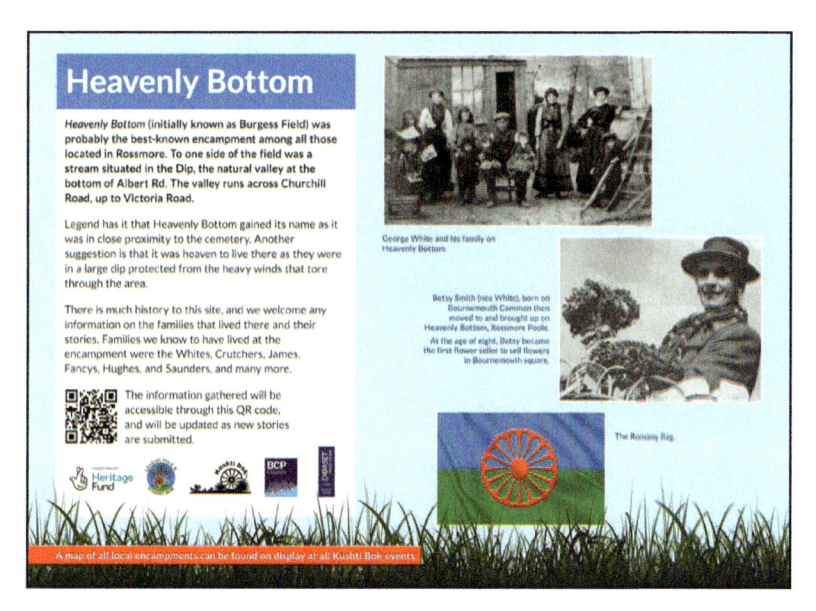

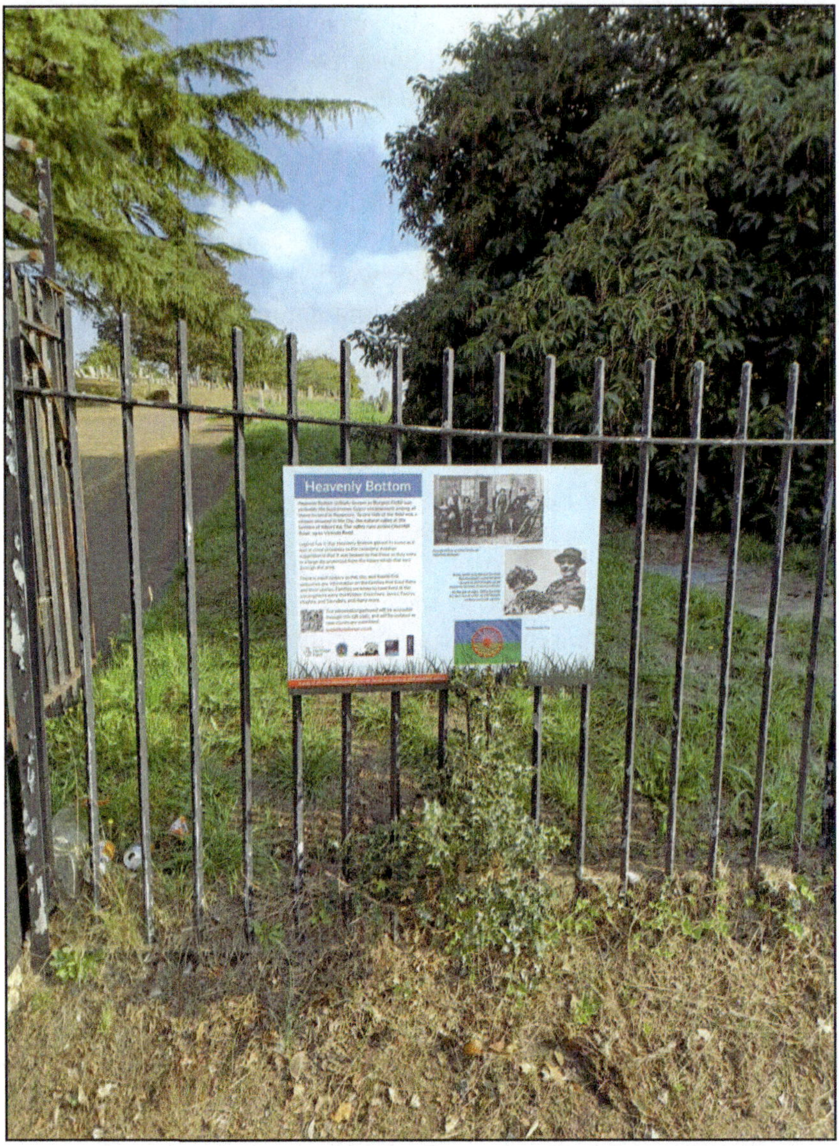
Heavenly Bottom

In recent years I met up with the late Jean Hope Matthews at West howe library in Kinson where I was giving a talk. Jean and I had a lovely chat, and she told me all about her childhood at the Heavenly bottom campsite. She told me that although she had been born in the family vardo by Christchurch railway station. Jean said. "We moved to Heavenly Bottom from the top of Churchill Road which was a place where the fair was held". "I can remember going around the fairground during the day with my brothers Peter and Freddie Carter this fairground was our playground." "We left there later for Heavenly Bottom which was known also as Burgess Field." "To one side of the field was a stream that ran through it. Where many a bucket was filled for various purposes." "At the bottom of the field there was a sawmill or wood yard"." I remember visiting with my mother's cousin Emma Hughes, nee Saunders" she said.

The Turners and Coopers families turned up each year assisting on the Shaftesbury estate. Mugos they pulled up by hand and hoed.

A regular here on Heavenly bottom was Major White Married M 42 1869 General Dealer, Emily Wife Married 14 years F 30 1881 Southampton, Rose Daughter 11 1900 Southampton, Silby Daughter 9 1902 Southampton Elizabeth Daughter F 6 1905 Southampton, Daisy Daughter (2 Months) 1911 Branksome RG number: RG14 Piece:12273 Reference: RG14PN12273 RG78PN694 RD261 SD1 ED10 SN165 Registration District: Poole Sub District: Canford Enumeration District:10 Parish: Poole

Address: Gipsy Camp Beresford Road County: Dorsetshire

Looks like the same family in 1901 with a wonderful address

Major White Married M 38 1863 Traveller Gipsy

Winchester Hampshire, Emily Wife Married F 25 1876

Basingstoke Hampshire, Rosie May Daughter Single F 1 1900

Andover Hampshire Piece:1978 Folio: 65 Page: 33 Registration District: Poole Civil Parish: Branksome Municipal Borough:

Address: Heavenly Bottom, Branksome County: Dorsetshire.

Major White lived with his wife Emma and daughter Elsie whose husband Leonard Sherwood fought in the war and was killed in Arnhem. Major would be seen siting on a log in their front garden chopping up wood then putting logs he would put them in an old pram and go selling them door to door. When he first moved into the bungalow he erected his tent in the front room. In the summer Emma would sit on the kerb smoking her clay pipe. Augustus John painted two of the James sisters as well as Rosie White. She was very dark skinned with hair as black as a raven. John wrote "I had made an acquittance with a family of Whites. Major White was an acentric but friendly character and was never seen without a red waistcoat, a family heirloom to judge by its quality. Rowley and his elder daughter had formed an attachment. She was dark handsome girl. Her red headed sister was also attractive but in a more robust style".

Navvy labouring gangs arrived in the upper Parkstone Branksome area and were quickly identified with their familiar thick coats and corduroy trousers tied with thongs beneath the knees and their cloth caps slanting over one ear. These men soon integrated and marred into the local community. Many moved to live in the developing Newtown and up on hill area of Parkstone which was built to accommodate them with their new families. There were now new craftsmen aside from the former agricultural workers and farm labourers. Such as brick makers, potters etc with new skills who worked n developed the new clay works, brickyards the railway station and viaducts at Branksome and potteries.

The Newtown St Clements Traveller church

In the heart of Newtown itself St Clements Gypsy family church. Its building was financed by Lord Wimborne. Gypsies were baptised, married, and buried in the local church cemeteries at St Andrews Kinson, St Marks Wallisdown, St Clements, and St Huberts Corfe Mullen. The St Clements church in Newtown was known as the Gypsy family church.

> Sacred
> TO THE MEMORY OF OUR BELOVED MEN
> OF THIS PARISH
> WHO DIED FOR THEIR COUNTRY AND FOR US
> IN THE EUROPEAN WAR 1915
>
> Pte HENRY CHARLES HOPKINS
> 1st cl. Stoker WILLIAM HENRY MEDLAND
> Pte WILLIAM MAURICE READHEAD
> Sergt. FREDERICK GEORGE CLARKE
> Pte SIMON FREDERICK FENDLEY
> Pte HAROLD JAMES TILLEY
> Pte HENRY JOHN SAUNDERS
> Pte EDGAR FREDERIC GOFF
> Pte IVOR HUNT
> Pte THOMAS CHERRETT
> Pte REGINALD HUNT
> Stwd HARRY DARLEY
> Pte TOM HAROLD WATMORE
> Pte REGINALD GEORGE YEOMAN
> Pte WALLACE PACKER
> Pte FREDERICK CHARLES VINE
> Pte ERNEST BREWER
> Pte THOMAS ROBERT CATTLE
> Pte LEONARD ROGERS
> Pte HERBERT C. BRACKSTONE
>
> "GREATER LOVE HATH NO MAN THAN THIS"

The St Clements church has two remembrance walls with the names of those local men who lost their lives in the 1914-18 and the 1939-45 wars. Many of whom were Gypsy Travellers. This is one of two plaques on the walls of St Clément's church with the names of those from Newtown including Gypsy Travellers. Who lost their lives fighting for the country in the two world wars.

Rogers

Many of those from the Rogers family over the years were Wardens at St Clements church for many years. One of whom gained a notorious reputation for turfing the congregation out of the church well before the service had ended. The Rogers family had contributed towards both the costs of building the Wesleyan/Methodist church at Newtown and the more modern evangelical church on the Ringwood Road. There were many Rogers families living throughout Newtown, Alderney and on the Trinadad estate.

Roger's Transport (Parkstone) Ltd owned one of the largest lorry fleets in the area. This picture was taken at the company's depot in Fancy Road in the 1960s. The workshops of Rogers Engineering, who were also specialists in crane hire, can be seen in the background.

The Rogers family were renowned for creating the red Rogers brick which were sold worldwide. William Charles Rogers and brother Alfred George Rogers were in partnership as Rogers Bros. They owned brickworks at Mannings Heath, Ringwood Road, Parkstone and Holt Brickworks Wimborne.

The Rogers family - Vale brickworks Fancy road 1925.

The Rogers family brickyards were known as the Albion Brick Company, Alderney Brickworks and Dorset Brick company which Emily Rogers husband William and his brother Alfred with their sons managed. All from Emilys humble beginnings with one pig!! And the success of their small holding in Newtown.

The partnership ended when Rogers Brickworks went bankrupt in 1926. Alfred George Rogers and son George stayed in the brick making business. With Charlie Rogers then focused on transport work including the hauling of bricks, timber and other building materials into the early 1950's.

Reginald Rogers (known as Bill) was born 2 November 1926 the oldest boy of 8 siblings (6 girls and 2 boys) at Reginald and Alice Rogers smallholding home known as The Mannings on the Mannings Heath at Poole. The Rogers family came from a long tradition of brick makers Bills father Reg and his three uncles being involved in the local family Rogers Bros with brickyards at Mannings Heath and Holt Wood, Wimborne. Bills fathers' mother (Grandmother Elizabeth nee Fancy daughter of Gideon) came from a well-respected travelling family who had lived for generations at one of the many local gypsy campsites of the Kinson parish on Canford Heath at Bourne Bottom. Bills fathers' family were cousins to the Stanleys, leaders of the travelling clan whose origins stemmed from the New Forest in the 16th century and before. Bill had attended the two local schools at Branksome Heath and Kemp Welch as a child, thus many of Bills school friends were from the local travelling community, like the Turners, Warrens, Stanleys, Phillips, Coles, Charrettes, Smalls, Coopers, Scott's, Crutcher's and the Sherwood's. The Stanley's being best known for their father Sammy Stanley's burglary exploits, Abe Stanley's world boxing championship bouts and in recent years Nelson's local thriving business success with his scrap iron company. As a child his playmate was his cousin Elsie Rogers, he lived in Fancy Road Newtown who later married Joker Hill. Bill Rogers is perhaps best known locally for his story telling often reciting long monologues at the drop of a hat. His range of rhymes, stories and funny quips are famous throughout the area. From simple children's rhymes to long adult renditions which seemed endless and have entertained and amused generations. As a child Bill had grown up with an interest and love of wildlife spending much of his free time when not assisting with the care of the animals on the family smallholding and its upkeep. Pastimes such as rabbiting on the Canford Heath along with his younger brother Tony and their gypsy traveller friends the Turners and the Warrens with many dogs and ferrets. They all were keen dart players and avid readers of cowboy books. Bill also in particular had an avid interest in goldfinches breeding them with canaries and their young were renowned as excellent songbirds. Like other gypsies he also caught gold finches in special trap cages he had created placing them and attracting them to areas of abundant thistles, for the wild bird's finches loved the thistle seeds. They bred them with canaries for their offspring in wonderful bird cages and nest boxes which they made. These young songbirds made wonderful bird song. Bill soon became adept at creating bird nest boxes, aviaries and lofts for his many canaries, pigeons, doves and songbirds. He was well known as a pigeon fancier, breeding prize racing pigeons and as a darts champion like his father Reg he had many trophies.. He built lovely bird aviaries and pigeon lofts on our Mannings smallholding. In his bird shed and aviaries he kept hordes of nest boxes full of young canaries, gold finches and miners. Folks came to him from miles away to buy these young birds who sang beautifully. He fed them on seed along with the wild chic weed which they thrived on. His Prize pigeons were taken on our excursions to Exeter in a large cane basket when we visited our relations the Thorpe's. Then he would set these free from the basket as we left Exeter with them arriving back at the Mannings pigeon and dove lofts well before we did. Uncle Bill had many girlfriends as a young man including a Gypsy called Roma. He took me out in his 'British Road Services' lorry, to collect coal from railway sidings at Southampton Docks. Then later when he drove for Uncle Sid's Rogers Transport in Fancy Road, and he often took me with him. When we drove back to uncle Sid's Rogers Transport yard in Fancy Road Uncle Sid often made a fuss of me and gave me a silver coin. The cousins Bill Rogers and Sid Rogers remained very close friends for many years. They were both good story tellers though Uncle Sid's stories were very rude compared to Bills. Uncle Bill married Winifred

Freebourn from Ferndown. I went to their wedding reception which was held in the Poole pub the Shovel and Spade. A young Victor Clapcott attended and played his piano accordion for us. My Mother came along with her landlord Gypsy Cedric Hughes from Wareham. Cedric Hughes Mother was a gypsy Queen she lived in a vardo. Cedric told my grandad that the Wareham White family originally came from and had their roots in Kinson Gypsies. Uncle Bill and aunt Win stayed in the front room at the Mannings till they got their council house in Trinidad estate. For many years Uncle Bill was a regular at the Labour club in Newtown playing cards with his friends the Turners. Bill sadly lost his wife Win suddenly to cancer and he never married again. Uncle Bills younger brother Tony Rogers worked as a labourer at E F Phillips for most of his working life. He hardly attended school spending his childhood on the heath with his dogs. He once drew me aside and told me. "Our Dads people the Rogers originally came to Kinson from the New Forest". "They went through hard times there and had moved to Kinson to make a new life for themselves." Tony had the gift of prophecy as he told me. "In years to come all of Canford heath land will be built on, there will be nothing but houses with cinemas close by and big shops." Years later the area became known as Tower Park, which is now a large estate with many shops and leisure centres. Uncle Tony was a heavy smoker he died at 61 years of age whilst living in his bungalow off Manor Avenue. He claimed to have known Johnny Cash the singer and that they drank together in the private bar of the local pub The Mountbatten Arms hotel when Cash was performing in Bournemouth. The pub had been officially opened by Lord Mountbatten. We often took large cane baskets full of pigeons when visiting our relations the Thorpes in Exeter letting out the birds from their large baskets before we left for home. Then when home we watched them, all returns out of the skies to land safely in their lofts. The Albion pubs snake pit area was often used by locals to set their differences and there were often frequent fist fights here and the pub soon had a reputation as a rough house. My uncles Bill and his brother Tony Rogers often returned home with tales of fights with the Stanleys and Uncle Bill Rogers was himself someone prone to a good scrap there. With a reputation as someone who could handle himself. On leaving school Bill had worked at the local garage before joining the 4th Dorset Regiment, spending time as a soldier in Italy and Gaza, Palestine and Israel. After the war Bill worked as a truck driver for British transport and in the local clay pits with his brother Tony. Before working for his cousin Sid (who at one time took part in the Monte Carlo Rally) and run Rogers Transport Company at Fancy Road Newtown. It was whilst working at Rogers Transport that Bill had first met Win, the lady who was to become the love of his life. Following their marriage they initially moved into his father's home the Mannings before him and Win moved into their own council home on the local Trinidad Estate at Newtowns Rossmore's Worbarrow Garden along with their daughter Lynda and son Tony opposite his sister in laws family the Mabey's. Bill became a keen popular gardener and regular supporter of the local Bournemouth (Cherries) soccer club who had many F.A cup runs over the years. His many interests included darts for which he was much celebrated locally, winning numerous competitions. Bill also enjoyed the occasional game of cards and shove halfpenny at local pubs such as the Albion and Newtown clubs with mates the Turners and had an interest in greyhounds and horse racing, visiting local cinemas to watch cowboy films, as well as enjoying the songs of country and western singer Johnny Cash. Card gambling was a regular feature of gypsy life. I recall card schools which were held each Saturday afternoons at my grandfather's home in the front room. Here Bill and all my uncles gathered to play card games such as 3 card and nine card Bragg games for hours. They all contributed to the kitty in the centre of the table till one won the high amounted score of pound notes and silver coins in the kitty. Then they started another game each person freely donated bets to see if he won. Often these pools amounted to perhaps a week's wages at their work. In the summer months they gathered out on the land laying on the grass using a large hardboard to lay out the cards and kitty's My uncles gathered here for years the Rogers, Castles, Kitchners and Dove. After 15 years of marriage his wife Win sadly passed away and he was left to bring up his two children Lynda and Tony alone, although fortunately with lots of help from neighbours and friends. Bill had over the years worked as a long-distance lorry driver carrying coal and pipes from Redlands pottery Branksome to and from the docks at Weymouth and Southampton and working for Hamworthy Engineering. As a child I often travelled with him with lorryloads of pipes from Redlands pottery across the new forest to Southampton. In his later years following his retirement, Bill spent much time on the local golf links on the Purbeck accompanying his cousin Sid Rogers and with his three grandchildren Lisa, Lee and Mark. He passed away just a day before his 90th birthday and on the day before he passed, his daughter my cousin Lynda read out an article to him which I had written about his life, published in Traveller Times. She told me that it had brought a smile to his face. He is buried at St Clements Church cemetery Newtown

Sidney Rogers ran Rogers Transport business in Newtown using old army lorries from the 1939/45 war.

Rogers and Fancy also managed successful smallholdings in the area. The Rogers family also contributed towards both the costs of building the Wesleyan/Methodist church and the more modern evangelical church on the Ringwood Road Newtown. Lester Rogers had also established himself as a haulage contractor based in Manor Avenue, Alderney, Parkstone. Manning's Heath, Parkstone, Ferndown and Wimborne which were sold worldwide. These included Alfred, Charles, Tien, Lester, and Reginald. A tragic accident took place in June 1935. Whilst reversing a lorry out into the main road, Lester Rogers had the terrible misfortune of running over his infant son, Frederick aged one year and seven months, killing him outright. At a subsequent inquest into the fatality, Lester was cleared of blame and the jury returned a verdict of accidental death. Whilst Harold Rogers was a successful house builder on the Ringwood Road Alderney. These were members of the Stanley tribe of Gypsies and families, including the Scott's, Bonds and the Cherretts.

The Newtown terrace

There was a neat row of cottages called the terrace on the Ringwood Road at Newtown Parkstone in the 1950s. Travellers and show people the Kings, Castles and Mabey's lived there before moving to live on the Newtown Trinidad estate. Mary Mabey nee Castle was the local flower seller. They were well known for making exquisite floral wreaths and wedding bouquets for the local community. Mary Mabey was the sister of George Castle her husband was Fred Mabey. George Castle married Macey Rogers the daughter of Reginald Rogers. Georges mothers Annabella White she married a king s family were the Kings. The kings were fairground people who had skills in the swing boat rides. Annabella king was known as Bella and was extremely attractive when young but was very dark and foreboding in old age and scary to a small boy. Jean Castle danced for Zena Martell's school and became Poole carnival Queen in the early 60s.

Brixey's

HENRY CHARLES BRIXEY

Henry was a brick maker and ran the successful family business Newtown Vale brickworks at Newtown Poole Dorset from 1906-1927. Brixey and Champion ran their Perfumed pottery, and tile works at Old Wareham road from 1927-1931.

The Brixeys built two cottages on the heaths long before the Trinadad estate. Barry, George and Ron Brixey established Brixeys Engineering. George and his wife Margaret lived in fancy road. The family set up their business in what became Brixey road

Newtown. Hughes in his memoir on Prior, in Journal of the Royal Institute of British Architects, for 15 October 1932, mentions how he persuaded makers of simple pottery on the shores of Poole Harbour to turn their clay to bricks of every colour from purple to vivid orange for his St Osmund's church at Parkstone. Poole, there may well have been a long discussion in those days which took place between Prior and Brixey about clays, moulding and firing techniques. Prior had a great feeling for local materials found on or very close to the site and had little time for "drawing board" architects. Whereas Maps and old photographs show that Brixey's works were well equipped with heated drying sheds, an arch-less continuous kiln of a type still used in India and Pakistan, plus a circular downdraught kiln and at least one scotch kiln.

Louise and Henry Brixey with daughters.

A Newtown Street party

The Albion pub encampment

There was for some years a stopping place for Gypsies on land at the rear of the pub where there was a gravel pit with a snake pit there. In 1841 David Stanley basket maker and Elia Stanley camped on the encampment with their children Henry Stanley, William Stanley, Solomon Stanley and baby Louisa Stanley.

The Albion pub was very popular with local travellers. It was run by landlords Mr & Mrs Arthur Loveless from 1930, Arthur died in 1940, Annie & Bill loveless were then landlord and landlady and ran the pub from 1940 to 1956, Fred Loveless & his mum were regulars.

Jack & Jill Sherwood ran a garage in Rosemary Rd, others included Albert and Charles West, Bill Kennedy, Shoey Sherring, Bouncer Barnes, Jim Ayley, Bill Hansford, Reginald Rogers, Iris Rogers, Sammy Stanley, Sampson Stanley and the strong man my grandad Jim Hansford. The pub ran a popular sports competition with awards. Activities including the popular darts and tug of war.

The public house was originally called the snake and was a popular attraction to Gypsy families.

The pub was well used by all the local Gypsies such as the Stanleys who were one of the most extended Gypsy clans and the most prominent Gypsy family in England. They considered Dorset as their home territory and Gypsies recognise the Stanley's as being of the royal blood line. They were very skilled in most of the Gypsy trades, including brick making and could speak well the Romany language. The Stanley family were recorded very early in Dorset, Hampshire and at Lyndhurst in the New Forest whilst many lived permanently in Dorset. These many local Newtown Parkstone Gypsies built local industries in haulage contractors, sand and gravel, scrap ironmongery, farming and caravans. Other became renowned local sports personalities, entertainers, and fairground workers.

There were other local pubs popular with the gypsy traveller community. Including Rossmoor Hotel and the New Inn.

Fox holes encampment

This encampment was just going down towards Oakdale from Newtown near the Pottery Arms. Joseph Rogers and his wife Louisa nee Phillips at one time managed the Foxholes brickyard nearby. Many traveller families lived here over the years. Including the Stanleys, Sharwood's, Wheelers, Whites, Buttons, Gillingham's, Domoney's, Raggett's, Bennetts, Trent's, Skinners.

Foxholes brickyard

The locals worked in these clay pits and brick yards at Fox Holes which had existed from the 1700. Joseph Rogers and Louisa nee Phillips married and ran Foxholes brickyard in Newtown from 1852.

Fancy road

Fancy road took its name from my great grand mother Elizabeth Fancy family. Fancy road was situated just off the Ringwood Road at top of old Wareham Road. Families living here included the Fancy's, Brixey's, Rogers, Sherwood's, Warrens and Hills. My Granddads cousin Henry Charles Brixey was also a brick maker. He ran the Vale brickworks from 1906-1927. There may well have been a long discussion in those days which took place between Prior and Brixey about clays, molding and firing techniques. Prior had a great feeling for local materials found on or very close to the site and had little time for "drawing board" architects. Whereas Maps and old photographs show that Brixey's works were well equipped with heated drying sheds, an arch-less continuous kiln of a type still used in India and Pakistan, plus a circular down draught kiln and at least one scotch kiln. Then later his three sons Barry, George, and Ron Brixey from Fancy Road, established Brixey's Engineering and built two cottages on the heaths, which became Brixey road at Rossmore. This was long before the present Trinidad estate was established

The Fancy's

It was at Bere Regis in 1686 Elizabeth and Mary Fancy daughters of Henry Fancy were first recorded. Members of their families were recorded there as varmint destroyers. By the 1700s many Fancies lived throughout Dorset.

EMILY ELIZABETH ROGERS nee FANCY

Emily Elizabeth Fancy was my great grandmother married to William Charles Rogers. Emily was born at the Bourne bottom campsite in 1850.Fancys were married to Cherretts, Bonds, Stanleys, Rogers and Crockers. The Fancies were also Quarrymen at Portland making the famous stone for the rebuilding of London's great houses at Westminster and St Paul's cathedral. The Fancy's had a reputation as brick makers and brick maker labourers both male and female working at brickyards throughout Dorset. Other members of the Fancies were stone masons and Quarry men on the Purbeck. Many of their descendants moved to the new world via the Newfoundland trade. Emily Fancy was born at the Bourne bottom encampment campsite in 1850. Her father was Gideon Fancy from Bourne bottom who was a child on the old original Mannings encampment. Emilys mother was Elizabeth Cherrett. Gideon Fancy and family later lived at the Gypsy encampments at Bourne Bottom and Heavenly Bottom and he was the father of my great grandmother Emily Elizabeth Fancy who married Willam Charles Rogers my great grandfather She was . Gideon's daughter.

Records show that 'Joseph Fancy of Arne was a, Brick maker'. His 3rd born daughter was baptised in Arne in 1790, but his other children were all baptised/buried in Lytchett Minster. After his second marriage in 1797 Joseph is shown as being a Proprietor/Occupier in Lytchett Minster. Two years later he took out a lease from the Lord of the Manor, William Trenchard on 12 Oct 1799 for an acre of land between Lytchett Bay and Poole turnpike road, adjoining his brick kiln. Joseph settled in Poole and moved his family from Dorset to start up a brickwork in Hornchurch in Essex. Unfortunately, the venture failed, but there are roads in Hornchurch that now have Dorset names. At Wareham David Fancy 1793- 1876. married Sarah and they had 5 children.

There were women brickmakers such as Mary Ann Fancy, Sophie Fancy and Daisy Fancy who lived in Wareham then in the 1800s and after they were at Heavenly bottom encampment in Newtown Parkstone. In later years he lived at Organford. He died in 1826 and was buried at Lytchett Minster.

Pembrooke road encampment

Many Gypsy travellers lived at the Pembrooke Road encampment at Rossmore. Living in wagons over the years. All their wagons were right next to Jeans Hopes Matthews grandmothers' yard, where she also had her wagon living hut. There were many caravans parked here and there was a great number of children and animals. Also living here was John Henry Walton known as Jack who was a circus bareback rider. Sampson James and his wife Kate James nee Collins originally came from the new forest. Before moving to Heavenly bottom then to Pembroke Road. Living in a wagon with their children, Sampson, Liberty, Peter, Cissy, Lily, Ida, Freedom and Hilda.

Sampson and Kate James were Jean Hopes grandparents. Jeans parents Golden Hope and Lily nee James. The Hopes were also living here in a wagon along with other families such as the Jeff's and the Crutcher's. They had strong family ties to the Couch, Griggs, Golders, Butchers, Coopers, Collins, Walton's, and Drapers. Sampson James and his wife Kate James nee Collins lived in a wagon with their children, Sampson, Liberty, Peter, Cissy, Lily, Ida, Freedom, and Hilda in the Pembroke Road encampment. Rossmore. They originally came from the new forest before moving Heavenly bottom encampment before Pembroke Road. There was a great number of children and animals.

Rossmore Days

We lived in our house wagons upon the Pembrooke Road
there were lots of Gypsy families there
like Hopes and James and even Nellie Old
they parked upon their old grandma's yard
they said they were as good as gold
least that is the story I've been told
there were lots of Gypsy folks in the Rossmoor hotel
and a sawmill down the road

The Circus ringmaster he had a whip
and the chavvies they all laughed
when ole Stanley did spit
we had a lot of fun those days
and bathed in old tin baths

There were quarries on the commons then
and lots of rabbit pies
the Kings and Warrens ran the lanes
and there was a stream a running bye.

We lived in our house wagons
off the Rossmore roads
there were lots of nappos and divvies around us then
and a co-op divi too
along with newts and toads

We caught the little flyer bus to Up on Hill
and walked to see the Regal flicks
there were lots of friendly neighbours then

we had our penny bicycles, and no one had a quid
but we were happy on the heath then
playing with our dustbin lids
The Sherwood's they were boxers
and it was where the Cacker Canyons
Arne Avenues Hurdy Gurdy man played
close by the Gypsy campsites with little Wally Cave
the Brixeys and the Rogers,
Smalls, Phillips folks and Trents

We had accumulator radios then
and lavender perfume scents,
the gal's they had their baskets of flowers for to sell
there were our horses on the heaths then
and turves with lots of peat as well.

Our chavvies were well behaved
though no shoes upon their feet
the school was down in Kinson village
n another towards Up on hill
whilst the Branksome Dartford warbler sang his song
and the slow was in the still.

Ray Wills

UP ON HILL KIDS

Once i lived in Churchill road
up on hill not far from the dip
where heavenly bottom camp once stood
where kids played soldiers with dustbin lids
near the monkey house and regal flicks
where we saw roy rogers hopalong and tom mix

The rossmore flier roamed these hills
and the Branksome heath was mixed
squirells scampering in the trees
seavew and the magicans shops box of tricks

Constitution hill was steep and rich in woodlands
with woodmans pub not too fars away
Branksome and heatherlands was our domain
was here we went to play

The gypsy travelling families all lived nearbys
with Tuckers, Johnsons and Frys
with old soldiers wooden legs and pirates with one eye

Walterman the bunkman rode a bike and the ferris wheel did spin
bumping cars and Stanleys cars and gals who passed you by
school bells rang and crickets danced and kids had a lot to say
in a world of simple pleasures and the mailman still did call
a friendly chat and a friendly smile we were kings above it all

Ray Wills

The Phillips

E F PHILLIPS YARD MANNINGS HEATH ROAD
Picture courtesy of Nicole Green, daughter of Michael Phillips.

For centuries the Phillips family had grazing rights on the Turbary common Kinson under the Doomsday book and kept pigs there. Percy Phillips carried on the family tradition of horse grazing on the Turbary common despite the council taking him to court on several occasions where he cited the grazing rights under the Domesday book and won his case many times.

Edward Frank Phillips originally started up the company E F Phillips thriving haulage business from a humble beginning of pony and cart after the war years of 1939-1945. Operating small sand and gravel pits on the Ringwood Road and on the Mannings Heath at the rear of my grandads Reg Rogers smallholding. It was the Phillips company who tipped lorry loads of building rubble into the swampy heath lands of Canford for the foundations of the large new housing estate now known as Tower Park.

They later expanded with a continental transport company to Europe in the 1970s, when Michael Phillips took on the business.

In more recent years his daughter Nicole Green became Deputy leader of Bournemouth Borough Council.

The Cherretts

Charrettes were recorded throughout Dorset at Shapwick, Morden Charlton, Wareham and Canford parish from the 1700s. James Cherrett was born at Newtown Poole in 1848 and worked his way up from brick labourer to brick maker to inn keeper to eventually to own his own farm estate owner in Kinson and employed servants.

The Stanleys

The Stanley's had first been recorded as vermin destroyers at Bere Regis in the 1600s and could speak well their own Romany language. The Stanley's are one of the most extended Gypsy clans and the most prominent Gypsy family in England. Being very skilled in most of trades, including brick making. Being recorded very early in Dorset, Hampshire and at Lyndhurst in the New Forest. Whilst many lived permanently in Dorset. They considered Dorset to be their home

Hercules and Parthenia Stanley lived at the gypsy traveller encampment at Okeford Fitzpaine in Wimborne 1764 with their 6 children. Benjamin Stanley was the brother of Levi who had emigrated with others to Dayton USA. Benjamin had chosen to settle down in New England site at Turbary common. Benjamin had been disowned by their father and it was said that a curse was put on him and the future families for the next three generations to follow.

On 17th November 1822, at the Church of Lady St Mary, Wareham, Moses Stanley, a razor grinder, married Ann Dory. He claimed to be the son of a Richard Stanley, Moses, appears to have four different wives over time, with very different ages. none of these many wives attributed to Moses are incorrect. Moses and Ann Stanley appear in the 1841 census, at Roper's Lane, in the parish of Lady St Mary, Wareham. Also, in 1841 David Stanley basket maker and Elia Stanley originally camped on the common at

Newtown with their children Henry, William, Solomon, and baby Louisa.

In 1900, Levi Stanley gave his birth as November 1808. In his obituary, his age was given as 96 (implying 1812). Levi was the son of Owen Stanley (1794–21 February 1860) and he married Worden (1793–30 August 1857), who preceded as King and Queen. Levi married Matilda Joles Stanley (1821? — 15 January 1878). She was the daughter of Ephraim Joles and was said to have a wonderful faculty of telling fortunes, when she pleased, and remarkable powers as a mesmerist. She was described in the press as a "plain, hardy-looking woman, with a touch of Meg Merrilee's in her appearance, and a manner indicative of a strong and pronounced character." Levi and Matilda had emigrated with others to Dayton in the USA in 1856—"when Buchanan was king," as they put it—along with others of their people and soon settled near Troy, Ohio. Shortly thereafter, they selected Dayton, Ohio as their headquarters for the summer months, and it became the centre for the Gypsies of the country. Contrary to common perception, they were reverent church people, and the reigning King and his son and heir, known as Sugar Stanley, were members in good standing of the International Order of Odd Fellows.

Mary Stanley was the granddaughter of Sarah who became famous for having had her portrait painted in oils by the famous new forest artist Amelia Goddard entitled "Mary Stanley in the Forest". Amelia records that the Marchioness of Waterford wrote from Highcliffe Castle in 1883 thanking her for the charming picture of a Gypsy which she was very glad to possess.

Charles Stanley laid the foundation stone of a Gypsy school at Farnham, Dorsetshire on Thursday the 24th of July. Around 500 people attended the ceremony including several groups of Gypsies. It was proposed at first to give education, food, and clothing, to 12 boys and 12 girls. Lord Ashley was the patron of this institution, and amongst its liberal supporters were the Lord Bishop of Salisbury, Marquis of Cholmondeley, Hon. Mr. Cowper, M.P., the Dowager Duchess of Beaufort, Sir Matthew Blackstone, Bart. The proposed school received a grant of 100 pounds from the committee of the Queen's Privy Council for Education. The building was undertaken with a view of gathering in the too-long neglected outcast Gypsy children from the highways and hedges, to be brought up *"in the nurture and admonition of the Lord"*.

The Rev. Mr. Crabb, in addressing the meeting, mentioned several instances of members of the Gypsy tribes becoming converted to Christianity, who go to Church regularly, and are most attentive in their religious devotions. The whole of the day's proceedings was of a highly animating nature, and likely to be long remembered by all who were present at this interesting scene.

Sampson Stanley and his wife, Phoebe Rowe married in 1889. Sampson and Phoebe with their large family were recorded in the 1911 census in Poole Dorset. They camped at the Talbot heath Wallisdown Gypsy encampments. Their children included Sampson Stanley born on 15th January 1911. Sampson in later years married Eliza they lived in Talbot and Newtown Poole Dorset. Sammy Stanley was a well-liked Gypsy with a pleasant cheerful manner. Sampson was a licensed hawker of flowers and clothes pegs and was also a local burglar. He was at one time a rag and bone man and gave children rides on his grey mare and cart. Sammy and Eliza lived with their children James, Cissie, Sampson, Thomas, Walter, Lizzie and Elsie on the Heavenly bottom and Beresford Road Gypsy campsites. He was the first Gypsy to move into a council bungalow. He loved a pint and along with family members was a regular at the local Albion public house in Newtown Parkstone Poole Dorset. By 1955 Sampson was an invalid and blind.

George Digger Stanley was the son of George and Cinderella Stanley and the grandson of Diverus and Naomi and the great grandson of Peter and Rebecca Stanley. (Said to have been the grandson of Gypsy queen Alice Stanley. George was the world bantam weight champion and first outright winner of the Lonsdale belt for boxing. He died in March 1919 in Fulham, London following a long illness. At his death newspapers recorded that the first outright winner of the Lonsdale belt had passed away in

Fulham following a long illness. He was the ex-England and Worlds bantam weight boxing champion.

William Proudly was the son of Rose Stanley. He was born 1800 and was an earthenware vendor. He was threatened to be transported to Australia for theft, but he was instead imprisoned at Poole. However, by 1881 he was a successful brick maker who owned his own farm and had employed many and was well respected.

Fairground boxer Abe Stanley married Jean Rogers, and they lived in Fancy Road. He was a professional boxer in the 1950s and 60s after previously boxing at Poole Fair and had 38 professional fights. Poole Fairground and world champion boxer and preacher.

Trent's

Trent's managed this yard with a large billboard outside proclaiming it the biggest scrap yard in Europe on the Ringwood Road at Alderney.

TRENTS SCRAPYARD ALDERNEY

The Sherwood's

The Sherwood family were recorded in Canford and Kinson from 1841 onwards and were in Parish registers long before then. Joseph Sherwood married Urania Burton who was the daughter of Henry and Priscilla Burton. Urania was born in 1855 at Sturminster Newton Dorset. Joseph and Urania lived in Kinson where they raised a family. William Turner is linked to the very large family tree of Sherwood's in the Poole area, traced back to George Sherwood who had married Eleanor Rix in 1740 at Kinson.

Ted Sherwood was born in Fancy Road, Newtown on 13th September 1910. (Fancy road took its name from the Fancy Gypsy family). As a boy had attended the Parkstone Heather lands school at Parkstone Poole near the Gypsy encampment at Heavenly Bottom. Where the Travellers lived in wagons and houses. Ted showed an aptitude for boxing, when he was a teenager Teddy regularly fought each year at the Poole fairground booths and training under the watchful eye of trainer Herbert Millett and becoming welter weight boxing champion. Following his boxing years Ted became addicted to alcohol but found salvation through religion, member of the Pentecostal church in Poole. Preaching in the open air at Sea View Newtown and from a soap box at Speakers Corner in Hyde Park, London. It was here he met the Reverend Dr. Ian Paisley, and they soon became close friends. When Ted preached, he used all the boxing movements which had made him famous in the boxing ring. Ted died in October 2000 in Poole Dorset.

Sidney Sherwood and his three sons Frederick, Alfred and Henry were all tragically killed in November 1940 when a large German bomb fell on their home in Fancy Road.

Brian Crutcher

Brian was born on 23rd August 1934 and became an international speedway champion making his debut for the Poole Pirates in 1951 at the age of 16 years managed a car repair business in sea view, Parkstone.

Mitchells

The Mitchells operated their haulage company in Poole. One of them Eddie Mitchell became director of Bournemouth football club. My former wife and I managed a dress shop for the Baber gypsy family at Wonder Holme parade Kinson in 2008. Before it became famous for making the dresses for the tv show big fat gypsy wedding. The Babers lived in Canford cliffs they came from Liverpool. Mr Baber was a car salesman.

Pidgleys

Oliver Pidgley married Edith nee Sheen they had 8 children. Edith sold flowers to the owners of the Dormy hotel who helped her to obtain a council house to prepare for the birth of her son Raymond who was born on 12th May 1935 at New England West Howe Kinson Bournemouth Dorset. He served in the Royal Marines Commandos as a sergeant and was Admiral Lord Mountbatten's bodyguard. He was also the lightweight champion of the royal marines and 3 commandos. Before the Act of 1871 all members of the Gypsy families were used as labour many often working 12-hour shifts. It was very labour-intensive hot work in brick yards with poor lighting and over the years a number were killed from suffocation and fumes. It is estimated that 30 million bricks were made in Poole where at one time there were over 50 brickyards. The potteries, brickyards and clay pits were the main employers the end of the Newfoundland trading days.

Queen of the Castles and Kings

She was a Gypsy sweetheart
one time Queen of the Castles and Kings
She rode the Canford commons
she made the starlings sing

She was beautiful when she was young
she made the young men heads turn

she was a rare breed Gypsy girl
within the heathers and the thorns
She rode the caravan's wagons of wood back then
When the wagon wheels did turn
She would dance and sing a melody
she made the young men yearn

Then when she grew older
she lost her youthful good looks
her darkness held her furrowed lines of age
She made the children feel uneasy n disturbed

She was the Queen of the Gypsies
she died upon the Canford heath
she was buried in her wagon's flames
Along with her belonging n her teeth
Her funeral was attended by hundreds of her clans

She was the Queen of the Gypsies
mother of the Gypsy band
She was the Queen of the Castles and the Kings
the Newtown clans of Gypsy families
She grew up wise in tooth and wisdom
When I was a kid, I remember
she was so kind to me

Ray Wills

Annabella King nee White known as Bella was Betsy Smith's elder sister. Her husband died, and she then married a showman called Castle. Annabella known as Bella was extremely attractive when young but was very dark and foreboding in old age and scary to me as a small boy. Her family the Kings were fairground people with skills in the swing boat rides. Mary Mabey was Annabella's Kings daughter she married George Mabey to become Mary Mabey. She was the Poole Flower Girl and lived in a terrace in Newtown.

Mary's brother George Castle married Macey Rogers. Sister-in-laws Mary Mabey and Macey Castle worked together making exquisite floral displays wreaths and wedding bouquets for the local Newtown community. They used to gather regularly outside Woolworths in Poole High Street to sell baskets of flowers with other flower sellers including the Crutchers. George Castle married Macey Rogers who was my aunt and the daughter of Reginald Rogers my grandfather. One of their daughters Jean Castle danced for Zena Martell's dancers and became Poole carnival Queen in the early 60s.

GYPSY LAD

She married a Gypsy with big roving eyes
he gave her his heather and told her his lies
he was born on the common one hour afore morn
he told her he loved her then left her at dawn

He worked in the fairgrounds and ponies he rode
he was a one for the ladies and the gal down the road
he drove a big cart and he told you a yarn
he was noble and famous but his breeches were worn

He wore those big earrings and talked diddy coy
he loved all the ladies and gave em the eye
he mixed with the coopers the mabeys and kings

though his name was castle he was the head of the ring
he could sale you a story and tell you a lie
say it was the real Truth then gave you that look in the eye

His family made flowers and kettles and tins
he was raised on old canford just where the ole warbler sings
he lived in a caravan with high wooden roof
he walked with a limp and his language was uncouth
he swore and he told some terrible lies
though the gals loved his blarney and his lovely dark eyes

They hung all their washing on the bramble bush free
they had a dozen dogs and lots of new forest ponies
his mother was Queenie and his father a king
he had him a fortune inside his gold ring
his pals came from London for that's what he said
as he told her her fortune then took her to bed

The bed it was bouncy and the springs they did squeak
he loved hers there twice nightly each day of the week
she was a dreamer pretty and cool
some say a diamond and some say a fool
but he was only a gypsy who grew up near Poole

Ray Wills

The Gypsy Childhood

My aunt Mary Mabey made the floral wreaths
the flowers for the shows
Aunt Maisie Castle read the tea leaves then
it seems so long ago

Uncle Bill Rogers he told the stories
yarns fit for a king
My Granfer Reg made the bricks back then
My great Aunt King was a Gypsy Queen

My great gran Emily Fancy was a lady
she wore her Fancy clothes
they made a roads name after her
it was so long ago

My long time granfer Jim Hansford
was a tug a war strong man
he lived upon the Turlin moors
my cousin Jean was a dancer
the Queen of Poole carnival shows

My cousin George was a choir boy
and school organ maker too
my uncle Sid rode in the Monte Carlo Rally
my aunt Vera was a Dominey
she lived in one of granfers houses
he had many from Newtown to Alderney
great uncle Harry was a house builder by trade
they say he had it made

My father was a romantic
he wrote letters and played the darts
he was a fine tree surgeon nearly fell to his grave a loss
My Mother served the military
waited on great folks at Wareham
Billy Wright the captain of the land
he played soccer and married Joy Beverley in Poole
with his one hundred caps in hand
our landlord was old Cedric Hughes
his mother was a Gypsy Queen

The artist John Augustus lived at Alderney Manor
He painted our house known as Heather view
before we all lived on the Mannings Heath
it had a lovely view of Poole

Ray Wills

In the 1960s Ewan Mc Coll and Peggy Seeger had discovered the Gypsy Queen singer Caroline Hughes on Canford heath and recorded many of her songs. Caroline Hughes family were living along with many other Gypsies.

Ewan (Miller)Mc Coll the Lancashire singer and scholar had taken a great interest in Gypsy lore. He travelled around the British Isles with his tape recorder and a notebook. Preserving stories and songs that were in danger of being lost as the Gypsy way of life which was threatened by modernization. It was while he was searching out Gypsies to record and talk to when he was writing one of his radio ballads called "The Travelling People". It was at Canford heath that he stumbled across Caroline Hughes on a lay by stopping place by the Old Wareham Road. Ewan Mc Coll visited her and recorded many of her songs which she had learnt from her mother Lavena at a very young age. Peggy Seeger and Ewan 'sat at the feet of "Queen Caroline" Hughes and heard her sing songs thought dead these hundred years.

MacColl took these songs of Carolines back to the U.S.A where they were published and can still be heard today from records held in the national archives. They were recorded by Eugene, Peggy Seeger, and Charles Parker, along with very many popular folk and beat groups of that era both in the U.S.A and in Britain. Caroline's son John made a wooden horse drawn vardo which became their home on the side of the road at Wareham. But it caught fire and Caroline said that's how come we moved here at Canford heath."

Dominic Reeves

Dominic came to Kinson downs
where Gypsies bedded down, and all young girls were heaven bound
the vardo wheels did turn there and times were tough on the common land of peat and bluff
he rode the trails of bracken down where birds did sing o'er rabbits mounds

Where folks worked hard when hours were long
amidst the days of swallow song
where Mountbatten arms doth stand today
afore shoulder of mutton along the way
where birch did grow amidst heathers sweet
with adder n lizards at your feet
near Alderney where Augustus John did paint
naked ladies so frequent

Where Sankey Ward built houses for the rich
and lady Wimborne's lodge was close to pitch
the writer stored his memories
of gypsy life neath sky and trees

Where crafts were rich in lore and pen #
where kids grew tall, and fern did bend
the local people in Kinson free
were rich in style and histories

The Longham bridge over the Stour
to Ferndown's haunts and village squires

the war had taken the youth its true
with tales of valour from Waterloo

The commons rich in gravel clay and stone
but to the Gypsy it was home
where grass was mean, and trails were sand
and fortunes told to open hands
where families came from new forest glades
to build their homes n get it made
Dominic wrote and his wife did paint
The Gypsy story oh so quaint

Till the Gypsies were all housed on West Howe land
with bricks of Rogers builders' band
where the chimneys grew tall upon the land
and pigs were sold in markets grand
the gaffers paid you each in hand
and the rich grew richer you understand

Those days of Gypsy life so free
were recorded there in histories
with Dominics books of fame and lore
he wrote it as it was after the war
the Gypsy families are still abroad
you can hear them sing with one accord
their heather sprigs are sold today
in Poole high street
just like it was yesterday

Ray Wills

Dominic Reeves in his book "Beneath the blue sky", also gav very illustrated account of a visit to the Parkstone's Old Wareham roads Canford heath site. Mentioning the site as being "a part of a vast estate laying in barren land near Poole". "A favorite of the old fashioned, travelers many still with horses and wagons". Dominic also met an old man name of Righteous in one of the old pubs in Poole backstreets. Righteous said he was nearing 82 and that he was a Romani of some 21 siblings. The many Gypsy traveler encampments which Dominic visited on Canford heath, this one was situated off old Wareham Road, had been there for decades.

SANKEY WARD

Sankey was born in London in 1893 he was the son of Thomas ward a laundryman in 1901. He worked for his uncle James Whittle a builder then during the First World War he was in the RAF as was his wife Florence Giles they were stationed at Grantham. They married there in January 1918 later they moved back to the Bournemouth Poole area. By 1939 Sankey was a master builder, brick maker and maker of clay products in the area. He died in 1978 aged 85 his wife Florence died in 1981. She was the sister of local builder George Rogers wife Frances Rogers nee Giles. Some believe Sankey was very sanctimonious so gaining the nick name Sankey Ward. Sankey had numerous clay pits at cuckoo bottom and broom road where he took over the Dorset Brick company site. Where many local Gypsies worked in the early 1950s including my uncles Bill and Tony Rogers, I would often go at weekends with them into the scorching hot kilns. Assisting with wheel borrowing loads of clay over the planks from the hot burning kilns. It was a hot task, and we came home with jeans covered in red clay. Sankey Ward who lived in Bournemouth and was at that time involved in the building of the Church of the Good Shepherd in Rossmore.

Christobel Cooper née duckett sister was Gertrude Hughes . Noah Bowers aka vanlo had a horse and cart and drank in the albion. Old Zena Bridgewater? was a quirky old Gypsy lady who came up to Wallisdown (Wally Wack) crossroads from the other end of Kinson Rd. She liked to raise havoc folks laughed at her antics but were scared at the same time She was often found sitting on the bench outside the Co-Op at the Wallisdown cross roads, drinking her beer from a jam jar kids were scared of her as she used to threaten them, curse and generally turn the air blue. She often used telephone boxes as toilets and was always drunk and very abusive.

Young Mary Gear lived in one of the Lady Wimborne cottage on Mannings heath road she was painted as a model for Augustus john which caused a outcry from the local Alderney church goers.

Fred Penny kept pigs down the bottom of Fancy Road near to the Gillingham family. He used to boil up the pig swill in a large pot on a fire outside on the ground, didn't smell too bad! Bill Eaton was the pig swill man who lived next to the church at the top of Old Wareham Road Bill kept pigs down the bottom of Fancy Road on a plot surrounded by an electric fence. Charlie Rogers kept his pigs in the back of the workshop where they repaired Roger's Transport Trucks. Ron Squires and Ted Belben' Gypsies would go Poole stadium near henry Harborne school and celebrate November 5th guy forks night with huge fires.

Gertrude King became a Rogers when she married George Rogers, lived at 606 Ringwood Road. Young Mary Gear lived in one of the Lady Wimborne cottage on Mannings heath road she was painted as a model for Augustus john which caused a outcry from the local Alderney church goers.

Isabella Dominey (née Trent, Charlie Trents eldest sister) died at the age of 41 in childbirth. The little ones in the family were all fostered out. when her mother Isabella died in childbirth, She was giving birth to her 17th or 18th child (not all survived childhood, there was a high rate of infant mortality in those days). Women then had spent most of her married life pregnant, by the time they had their last child they were literally worn out. Hard times in those days. Gypsies would go Poole stadium near henry Harborne school and celebrate November 5th guy forks night with huge fires. There were Chinchenn cottages in Newtown. The Chinchenn were quarry workers at the Purbeck.

1939 PARKSTONE CENSUS

CANFORD HEATH LOSS

THE JOHNSONS FAMILY ON CANFORD HEATH

The removal of the gypsy travellers from all their encampments on the Canford heath.

Canford Heath was to become Tower Park estate and others, Most of these local Gypsy families were eventually housed on the numerous local housing estates. Which were built at Rossmore/Trinadad, Branksome, Bourne bottom, Arne Avenue, Alderney, Trinadad, and Kinson/West Howe and to accommodate the growth in the local Gypsy population. The West Howe estate was the largest housing estate in the south. At one time in 1976 it boasted excess of 2000 children per square mile. Many Gypsy travellers adapted well to their new brick-built homes though still retaining the delightful artistry of interior furnishings and their cultures and identity. Though at that time 1960 there was a question and uproar in the House of Lords when it was announced that Lord Wimborne had made millions of pounds of profit overnight from the sale of the land to Poole Council.

Article courtesy of Michael Johnson

CHAPTER SIX

SIR GUSTAS

AUGUSTUS JOHN

Augustus John and the Gypsies

Folks say that Augustus
was fascinated by Gypsies
and that is why e drew n painted them every day
some in their fine and dandy clothes
some others naked in the hay

John was a roving bohemian guy
with his paint brush ready in his hand
he slept n lived upon the local common lands
with his vardo set in clay and dens

He at one time painted our Lady Wimborne rented house
called Heather View
with its pretty pink roses around its windows and door
with its red and its white bricks of the land
Where Crusoe came to call

They do say that Whistler the artist
was a friend of his
n Picasso he knew
Along with Llyod George too

he sketched the Gypsy chavvies
with local charcoal then
guess he knew Sid Rogers too

Now the famous London art museum
stores his scenes to view
some are of the common Gypsy folk
others lost at sea in Poole

His wife was Ida and his sister was Gwen
plus, all his lovely maids lived within the manor road
close to locals like Wally Cave
His art studio there was made of glass
though his farm life was basic mean
for he kept lots of goats n pigs that he would wean

His looks were dark and foreboding n ugly then
with his long coat and his beard
folks said he was eccentric whilst others thought him weird
the art world though him a master stroke
with his flair for all things bright
he painted local girls in the nude in the naked light
but I guess he was alright

Ray Wills

Augustus John the artist 1878-1971 was born at Haverford west in 1878 into a somewhat intimidating household. \His father had warned his children that if they walked abroad on market days they should be kidnapped by Gypsies and spirited away in their caravans to no one knows where. Augustus had longed to be someone other than his father's son. This had a great bearing on John and as a result- their grandfather exhorted his grandchildren to " Talk! If you can't think of anything to say, tell a lie!' and 'If you make a mistake, make it with Authority!' John and his siblings were looked after by two aunts, Rose & Lily, who rode round the neighbourhood in a wicker pony trap known as 'the Hallelujah Chariot'. They were both officers in the Salvation Army and followed the doctrines of the Quakers, Joanna Southcott and. Howell Harris. Johns' family moved to Tenby in 1884 where John enrolled at the Slade School of Art in 1894.From the art world he was the eccentric Augustis John who gypsies called Sir Gustas. He was a great supporter of the Gypsies and spent much time amongst them. He lived for a time at lady Wimborne's Alderney Manor renting it as his studio. Whist fashioning the Manors grounds on the same as the Gypsy encampments. Augustus John was in the 1920s Britain's leading portrait painter and a great defender of New Forest Gypsy rights.

In a summer between terms studying in London two incidents happened that would have a large influence in John's life - on a walking trip around Pembrokeshire he had his first encounter with Irish tinkers which would lead to a lifelong fascination with Romany culture and way of life. And in the summer of 1897, he suffered a severe accident hitting his head on a rock whilst diving into the sea, this seemingly resulted in a radical change in character - later leading to the myth that he had dived into the sea, hit his head on a rock and emerged from the water a genius. It was during this time that first met John Samson, the Romany scholar it was Sampson who introduced John to the Romany Gypsy culture, language & lifestyle. From then on and throughout his life John would seek our Gypsy encampments travelling in his own set of horse drawn vans. John spent much of his life painting and etching the local Gypsies and was regarded with much respect by both the Gypsy community and the wider art world. He was called "Sir

Gustus" by the Travellers. He developed a nomadic lifestyle based on the gypsy way and for a while he lived in a caravan and camped with and amongst the Gypsies. He had his own repertoire of Romany songs & dances. Joining them round their campfires at night, penetrating behind the veneer of romantic glamour, John saw the Gypsies as having true freedom, not restricted by modern life. In turn they soon came to accept John as an honorary Gypsy.

During his life he was seen as perhaps the greatest bohemian portrait artist of his time. As well a campaigner on behalf of Gypsies. At the outbreak of the First World War John was perhaps the best-known artist in Britain. Seen also by many as a promiscuous, hippie, early new age traveller and commune patriarch. In 1936 he was honoured to be elected president of the Gypsy Law Society.

It was in August 1911when John, and his lady companion Dorelia had rented Alderney Manor at Parkstone, Poole. The manor was a strange fortified pink bungalow built by an eccentric Frenchman within 60 acres of heath and woodland in Alderney Parkstone, Poole. With its large low house with Gothic windows and a castellated parapet, additional cottages, and a round walled garden. John moved there at the suggestion of his close artist friends and former students at Slade's school of Art John and Katherine Everett who lived in Wool. It was rented from Winston Churchill's Liberal aunt, Lady Wimborne, who was "pleased to have a clever artist as a tenant." All for the rent of £50 a year.

Katherine Everett described Alderney manor as 'an unusually attractive house built by a Frenchman, set in woodland, on the Wimborne property'. The John entourage arrived in a colourful caravan of carts & waggons with children singing as they came down the drive. They set to, turning it into the very picture of a bohemian commune. The coach house was converted into a studio, the cottage converted to accommodate the seemingly endless stream of visitors, some invited, some who just dropped in and would stay for days, months, even years. Others stayed in the blue & yellow Gypsy caravans dotted around the grounds and when numbers swelled for weekend parties, in Gypsy tents or alfresco in the orchard.

John was one of many young Slade artists who lodged with Augusta Everett at Fitzroy Street on his way to becoming England's pre-eminent painter of portraits, John made many visits to Swanage and Purbeck with his sister Gwen and painter Charles Conder. With their flamboyant Gypsy dress, beards and earrings, he and his friends became a familiar if somewhat unusual sight across the towns of south Dorset. During the 1920s he also painted two famous Dorset residents, TE Lawrence, and Thomas Hardy. The years at Alderney were the peak of John's artistic career. Everyone who was anyone seemingly wanted to have their portrait painted by the erstwhile King of Bohemia. Thomas Hardy on seeing his portrait painted by John in 1923 remarked "I don't know if that's how I look, but that's how I feel. John based his land on the Gypsies encampments. Whilst spending a lot of time amongst the families on the nearby heaths at Alderney and within the Kinson area and painting his famous portraits in his art studio at Manor Avenue. When Augustus painted his "The Mumper's Child". John persuaded a West Howe Gypsy girl to pose for the painting The Gypsy Girl. Augustus wrote that she was a traveller child who belonged to a family of travellers who camped near Alderney Manor which was almost opposite to where Alderney Hospital is now, and the John family lived a very Bohemian existence. John's children played a natural part in the community when not joining in with chores. Dorelia helped organise their education and even designed and made their clothes which were strongly influenced by the Gypsy culture they all admired. The children were full of natural mischief and freedom loving although said by some to be completely without discipline. Between private tutors for the girls and school for the boys, they ran wild over the heathland and through the woods. They bathed naked in the frog laden pond there and to the distress of the local parson dashed naked about the place until dry. They would shin up trees in bare feet and run around with a pack of red setter dogs They spent most their leisure time playing in the local broom road Dorset Brick Company brickyard and the E. F Phillips sand and gravel pit on The Munnings. They attended

Dane court school in Parkstone which had only eleven pupils till the arrival of Johns children.

John led a very eccentric life holding regular noisy parties for all his many radical art friends from the art and literary circles in London. John was painting and sketching the children and guests - taking part in afternoon jazz sessions - and presiding over the many parties, bonfires & trips to local pubs. All the usual suspects from the Bohemian art scene would make their way down to Dorset to spend time at Johns home. Johns many visitors at the Alderney Manor would often stay for days, months, even years in the blue & yellow Gypsy caravans in the grounds of the Manor and often Gypsy tents or alfresco in the orchard. Johns' children played a natural part in the community joining in with chores. And, between private tutors for the girls and school for the boys, they ran wild over the heathland and through the woods & bathed naked in the pond. His children played regularly on the Rogers and Phillips family brickworks and sand and gravel pit on Mannings heath. The communal chaos was presided over by Dorelia in pre-Raphaelite robes looking as if she was constantly about to pose for a portrait - busy organising guests and making the house run smoothly, dressing everyone in handmade clothes - helped by her sister Edie who ran the kitchen. Over the years at Alderney, they acquired all the trappings of a back to the land community; cows, a breeding herd of saddleback pigs, various donkeys, New Forest ponies, carthorses, miscellaneous cats & dogs, 12 hives of bees that stung everyone, a dovecote from which all the doves flew away and a 'biteful' monkey. Even in his own memories, John's fame as vagabond, philanderer, and dweller in Gypsydom had grown to be so overwhelming a stereotype to obscure the early originality of his artistic merits and the fresh modernity of his best 'gypsy' painting.

Despite his promiscuity lifestyle and the claim that he had fathered some 100 illegitimate offspring which is probably an exaggeration. It being fashionable at one time to claim to have had a child with him. They said he had a way with the ladies and had romantic ways. Although he himself was rather a frightening figure in appearance with his long dark hair and beard. At one time he painted nude a young local girl Mary who lived close to me on Manning's Heath

Road in one of Lady Wimborne cottages. This event caused quite a scandal at that time within the local church going community. Augustus also painted our Rogers families first home the delightful Heather View on the manning s heath road with a view of Poole quay in the distance. A house which grandad Reg Rogers had rented from Lady Wimborne prior to having his cousin Harold build our home The Mannings. John lived at his studio until 1927 before they moved to Fryern Court, Fording bridge - a 14th century friary turned farmhouse. The house on the edge of the New Forest became a stopping-off point for artists travelling to the West Country from London and developed into more of an open house than bohemian commune. In the less hectic lifestyle at Fryern where he entered the twilight of his artistic career. He pestered MPs on behalf of Gypsy & travellers' rights and was honoured to be elected president of the Gypsy Law Society in 1936. He was increasingly drawn to anarchism, both as a philosophy and a social system. eccentric. He launched an attack on hedges. `Hedges are miniature frontiers when serving as bulkheads, not windscreens. Hedges as bulkheads dividing up the Common Land should come down, for they represent and enclose stolen property. Frontiers are extended hedges and divide the whole world into compartments because of aggression and legalised robbery. They too should disappear and Dorelia lived out the last years of their lives at Fryern, interspersed with occasional trips abroad or up to London - where John would proceed, even into his eighties, to out-drink, out-party, and out-flirt his considerably younger companions. John made his way up to London on September 17th, 1961, hiding himself, somewhat appropriately, inside the National Gallery until the demonstration started. At 5 o'clock he emerged, walked across the road to Trafalgar Square and sat down, joining the unprecedented numbers who had gathered to protest the lunacy of atomic weapons - and declaring that he would " go to prison if necessary." Few there recognised the sick old man, but later when Bertrand Russell heard of John's attendance, he described it as a "heroic gesture." A month later 31st October 1961 Augustus John had died.

CHAPTER SEVEN

THE MANNINGS HEATH

The Mannings Heath encampment

FREEDOM CALLS

My thoughts lay scattered on the Gypsy camp
old Calor gas bottles shiny new lamps
yappy dogs barking warning sounds
night sky sparkling all around

Wagons parked neatly circled and free
horses cob a grazing contentedly

nippers playing blind man's buff
ole folks chewing baccy n sniffing snuff

Yogs a burning charcoal remains
flames a roaring caste a look down the lane
gal's sat grooming combing their hair
fancy skirts nights at the fair

Young men gathered on the green
chavvies talking boxing scenes
storytellers sat around cushions
scattered upon the ground

Old Ma dukkerin she won't change
fortunes me dear love on the grange
masters in his lordship's domain
lands and properties fortunes gained
toss of the coin tells me again

Bartered contracts spit and shake
Gypsy's word doesn't hesitate
who's that standing at the pearly gates
wagons roll down some ole lane
freedom calls and were off again

Ray Wills

Travellers such as the young Gideon Fancy and family camped here. The Mannings heath commons encampment was within the area known then as Canford and now known as Tower Park. Mannings heath may well have got its name when the Welsh travelling family changed their name from Welsh origin to Mannings and may well have settled in that part of Canford heath. The young Gideon Fancy and family camped there some years prior to the establishment of the council's permanent site in the 1950s. The Gypsy Basil Burton was employed here then by Dorset County council as warden. It was the very first local authority gypsy site in the UK. Gypsy families who lived there including the Bonds and Sherwood's.

Mary Bond lived there she was affectionately known as Queen of the Gypsies she was the eldest of Caroline Hughes's eight children. born in Sherborne in a bender tent. In her childhood her family all worked on farms. She loved cooking, making bacon and meat puddings in two-gallon pot. She went to the Dorset steam fair each year and to the Epsom Downs.

Mary Bond

Amongst those also living on the Mannings heath encampment over the years was the Gypsy Folk Singer Caroline Hughes. Who was born at Gallows hill encampment Bere Regis. Caroline Hughes was one of 17 children she was born in a Vardo at Bere Regis. Her mother Lavina Bateman was a hawker, and her father Arthur Hughes was a rat catcher. The Hughes family also camped at Corfe Mullen, "Downy" encampment on Colonel Georges land by the woods. When Diana and Johns married the family were staying at Blandford and didn't attend, neither did they approve of the marriage. They lived from 1973 until Carolines death on Mannings heath site. Caroline died at the Mannings heath encampment in 1973.

The Mannings encampment eventually became Dorset's permanent gypsy site in the 1950s. The camp wardens over the years employed by Dorset County council included Gypsies Sheilagh "Celia" Johnson and Basil Burton as Gypsy liaison officers for 15 years. Gypsy traveller families lived here over the years including the Hughes, Bonds, Turners, Burtons and Johnsons.

Basil Burton the Mannings camp warden often dropped in us at the Mannings to chat with my Grandad at our Mannings home. He was quite a character and often spoke up in defence of the Gypsies on.

"This site is uninhabitable. It is full of rats and some of the rubbish here has been left by fly-tippers," said Mr Burton, chairman of the Southern Romani Rights Association.

According to Mr Burton the yearly strife between travellers and householders could be avoided if councils provided designated camp areas.

"All the onus is being put on the Gypsies, but the councils are not fulfilling their obligation to provide land for the Gypsies. "It is about time the public knew what the councils aren't doing before they start screaming at the Gypsies." Shaun Robson, Borough of Poole consumer protection manager, said the Mannings Heath Road site was being put under surveillance to determine who was responsible for the fly-tipping. Mr Robson added: "The instance of

Travellers within Poole is relatively small compared with the rest of the Southwest, so there is not a strong demand for a permanent site." No doubt he had limited knowledge of the rich Gypsy area.

Mannings heath in the local press.

According to Basil the yearly strife between travellers and householders could be avoided if councils provided designated camp areas. He said, "I pointed to all the items of rubbish which didn't belong to the Gypsies." "It was local people who were dumping their household rubbish on the site and the Gypsies took the blame." he said, "It happens all the time". "The dam press and their lies". "Gypsies would not burn down their own amenities either." "That would be daft." "Gypsies would not ever think about setting fire to the roofs. For roof tiles are worth a lot of money and if so, they would have surely, they would have taken the tiles off before."

The following is from a Bournemouth Echo article of 2001:

WHAT a cheek! Fly-tippers are dumping their rubbish at a Gypsy site. Mountains of household and garden junk have been piling up for years at a designated Gypsy site, turning it into an eyesore. Residents of Bournemouth and Poole have bemoaned the mess left behind by travellers setting up camp in public parks and beauty spots. But the problem is far from one-sided, according to former county council Gypsy liaison officer Basil Burton. He showed the Echo around the site in Mannings Heath, Poole, and pointed to items which he claims were categorically not rubbish belonging to Gypsies. A change in the law in the mid-1990s that made it no longer a duty for local authorities to provide for travellers has left the conurbation with only the semi-barren Poole site for Gypsies. "This site is uninhabitable. It is full of rats and some of the rubbish here has been left by fly-tippers," said Mr Burton, chairman of the Southern Romani Rights Association. According to Mr Burton the yearly strife between travellers and householders could be avoided if councils provided designated camp areas.

"All the onus is being put on the Gypsies, but the councils are not fulfilling their obligation to provide land for the Gypsies. "It is about time the public knew what the councils aren't doing before they start screaming at the Gypsies." Shaun Robson, Borough of Poole consumer protection manager, said the Mannings Heath Road site was being put under surveillance to determine who was responsible for the fly-tipping. Mr Robson added: "The instance of Travellers within Poole is relatively small compared with the rest of the Southwest, so there is not a strong demand for a permanent site." No doubt he had limited knowledge.

Basil recalled the lifestyle. "My father left the area for Kent for the whole of summer it took 3 days to get there by caravan and then we spent the season working on the farms and harvesting strawberries potatoes and hops". As the summer ended, they made their way back home stopping enroute to help at various farms with the ploughing. "It was our horses he said that were so important to us, they gave us the transport and were the reason for means to earn a living. When we arrived back home in the Autumn my father took out all the monies out of his pocket that he had made during the summer and distributed it around the family/ Basil was one of those characters with endless stories. He was born into a gypsy family he served in the war. At that time, he could not read or write but his sergeant said he would teach him if he remained in the Army after the war and play football for the regiment. This he did so successfully that he in 1950 signed professional forms for Southampton and was their striker for many seasons.

Celia Johnson was born in a tent in Ropers Lane Gypsy travellers encampment Wareham. From the age of six, she was mother to the seven other children in her family, rarely going to school later in life she learned to read and write. She was so determined that her children should not miss out on an education the way she had done that she gave up travelling for them to settle in one school. Celia was a mother-of-six from a previous marriage. When Celia Johnson died more than 1,000 Gypsies from all over the country made their way to Poole to pay their last respects to a Romany "Queen". She returned home from the undertakers in an American-made coffin. Her huge, extended family brought along birthday cards and presents, which were buried with her, along with treasured photographs and mementoes. Her funeral procession comprised a silver hearse and eight similar coloured limousines, all brought in from Sussex. Celias funeral service was held at the Church of St Peter and St Paul in Blandford. Celia" Johnson was so revered in her widespread community that she "lie in state" for a week in her four-bedroom home in Twynham Avenue,Rossmore. Travellers trekked throughout this week from every corner of the UK in a pilgrimage to pay homage to the woman widely regarded as the heart and soul of the traditional Romany clan. Celia was so obsessive about cleanliness her grave was totally bricked in - top and bottom and all four side. It was said that when was lived that she even Hoovered the drive and parking space outside her house every day," said her niece, Hayley Turner, aged 22. "So, it's important there no dirt should ever get on her coffin." Celia, a mother-of-six from a previous marriage, was returned home yesterday from the undertakers in an American-made coffin for her huge, extended family to bring birthday cards and presents, which will be buried with her, along with treasured photographs and mementoes. A portable cabin had been rented and parked outside the house for mourners to meet and reminisce, while waiting their turn to say their farewells to the woman who was their inspiration.

Celia's husband, George, aged 63, said: "She had always talked of being buried in one of those shiny, silver American caskets, the sort in which film stars go to the grave." But the undertakers told us they're forbidden in this country, so the next best thing was an American wooden one -ornate and elaborate." Funeral directors H.J. Cole and Sons had one in stock at their central depot in Manchester. Husband George had his own epitaph for her: "She loved the world, and she should continue her travels with the world showing its love for her. The cortege comprised a silver hearse and eight similar coloured limousines, all brought in from Sussex. The funeral service at the Church of St Peter and St Paul in Blandford. Police escorted the cortege on every inch of the route from Poole.

Diana Turner attended the Great Dorset Steam Fayre each year telling fortunes. When Diana died in 1999 many Gypsies visited the Canford Heath Travellers site to pay their last respects.

Amongst those many Gypsy traveller families who lived on the Mannings heath Gypsy encampment next door to the Rogers family Mannings house were Grandads Reg Rogers cousins the Bonds. Mary Bond was the eldest of the eight children born to Caroline and John Cooper in Sherborne in 1921, Mary was born in a bender tent daughter of Caroline Hughes. Mary and her family had moved there in the early 1970s. She was affectionately known as "Queen of the Gypsies". Mary had married her husband Harold Bond on January 9th, 1939, at the Blandford parish church. They travelled with her parents when they first married to Bridgewater to work on the pea fields and cut sugar beet. They lived in Carter Down in a shepherd's hut while Mrs Bond worked on the land there. They went hawking lace, heather, scrap metal, rabbit skins and more, travelling as far afield as Winchester. Then in the 1950s they settled in a house in East Street Blandford Dorset. In later years their son John made a wooden horse drawn vardo which became their home on the side of the road at Wareham. Until it caught fire, and they moved to Canford heath. Harold Bond died in 1965. Mary often travelled into Bournemouth with her friend Tilly Johnson selling lucky heather and charms in the square, being part of the famous Gypsy lady flower sellers. She visited the Great Dorset Steam Fair. She died a great great-grandmother in January 2015. Hundreds of folks turned out to bid farewell to Dan Turner's aunt who passed away at the age of 94. A large funeral cortège including three horse-drawn carriages, wound its way from her Alderney home to St Clement's Church, Newtown, for the funeral service.

CHAPTER EIGHT

THE ALDERNEY AND WALLISDOWN GYPSY TRAVELLERS

The old clay cutters

There were gangs of clay cutters on Mitchell's site
cutting clay by day and night
the work was tiresome and the hours long
but they we're mean, and they were strong

On the alder hills they dug the quarry
their kids to feed and waif's they had married
the Talbot land was rich in clay
with a good day's work for a poor man's pay

The brickyards stretched across the land
from Wareham Road to Turbary's sands

Old Meg the Gypsy lived in her cottage on the heath
where tinkers blessed the turf's so deep
to cut their turfs was o survive
in wintertime when love was wild

The warblers sang their songs for free
whilst the adders and lizards squirmed beneath birch trees
the common land was fit to roam
with Gypsy vendors with high curved domes
the sacks were plentiful on the ground

Where fir cones dropped, and beggars scrounged
    the Talbot sisters heard their pleas
the working men and poor widow's pleas
    they built a village to be proud
like Winton soil the land was loud

Ray Wills

When

When Wallisdown was just a roman track
for heavy wooden cartwheels
when just rabbit's habitat-ed all the downs
the Gypsy kids played in Gypsy town.
a fortune then was half of a crown.

When Ensbury park was an old horse racetrack
the grass was tall and spread out and back
across the Talbot Heath woods gravel tracks
he heathers song was buzzed.
by hordes of merry bees in the fuzz

The church bells rang out.
across the village green
from Millhams Lane to Ringwood Road
little wayside country inn
home of rest to all that were a traveling.
It was quite a scene

When many walked the gravel track to Wimborne bridge
across the lanes of hills n ridge
cows brought back from the market towns stalls.
through fern down haunts and Kinson moors
they called out to the heifer crews.
along that road that led to Poole

The pines were oh so tall n proud.
all their branches wore a shroud.
of green n browns n pollen flowers

to delight young girls for many hours

In days long afore the cars took oer
those lanes n gravel tracks that were.
Dartford warblers were fine birds.
Their songs were often heard.

Now all that's left are memories.
Of all those walks that used to be
before the Tower Park complexity
covered up what's left by Alderney.

Ray Wills

Such Majesty

We tided and tethered all our ponies and cobs with wagons
standing bye
next to Alders windswept lanes and bracken
whilst we drank within the Kings Arms
on the hillsides of Wallisdown

All its heavy iron rings were fastened to its wall
Where the wind blew over the bracken
where the sisters Talbot built their village and the dwellings
for the poor downtrodden masses
in the time of John Augustus
in the days of Lady Cornelia Guest

Where the heather blessed the commons
and the Gypsies rode the lanes and blessed
the encampments on the common then
were rich in stories n true in faith
With all their chavvies running free
All their wisdom shared around their yog fires

All the virtues of the tribes
Ayres n Sherwood's, Coles and Stanleys, Jeffs and Coopers
Bless the bride,
sprigs of our heather for your luck dear
Off to Woolworths in Poole

Once we saw the dolphin's ride
upon the quayside tide there

Where the ships sail out to sea
Bound for to gain their fortunes in Newfound lands
Rich in bounty in another time
Such Majesty

Ray Wills

Wallisdown encampments

Wally Wack was a term used for Wallisdown where there were many encampments including one on the corner of Ringwood Road and Wallisdown Road as well as on the site of the present public house restaurant was previously known as the Mountbatten Arms. With another on the opposite corner where the petrol service garage is today. 36 children from local encampments at Wallisdown at one time attended Kinson village school in 1928 and some locals complained. Although at the time the head teacher Miss Ward remarked that there was no problem with them mixing with the other children or from the village parents about their behaviour. Many of these families also worked in the local factories in Wallisdown at Max Factors or Websters, Pineland laundry Chalwyn Lamps, Ryvita and Bluebird Caravans. Whilst many would take sprigs of heather, create artificial paper crape flowers or floral bouquets, and wreaths and sell them privately or outside of Beales store in Bournemouth square and Woolworth's stores in Poole high street.

THE KINGS ARMS WALLISDOWN

William Sherwood and family were the landlords of the Kings Arms pub at Wallisdown for many years around 1870. The pub had iron rings on its outside walls for the Gypsy horses to be tethered to and there was straw on the floor. It was a popular Gypsy pub it was near the Talbot encampments. William Turner was also linked to the very large family tree of Sherwood's traced back to George Sherwood who had married Eleanor Rix in 1740 at Kinson. Poole council bought land off of lord Wimborne in 1962. Some 230 acres at Canford heath. Its first house was built in wrong place and had to be demolished and built again. Housing estates were built at Rossmore, Trinidad, Branksome, Bourne Bottom, Arne Avenue, Alderney, Kinson, and West Howe. Many Gypsy travellers adapted well to their new homes though still retaining the delightful artistry of interior furnishings reminiscent of their culture and identity. Tower Park as built on swampy ground Phillips sank lorry loads rubble there for foundations.

A Mitchell family operated clay pits on Alder hills

Bill Knott Manager of the Bluebird caravans originally lived in a bungalow in Broom Road Alderney before he became an entrepreneur and millionaire. Bill started his road to self-employed selling shoelaces and match boxes on the streets of up on hill at Ashley Road Parkstone. Before building his bluebird caravan industry grew out of the local Gypsy caravan concept locally, his mother being a Gypsy lady. My aunt Ivy Thorpe nee Rogers worked there as a child minder for the family.

Despite their earthy sometimes muddy surroundings Gypsies and Travellers tents, benders, caravans were kept spotlessly clean. With highly polished brass lamps, cut glass mirrors. Cooking was done outside, over an open fire, washing was boiled outside in big iron cauldrons. Romanies preferred to marry into other Romany families, although in time they started to marry outside their community.

The Bourne hill encampment

This was also known as top common Gypsy encampment. This camp was situated at the rear of the Saunders Homes of Rest on the

Ringwood Road West Howe known as Hoopers gravel pit and top common encampment. It which was a short distance from the Mountbatten Arms pub on the Wallisdown Road. This was the higher Gypsy encampment which held up to 15 Gypsy families and was owned by a Mr Hooper. Here the Gypsies paid 1 shilling rent a week to Mr Hooper. The writer Dominic Reeves and the artist Augustus John also stayed here on numerous occasions and made friends with many local Gypsy families here. It was here where Augustus John the artist stayed here on occasion where he painted a gypsy child from the camp for his Mumpers child. Dominic Reeves who was a prolific writer of tales of the Gypsy life also wrote about the Gypsies he stayed with at the higher encampment at Bourne hill, at the rear of Saunders homes of rest on the Ringwood Road.

Many of these encampments contained flimsy homes of sacking some cut out of the mud with basic bender roofing. When Mr Hooper died the land was sold and developed.

Annie White married Walter Dane Matthews in 1934 whose family lived on the Bourne hill encampment. Annie White and family were originally from Bristol before moving to West howe where they lived for a few months in Mr Coopers rented Vardo. Before moving into a shack in fern heath road then into Acres Road. Most of these camps contained flimsy homes of sacking some cut out of the mud with basic bender roofing. Brittania Keets lived there and is buried in Kinson St Andrew's cemetery where there is a grand angelic monument dedicated to her. There were other encampments on the corners of Ringwood and Wallisdown roads and on the Common by lady Wimborne bridge.

Nelson Stanley Scrap yard Alder hills
Nelson has operated his very successful scrap metal business on the Alder hills for many years.

Lodge Hills encampment

This encampment was situated on the higher ground high above Mannings heath towards Magna Road at Bere Cross and all the caravans here were very exquisite.

Many of these traditional stopping places and encampments were taken over managed by local councils or by settled individuals decades ago. These have subsequently changed hands on very many occasions; however, Gypsies have long historical connections to such places and do not always willingly give them up. Most Gypsy traveller's families are identifiable by their traditional wintering base, where they will stop travelling for the winter, this place will be technically where a family is from.

Talbot encampments

The 1840s and 1850s had become a time of high unemployment for many. Whilst just a few miles away on the Wallis downs the Talbot family sisters the wealthy Talbot sisters from Surrey, Georgina and Mary [Marianne] Talbot, who had visited the area as children were creating a community in the local woodlands. Providing work for locals with housing needs within a community of church, farm outhouses and even a school for the children with land for Gypsy encampments in their Talbot village. The village provided employment for many traveller families plus areas to graze their horses. The sisters had originally come to Wallisdown Bournemouth in their school holidays staying at Hinton Wood House on the East Cliff. The sisters were touched by local poverty and unemployment the plight of some of the poor in the locality many of whom were from the local Gypsy communities. They saw poor people begging on the streets in filth with not enough money to provide for their families and vowed to do something to help in the future. Then later in 1850 when their father died and left them his estate the two Sisters come to Wallisdown and worked to fulfil their dreams and philanthropist ideals. They set about acquiring several parcels of land using the money at their disposal. To build cottages, with smallholdings of 6 farms each covering some 20 acres, with alms houses, a church and a school. In all about 70 acres was reserved for their Talbot model village. With an area of 150 acres retained as common land to provide animal grazing for new tenants. Initially locals many of whom were Gypsy brick makers and labourers were employed to clear the land and to build cottages. Each one on an acre plot and each had a well, animal pens and fruit trees, plus free areas to graze their horses. Some of these workers were from Gypsy encampments at Kinson, New England, Bankes common and Wallis downs high moor. Once the 19 cottages were built the workers lived in them and were charged a rent of between 4 and 5 shillings per week. The cottages were in a style that was influenced by John Nash's designs Tenants were expected to develop sustainable lifestyles by keeping animals, such as pigs and chickens, and by growing fruit and vegetables.

The Kings Arms encampment

The encampment was opposite where the petrol service garage is today. Many local Gypsies tethered their ponies outside this Wallisdown pub fastened to the large metal rings on the outside walls. The Gypsies who camped on these Wallisdown encampments were regulars at the local Kings Arms public house with its straw lined floor.

Alderney Common encampment

This popular site was situated on the Belben Road and Ringwood Road area near to lady Wimborne bridge and which is now the site of the local corner shop.

There was another large encampment on the junction to the left of the Mountbatten pub. It was close to the golf course and now it is a caravan site.

John Ruffle married Rebekka Keets from Wallisdown in 1874 as recorded in the 1911 census. One of the encampments was on the site of the present public house restaurant previously known as the Mountbatten Arms which was originally opened by Lord Mountbatten.

There were Gypsy stone masons at Wallisdown as well as blacksmiths.

CHAPTER NINE

AFTER POOLE HEATH

The Gypsies flower girl's dream

Youl see them there on Saturdays
outside Bournemouth town great square
With baskets full of daffodils, lilacs and roses by the score
their braided hair and darker looks
with their dresses oh so gay
from heather sweet terrains they came
to while the hours away

Their dialect was course with melody
though their words were plain
they spoke the true Romani like children once again
they promised wealth good health and more
to people passing by
with smiles to warrant fortunes gained
with wisdom in their eyes

The homes of vardos on the heath and songs of yesterday
with accordions playing songs of love
with rabbits in the hay
with ponies small and dog juk packs calls
with heathers sweetly laid
amongst the hills where myxomatosis killed the food of yesterday

Ray Wills

Before the houses

From Bourne Valley bottom and along the dirt track
the caravans rumbled to Lodge hills and back
though thick hedges laden full of bramble and gorse
with lovely chestnuts to nibble by our little horse
there at Coy meadows we drank from the stream
little fresh springs and wonders to dream

There were Gypsies at Beales in Bournemouth today
so, we tell you your fortune then be on our way
the village kids saw us, and they gave us the eye
in our caravans' homes which smoked right up to the sky

With rabbits to ferret and hedgehogs to eat
With songs around the campfire and family to greet
the wheels rolled their daily whilst the stars shone at night
there were folks in their glory with clothes to delight

There was food on the table and rugs on the floor
the candles n lamps lit with designs on the doors
Whilst the music was played with accordion Joe
whilst the songs that we sung were older than dough

There were times which were hard then
and folks they did stray
But we were far wiser than many today
the grass grew so course and the daisies were spread
like creation was labelled for the good and the dead

The Queen of the Gypsies was dark and so rare
she had braided long hair and spent nights at Poole fair
the wagons were rich and the lamps they were gold
whilst the little chavs all danced naked upon their tip toes
the chaffinches sung at the break of the day
as we ambled along our stories to say

Now there's just tarmac on Tower Park ridge
where there was once magic with our uncle Sid
For we lived on the heaths then
when the land it was free
Before Lord Wimborne sold it to Poole council
for houses for thee

Ray Wills

Bournemouth encampments

Bournemouth was originally known as Poole Heath. It was an area of acid sandy soil and gorse, criss-crossed by tracks, with a stream called the Bourne running through into the sea and wooded chine's cut by other streams. Here there was Gypsies and a few fishermen living in timber-framed cottages.

Holdenhurst common encampments

Here there were gypsy encampments in the late 1950s. This was where the Sherwood's, Bonsais and Coopers families lived.

Five Ways encampments

These were situated on the Turbary Allotments now known as Queens Park Avenue part of the present golf course. These included Camels hump, Devils drop and Wall of death.

Many camped here from the late 1800s. It was Situated between two hills with tents and vans. George and Louisa White nee Crutcher lived here. Their daughter Betsy Smith nee White was born here in 1890. She was one of eleven children and the original Bournemouth flower girl. The family and others all moved to Parkstone's Heavenly bottom campsite when the site was developed in later years end of the 19th century.' Here there were Dark men lounging about smoking short pipes, several children, a few horses and one or two lean and hungry looking dogs.' These gypsies, it seems, were the first inhabitants of the Queens Park Avenue region. 'The tents are very curious and un-English in appearance, patched in places with pieces of gawdy material. One or two of the women home from the town after selling flowers are turning in at the gate, and from the caravans rise a few curls of bluish-grey smoke.

Jean Matthews was born in the family vardo wagon close by the Christchurch railway station on 10th October 1928. Jean recalled that "We moved to Heavenly Bottom from the top of Churchill Road Parkstone Poole. A place where once the fair was held. I can remember going around the fairground during the day with my brothers Peter and Freddie Carter this fairground was our playground. We left there later for Heavenly Bottom which was known also as Burgess Field. To one side of the field was a stream that ran through it. Where many a bucket was filled for various purposes. At the bottom of the field there was a sawmill or wood yard. I remember visiting with my mother's cousin Emma Hughes nee Saunders.

Redhill encampment

There was a popular Gypsy traveler encampment in the late 1950s at Sandy Lane Red hill common. It was based in a gravel pit and managed by a Mr. Luther. There were many horses within this camp.

British born Charles Parker explored the lives of England's 'Travelling People'. Charles admitted 'As a boy I roamed the heathlands of the Dorset Hampshire border, but of the people who had roamed these heaths for five hundred years, I knew nothing'.

Indian hut

Indian Hut stood as a landmark in Bournemouth a century ago and was even marked on maps of the time. But, since it disappeared, generations of Bournemouth people have puzzled over how it came by its name. Now a Bournemouth woman, Mrs Pearl Hoar, thinks a friend of hers may have the answer Tom Rees reckons the hut, situated in a then lonely spot near what is now Fiveways at Charminster, gained its name when Buffalo Bill's Wild West Show came to town.

Mrs Hoar, who lives in Austin Close, is the granddaughter of Mark Loader, the contractor responsible for making many of the roads on the town's housing estates. His yard was situated where Indian Hut had stood.

She mentioned to Mr Rees that her grandfather was Mark Loader and he at once replied: "His place was where Indian Hut stood in

Charminster." Mrs Hoar possesses an old cutting of the Echo, dating back to 1973, that tried to trace the origin of the name Indian Hut, and she realised Mr Rees may have given the answer to the old enigma. Although that cutting of 1973 suggests the hut was built around 1870, it may have been much older

Mr Rees, of Spring Road, who like, Mrs Hoar, is born and bred in the town, told the Echo: "When I was a boy my mother told that when she was a child, Buffalo Bill's circus came to East Station Common, which stood between Bournemouth Station and the cemetery. "She was about eight at the time and the circus recruited youngsters to go into the covered wagons to be chased round by the Indians. "She was one of the children and told me there were about 30 Indians, some of whom were billeted at that hut."

Bournemouth librarian Jan Marsh said a book by Pascoe Marshall, who lived in Throop, referred to a primitive wattle and daub hut at Fiveways, which was used as an isolation hut by smallpox sufferers who had to fend for themselves.

The Echo cutting of 1973 says Indian Hut is clearly shown on several maps published around the end of the 19th century. It suggests Indian Hut stood in "splendid isolation" at Fiveways from about 1870 to 1907 and quotes from a 1905 report in the Bournemouth Graphic newspaper of the time that, even then, could not explain how it got its name.

The Graphic writer described it as being in a wooded area of pines and past a gypsy encampment. It had one floor, a thatched roof and a square chimney was the only brickwork. "The walls are rough, the windows low and square and painted, by some unhappy inspiration, a bright yellow," the writer added.

The writer also told how he had met an elderly road mender who told him: "No zur, I don't know why it be called the Indian 'hut. It work put up for a cripple that came to 'Olderness (Holdenhurst)."

He added: "No zur, I never see no Indians." By 1907 the hut had gone.

The 1973 Echo article quoted one reader, William Mist, of Winton, who said: "My father told me the name Indian Hut came from the fact that there was, at one time, an old hut which was used by a tramp who either originated from India or was an ex-Serviceman who had served in India." Other readers recalled how it had been a popular play area at the turn of that century, that it had been used by "some rough-living character" and it stood on the spot then used as Mark Loader's yard.

In 1957 David Young, a Bournemouth librarian, who, when writing about Bournemouth in 1895, wrote: "Charminster Road continued as a narrow lane, the land on either side still covered with claypits, lime kilns and brickyards, the only habitation within a mile save for occasional encampments of gypsies, the lone Indian Hut, situated in the area now known as Fiveways at the junction of the lane with the track which later became Green Road.

"The brickfields of this district were the property of Mark Loader who was responsible for making the roads on many of the new building estates in Bournemouth and introduced the steamroller into the borough."

Snapshots of the Past, two years ago, asked if anyone could throw light on the origins of Indian Hut and its occupants and readers reminisced about a former Fiveways newsagents that used to be known as Indian Hut, after the building that had stood nearby and which outside had a full-sized wooden figure of an Indian in headdress, marking the shop as an agent for Ogden's Flake tobacco.

The year 1894, which Tom Rees reckons is when Buffalo Bill's circus came to Bournemouth, pre-dates the launch of the Echo in 1900 but his outfit certainly came to the neighbourhood. In 1904 local papers reported Colonel W F Cody, and his troop of 1,300 men and horses put on a display at Poole's Ladies Walking Field.

Pearl Hoar and Tom Rees are pretty sure they have the answer to the riddle of Indian Hut. "I imagine it's true," said Tom. "Why else would my mother have told it to me?"

Down one side of a hill. Into a narrow and rutty lane.' (The Graphic author seems to have entered the top part of Mallard Road, or Strouden Lane as it would have been then, at a point where it is now Queens Park Avenue. The next stage of his journey will take him up Howard Road to Strouden playing fields.)

'Up another slope and we get our first view of what appears a new part of Bournemouth. The new roads are hidden now, and to the south-east rise pines and firs, firs and pines stretching away back further and further until the ground rises and finds a background in the slopes above the new golf links.'

(From the top of Howard Road, it would indeed be possible to turn and look south-east to Queens Park golf links 'If it wasn't for the 'houses in between' as Gus Elen might have sung.)

'Close at hand the ground is covered with bracken, brown and faded. It spreads outward from the lane, drops suddenly down the slope and is lost among the trees. The month is December, and it is a December mist that lurks among the bushes and, back in the wood, where the pines are closer and thicker, forms itself into a shadowy grey wall.'

With forgivable whimsy, the author is distracted from his search for the Indian Hut, by some local colour.) 'Behind us there is a different scene. Between the two hills stands a gipsy encampment comprised of about half a dozen caravans, four or five tents, and the striking and picturesque accessories usually attendant, consisting of dark men lounging about and smoking short pipes, several children, a few horses and one or two lean and hungry looking dogs.' (These gypsies, it seems, were the first inhabitants of the Queens Park Avenue region.)

'The tents are very curious and un-English in appearance, patched in places with pieces of gawdy material. One or two of the women home from the town after selling flowers are turning in at the gate, and from the caravans rise a few curls of bluish-grey smoke. Beyond, the skyline is broken with the tops of tall trees, and above a mass of soft and snowy clouds float low in the air with a yellow sun shining into their fleecy depths.'

(It's all very poetic, but studying the fleecy depths of the clouds, rather than consulting an Ordnance Survey map, will have consequences.)

It isn't clear if the properties Tregonwell built and bought were for friends staying as invited guests, or to be leased to paying visitors. In 1815, Mrs Sarah Grosvenor was visiting: Sarah Frances Erle-Drax (c1761-1822) heiress to the Charborough Park Estate in Dorset married Richard Grosvenor. A close friend of the Tregonwells, Mrs Grosvenor, during her visits to Bourne, sketched and wrote about the place. Her 'A Peep into Futurity', took an amusing view of Bourne as it existed in 1815, and the town she imagined it becoming sixty years into the future. Mrs Grosvenor's works constitute our earliest pictures of Bourne, and our earliest evidence that anyone considered it growing into a town.

Mrs Grosvenor alluded to smuggling activities, with barrels of rum appearing in some sketches. One shows the terrifying gypsy, Meg or Peggy, rushing down 'Meg's Hill' (the West Cliff) waving a knife. The gypsy reference is significant, because the travelling community were missed in the enclosure process. There was no recognition in the 1805 Award of gypsies' rights to their camps; which of long tradition had been at Queens Park, the West Cliff, Wallisdown, etc.

By 1820, Tregonwell had gone beyond simply having friends to stay at Bourne, he was actively advertising 'The Mansion' through newspapers, where it was described as a Marine Residence 'at Bourne Cliff, near Christchurch, Hants'. This was an amended version of 'Boorn Cliff' from the 1809 adverts, as the name of the place.

Lucy Kemp Welch

Lucy was born in Bournemouth in June 1869 and her childhood was spent in Bournemouth. She was an accomplished painter who specialised in horses. When she was 19, she moved to Bushey, Hertfordshire, to study at the art school of Hubert von Herkomer. She lived most of her life in Bushey, the New Forest was a rich source of material for her.

Lucy's first encounter with gypsies was purely by chance that she saw, from her window at Bushey a group of horses going up the muddy road to Barnet Fair. She wrote about what happened and said "They were shepherded and driven by wild-looking gypsy men on horseback, with frequent rushes to prevent the outliers from getting through the gates or turning up the side lanes. "She went on to explain how she rushed out of the house with her palette in excitement and part of the wooden slide from her paint box to draw on and ran after the group as fast as she could. Fortunately, they had stopped on a green by the public house." There I made a lightening sketch of the scene- my long training of quick sketches in the street helping greatly".

This initial drawing developed into what was to become her first submission to the Royal Academy exhibition titled "Gypsy Horse Drovers", received much acclaim and was hung in choice position just over 'the line'. Both the sketch and the huge exhibition work are now in the Russell-Cotes collection in Bournemouth. In 1922, Queen Victoria's granddaughter, Princess Marie-Louise, asked Lucy to make a miniscule painting for the Queen's Dolls' House. The postage stamp-sized painting can now be seen with the other miniature furniture at Windsor Castle.

Lucy spent several of her summers in the 20s and 30s following Lord Sanger's Circus, recording the horses in sketches and paint. She focussed her work on the scenes of Gypsy and circus life, wild Exmoor ponies, heavy horses and farm horses. Sanger's circus was one of the biggest inter-war circuses and for months at a time Lucy lived in a caravan hitched to the back of her car. During this time, she expanded her painting repertoire to include lions, seals and elephants. In later years she also painted pictures of gypsy caravans. In 1935 she won a local competition in Bushey with her design for a triumphal arch and float to celebrate George V's Jubilee. The arch was erected at the entrance to the village across the High Street and a parade was held in the King's honour.

'Herkomer was so impressed by 'her picture The Gypsy Horse Drovers' taking horses to a fair that he recommended that Lucy submit it for the next Royal Academy Exhibition. This she did, and it was hung in a good position just above the line and was quickly purchased by Sir Frederic Harris for £60.00. At that time £60.00 represented a significant sum; Lucy would have been overjoyed. 'She took over the management of the school in 1905, and ran it until 1926, first as the Bushey School of Painting, and later as the Kemp-Welch School, when she moved it to her own house. She was a good friend of Robert Baden-Powell and helped him with a horse that had been presented to him by the people of Australia. The horse, Black Prince, was intended for ceremonial parades. Unfortunately, unlike Baden-Powell, Black Prince detested soldiers and was terrified by the sound of gunfire and drums. Following several 'incidents' on the parade ground, the horse's future was in doubt until Kemp-Welch stepped in. Able to calm the 17.5hh stallion, she looked after him until his death in 1922. Kemp-Welch immortalised Black Prince in the illustrations she did for Anna Sewell's 'Black Beauty', This was just the beginning of Lucy's career, which included illustrating the children's book. At the age of 80, though her eyesight was failing, Lucy was still able to exhibit one painting at the Royal Academy in 1949. During the 1950s she became something of a recluse and died in hospital in Watford in in November 1958.

By the 18th century Poole was dominated by the Newfoundland trade and it was a prosperous and growing town. Dorset had over 100 brickyards with Poole alone having excess of 50 and it was estimated that at its peak 30 million bricks were made in Poole providing regular employment throughout the area. Clay was exported to the Minton and Wedgewood potteries. By 1812, up to 20,000 tons of clay was being shipped from Poole to Liverpool for the Staffordshire potteries. With export had risen to 69,286 tons in 1851. The heathlands including Poole heath and Canford encompassed the community of Newtown at Parkstone Branksome in Poole. With acres of heather lands scattered over the land in which local Gypsy Travellers lived in their numerous encampments. At one time it seemed that the whole area of Canford heathlands was but a massive encampment. The area was rich in clay, gravel and sand which provided growing numbers of clay pits, sand and gravel pits, potteries, and brickworks. Providing much needed work for local people with a great local natural seaport at hand at Poole. Here ships exported locally made exquisite pottery, bricks, tiles and other commodities which were renowned throughout the world. Poole had in earlier years been a highly profitable dock with its rich trade with Newfoundland. There was what was known as Turbary rights granted in 1248 which ended in 1822 with the Enclosure Act.

All members of the Gypsy families were used as labour many often working 12-hour shifts. It was very labour intensive and hot work in brick yards with poor lighting and over the years a number were killed from suffocation and fumes

Bere Cross Encampment

The encampment was to the left of Bere cross pub. Gypsy Travellers families here on this encampment included the Sherwood's, Barnes, Barneys, Brewers, Budden's, Burdens, Coles, Coopers, Crutcher's, Croucher's, Crockers, Does, Fancy's, Hanford's, Harris, Harrisons, Hawkins, Hughes, James, Jeffs, Keets, Lights, Matthews, Mitchells, Phillips, Pittman's, Pidgeley's, Sherwood's, Smiths, Stanleys, Tillys, Turners, Warrens, Whites and Willetts. These were skilled artisan's, horse trader's, brick and pottery makers, floral and wreath makers, tinkers, fortune and story tellers, fairground people and farm labourers. Many worked for Carters, Budden's and Elliotts.

Gypsies helped to establish many new work sites like Harold Rogers brick works at Fortescue Road /Dorchester Road 1878-1900. Alpen way Bourne valley pottery clay pits in 1886 and Dupes Brickworks 1887–1967 Daccombe and T Rabbetts had brickworks 1923-58. C Mitchell Downton's.

There was an Alder Road brickwork in 1927-1974.George Rogers at Church Road, Upper Parkstone R.S.O. Rogers Brothers Brickworks at Mannings heath 1926 and Broom Road Dorset Brick Company in 1923. Henry Charles Brixey Newtown Vale brickworks in fancy road 1906-1927.Warboys was also a big employer in the area.

The Bear Cross pub

It was originally called the brick makers arms. It was originally a thatched cottage a little behind the site of the present hotel. The first landlord of the pub was George Ware. George was a brick maker by day, as were most locals. When Ware died in 1883 the inn's license had passed to the Lane family, among them Frank Lane who worked as a carpenter by day building coffins for the Gypsy community at Alderney Common encampments. His son Arthur Lane had been born above The Bear Cross Inn in 1913 and could recall Augustus John who would spend noisy evenings on the premises, plus similar evenings at The Shoulder of Mutton in West Howe. The present Bear Cross Hotel was built in 1931 in front of the old inn which was then pulled down.

There were many stories of pugilist bare knuckle boxing fights there attracting hordes of folks to their illegal gathering's.

CHAPTER TEN

KINSON VILLAGE

The Village

Mural Hub Kinson designed by Devon-based artist David Harbott.

Romany Roots

He had travelled through those Romany roots
where cultures and heartaches were seldom foolproof
he'd walked o'er the footpaths where thorns tagged your toes
where rabbits and foxgloves bridled your clothes
he'd stumbled on wise folk who'd been through the wars
when peace was a haven and Truth was one's word
his clothes they were tattered, and his language was rich
he'd laid in the gutters the sideways and ditch

The lore of his nation was caste to the winds
where freedom was gifted with Romany rings
where the sun hit you blindly each morning at dawn
where the heavens were open, and your ways were forlorn

The paths that they had ventured o'er valley and dale
with scent of the flower and the rich golden smells
where your fortune was told through the wink of an eye
where fairgrounds were rolling, and spirits were high
like days long ago when the soil was rich
they travelled their wagons through mud and low ditch

Where heather and fern stretched for many a mile
where the Romany roots were a haven a while
where the man was renowned for the good in his smile

Ray Wills

Kinson village is situated within the old parish of Greater Canford and it pre-dates the Doomsday book where it was recorded as Chines Tu. After many name changes over the centuries, it was eventually known as Kinson in the 1800s.

Kinson Potteries.

In the early days the wide Kinson Parish area, all its brickyards and potteries were thriving from the 1800s. It was situated in the south-west corner of the parish towards Poole. It had 27 acres of clay of three different qualities, some beds being as much as 40 feet thick although all were under a great depth of sand. The pottery works here were started early last century but received a fillip with the increase in building around Poole and Bournemouth.

The Kinson Clay fields and Fired Pottery Company was established in 1854 with a capital of £40,000. The money was raised by a business group from 'up country' and the potteries leased locally. By the 1860s the works had twelve kilns, a boiler, engine house, drying sheds, stables, and offices. Bricks, tiles, chimney pots and drainpipes were made. At about this time oil had been found in Canada and an oilfield established at Collingwood. Good firebricks were required for the processing and the potteries at Kinson manufactured refractory chimney flue bricks which suited the purpose. Orders for them were sent back home and the goods duly despatched. Their progress was recently traced and went thus: by horse and cart from the potteries to Poole Quay, by barge to London or Southampton, across the Atlantic to Quebec or Montreal, by raft or barge up the St. Lawrence River to York (present Toronto), by railway to Collingwood harbour, by raft along the southern shores to Nottawasaga Bay to the beach nearest the site and by hand the rest of the way. Cheaper oil was found elsewhere and production at Collingwood ceased in 1861. Recently some of the bricks, each bearing the words KINSON, POOLE, were found in a field there. One was returned to England.

The landscape in the early 1800s was very similar to The New Forest of today with vast areas of heath lands. Kinson was then part of Canford Magna estate with the higher grounds were known as Howe's and the main valley referred to as Bourne Valley.

The locals had been reliant on pigs for their livelihoods which were mainly pastured in the woodlands. In the Kinson village there were prominent groups of Gypsy traveller families some of whom were flower gatherers, basket makers, brick makers, broom makers and fairground people, many worked with horses, and some dealt in scrap and rag and bone. There were many local gypsy brick makers in Kinson all part of this great workforce at Burdens brickyard Ringwood Road and Poole Lane and at Alder Road brickyard on Talbot heathlands.

Frampton Terrace

It was built specifically for the brickmaker families.

Local brick and pottery company's workers included E Fancy brick maker East Howe Kinson. James Rogers brick maker at constitution hill, George Ware brick maker Kinson, Phillip Hawkes brick maker Kinson, Alfred Carters bricks and tile works Kinson, W T Budden's brick works west howe Kinson, and E A Elliott's Kinson brick works. Bricks had been handmade in Dorset since Tudor times going hand in hand with Agriculture.

Elliot's potteries started at Bear Cross. Mr. E.A. Elliot, farmed extensively in the area, discovered good brick clay when a well was sunk on his farm at Condell. A brickwork was started here where the farmland met the crossroads, and hand-made bricks were made from around 1880 to 1900. The When the clay at Bere Cross ran out the brickworks was moved to the rise of land at West Howe in Poole Lane.

The clay here was a much better-quality Ball Clay. Later, in 1912, drainpipes, terra cotta ware and roofing tiles were manufactured in addition to bricks. In 1922, Mr. N. T. Elliot entered the firm and by 1927 the manufacture of bricks fir domestic fireplaces was started and these together with stoneware drainpipes, were made until the potteries closed in 1966. Bournemouth Corporation and Max

Factor's (local light industry) bought the land. To the east of Elliot's stood Painter and Ropers 'Kinson Steam Brickworks', later owned by Burdens. This was a smaller concern where hand-made bricks were manufactured. (Taken from Old Kinson by S.J. Lands).

For well over half a century the Arnolds, Edmund then Thomas, were the Kinson village blacksmiths with their smithy where Home Road now joins the main road. The Pound was on the triangle of land formed at the junction of Pound and Millhams Lanes. The pound keeper's cottage stood next to it. Here were brought any cattle, horses or goats straying or causing damage. They were rounded up by the pound-keeper and here they remained until their owners paid for any damage done, for their keep and the impounding fee.

Gypsies Walter Barnes and Selina Light were fined sixpence with 2s. 6d. costs in 1895 for allowing their horses to stray.

Fanny Cole (nee Longman) lived in her cottage next door to the Dolphin public house in Kinson, which is now known as Gulliver's. Fanny ran her coal delivery business from her coal yard with her pony and cart. Then shortly after the death of her husband in 1897. She bought the coal at Poole Quay and delivered coal all around the Newtown area.

The Cole's were show people who managed fairgrounds along with a history of work with elephants at circuses. They were a dark race said to originate in Spain.

My mother Iris Rogers and her friends the Sherwood's when teenagers cycled from Alderney then down Poole lane to attend the Kinson hairdressers.

On the village green in Kinson in olden times was where they put the local villains in the stocks and where the village girls danced around the maypole. It was where Revd Sharp once played cricket with his young talented lads who were chosen to play for England but 1914-18 war made that unlikely. The village school nearby was where in 1928 some 36 bare footed Gypsy children from Gypsy encampments at Wallisdown had descended on the headmistress Miss Ward one cold Monday morning. All of them wanting to be schooled, yet some locals complained. The head teacher remarked at the time that there was no problem with them mixing with the other children and the village parents never complained about their behaviour. Many Travellers who made Kinson their home, still returned every year to popular stopping places at Alton, Medstead, Binstead, Horton Heath, near Cranborne and the West Moors Common for the hopping and strawberry and pea-picking. Many of whom lived in tents or benders in the early days, then later in caravans or Vardos or simple houses.

Millhams Mead encampment

In the Kinson village there were prominent groups of Gypsy traveller families some of whom were flower gatherers, basket makers, brick makers, broom makers and fairground people, many worked with horses and others dealt in scrap and rag and bone. There were over the years numerous encampments at Kinson Common and Millhams Mead.

THE FLOWER GIRLS

NANCY CRUTCHER

In Kinson there was a large white stoned house on church lane itself where travelling families the Crutcher's, Jeff's and family lived with their pig sties in the grounds. Whilst in the centre of the village was the village green where the local Revd. Sharp was busy with his young team of cricketers some of whom were chosen to play for England. The Kinson village green was used for local events. Such as maypole dances on maypole days and here local criminals' wrong doers from the locality were put in wooden stocks and local folk were able to throw rotten vegetables at them.

The Crutcher's had made floral tributes and buttonholes for weddings and sold flowers in Bournemouth square with others of the Bournemouth flower girls. All Kinson people went to Nancy,

Gerty and earlier her mums when they wanted flowers or wreaths made. The Jeffs sold flowers on the streets of Christchurch for very many years (Violet Jeff nee White). Nancy Crutcher lived at the large white house in Millhams Lane in Kinson where she ran her flower business. Nancy lived with her mother and her brothers. Nancy's mother was widowed and remarried a Jeff; therefore, Nancy was well known as Nancy Jeff. She was well-known and well-liked lady, and she had a thriving flowers business, growing and selling flowers, making wreaths and bridal bouquets.

Nancy is also related to the original Flower Girl Betsy Smith (nee White) from Heavenly Bottom. In the later years after Betsy's death when only a few of the family (Betty Smith nee Cooper, and Daisy Wheeler nee Hughes) were still flower selling, Nancy and her brothers saw an opening and came into Bournemouth Square where she sold for many years. Nancy became very popular with Bournemouth Folk, as Betsy had before her.

Job Jeff as a child had lived on the Bankes common encampment Kinson with his mother Macey and his father also job jeff and his siblings Sam, Lousia, Walter, and Lizzie. Whilst Nancy was well known by all those Gypsies who lived at the heavenly bottom campsite in Parkstone Poole. The Jeff's sold flowers on the streets of Christchurch for very many years. They all lived at the large house in Milldams Lane in Kinson. The Crutcher's had made floral tributes and buttonholes for weddings and sold flowers in Bournemouth square with others of the Bournemouth flower girls for many years. Taking over the family head role at Millhams Lane when Granny Jeff died. Nancy loved the occasional flutter on the horses and driving her car. She was a kind and generous woman. I recall in the late 80s when I was at St Andrews church Kinson operating the Kinson renovation of the churchyard project. Nancy visited me and gave me a bottle of stout for tending one of the family's gravestones.

THE GYPSY CLAN OF MILLHAMS

I see her even to this day in her rocking chair
Drawing on her pipe of clay
With six fingers on each hand shed wave
Beckoned me from the door.

Her blanket lay across her lap and dangled on the floor
Then Shed say Come my sweet,come sit and talk awhile
Then shed give her all knowing smile
As a little girl I could only stare
At Granny Jeff in her rocking chair.

Then there was the family
Joe and Walt,John and Henry
Yould see them in the street r find em in the pub
A bunch of rogues like yould ever meet
But they were always good to me
And Gert, God bless her. But I never really knew
Who exactly she was married too
She wasnt very often seen
But her daughter went to school with me.

Then there was Nancy the head of the race
When Granny died she took her place
Nancy sold flowers in the town
Come rain or shine she could be found
No matter the custom or how busy shed be
Nancy always had time to talk with me
I still see her smile and her weathered face
Each lime a memory could be traced

When my first born died she made wreaths for me
And one from all her family.

I saw Nancy often as i grew old
To talk to me or in her car, driving up the road
She could just abut see over the steering wheel
Nancy was just pure gold to me
She would cuss and swear F and blind
But from her Id never pay a mind
She liked a flutter on the horses and dogs and more than a brandy
or two
Dear Nancy I remember you
She never had it easy had cancer twice, a heart problem yet
survived.

I recall one night there was a burglary
Nancy stood her ground for the family
The thugs ransacked the place looking for cash
Her little dog they threw on the fire
I think the shock took its toll because soon afterwards she retired
Nancy died in 2006
Her brother Henry died soon after in a local hospice
The house stands empty in Millhams lane
Just a derelict property will remain
A memory nothing else to see
With just these few lines of poetry
To honour the family who were good to me

JANET ROGERS

James Cherrett was born in 1848. He became a wealthy brickmaker then an Inn keeper before eventually managing his very own farm in Kinson and employed many. The Dolphin pub At Kinson became Gulliver's, it had many gypsies' traveller as regular clientele.

Gulliver

HOWE LODGE GULLIVERS HOME ON BROOK ROAD

Isaac Gulliver (c. 1745–1822) was a smuggler. He was born 1745 at Semingtom Wiltshire. He was well known to all the Kinson gypsy travellers. Gulliver and his gang smuggled gin, silk, lace and tea from the Continent to Poole Bay Dorset to Devon. He was known as "King of the Dorset Smugglers" and was often referred to as "the gentle smuggler who never killed a man". He lived a life as a very wealthy gentleman landlord with numerous properties very fine houses and farms, He married Betty Beale an inn keeper's daughter at Sixpenny Handley. Among his properties was 'Howe Lodge', in Kinson which was a purpose-built smuggling stronghold. When the house was demolished by Bournemouth Borough Council in 1958, several hiding places were found within, including a secret room only accessible through a door 10 feet up a chimney. At Howe Lodge it was said that he faked his own death to avoided being caught by the custom men by allegedly covering his face in white powder and laying in an open coffin. When the customs men arrived to arrest him, his wife told them he had died during the night and showed them the 'body'. Then when they left, he got out of the coffin and escaped and then later, a mock funeral was held using a coffin filled with stones. Following a Report by Customs house Poole he was pardoned in 1782. He dropped that branch of smuggling and confined himself chiefly to the wine trade and became a respected gentleman banker. He retired to Gulliver's House, West Borough Wimborne. He died 13 September 1822, leaving an estate of £60,000, with properties across Hampshire, Wiltshire, Somerset and Dorset. He was buried at Wimborne Minster.

Britania Keets in St. Andrews Church cemetery.

St. Andrews Church

CHURCH YARD DAYS

I was down at the churchyard in old Kinson town
attending the graves and looking around
when a gypsy addressed me with braids in her hair
she requested my help for her graveside to care

She offered me kushti and smiled with those eyes
so i tended that grave for her Roma family wise
then later she brought me the finest of ale
brought a smile to my face and my belly as well

The church had a tower and the bells they did chime
each hour of the day i tended the vine
the lads were a team of local so true
though two came from old Liverpool

We cultured the landscape and tidied the grounds
gained the rose award prize with looks that astounds
there were burials there daily and christenings too
then a party to crown it in the parish of Poole

Old Gulliver haunted all this terrain
long summers past in the winds and the rains
the zunners did play here down at the green
down old Millhams lane with the old gypsy queen

Ray Wills

CHAPTER ELEVEN

WEST HOWE

New England encampment

LIVING IN NEW ENGLAND

I'm living in New England by the Fern heath valley spruce
where the heather and the brambles roam across the paths aloof
I'm walking down the same ole tracks where once the folki roamed
where the Dartford Warbler still doth sing
and the sand lizards have their home

I'm sat here reminiscing of how things used to be
when the travellers lived upon the heath
not far from Alderney
where the peat, they cut in turves so clean
and the blackberry was rich
close by the birch and ferns
where they paddled in the ditch

The Longham walk was rich and free
and the Stour was rushing ore
where the waterworks gave out its roar
and the ponies bridled poor
where the rich man and the poor man
said prayers

They bought their floral wreaths
from Nancy at Millhams lane
where the church still stands seems so far away

The gorse was thick and noble,
and the fuzz was rich in perfumed flower
where they lived upon the common then
and sold heather n flowers
where their baskets were so awesome
and the town it clock did chime
where Jeffs and Whites were settled
in the land of Gypsy rhyme.

Ray Wills

New England Gypsies

I journeyed back to West Howe many years ago
when winter time was hard
with cold wind freezing snows
i gathered all my memories
and stored them in a trunk
composed a poetry book of rhymes
to tell one of those times

The ladies rode their bikes to work
through Poole lanes dips n dales
there were Gypsies on the heath lands there
and heather for your luck

The co op grounds were rich in grass
and the trees were young and prime
the Canford warbler sang his song
and the adders were all fine

The coppice was rich in green
and the dew was on the ground
the fairs were rich in didykoy
and the big show was in town

Long before the houses built
for Gypsy family
long before the common land
was sold for ladies sprees

The goldfinch chirped on fuzz bush thick
and the broom was rich with flower
Gypsies grazed their ponies there amongst the gorse
and close by the river stour

The Smugglers Arms was tall and proud
and the gaffers took their pride
in Workman's labouring skills
and the young men took their brides

The land was rich in gravel,
clay and sand was free
there were many church bells ringing proud
on Sundays by the lea

The village children danced their reels
and the schoolmaster was strict
they say that councillor George Spicer saved the trees
and Sankey Ward took the bricks

There were many folki around this day
can all recall those days with pride
when Turbary and Kinson
were rich in trees and wide

Where rabbits ran upon the copse
and the zunners went to play
at scrumping fruit from Alderney orchard
and rabbiting with ferrets along the way

The knuckle boxers showed their skills
like Freddie Mills to-shay
where Bear Cross stood with brotherhood
of guests and family May

The Crutchers and the Dibbens
with Sherwood's and the Whites
played darts and sported game

Whilst Jeff's gave chase along the race
with names handed down with pride
of Gypsy clan and tattooed man
with Giorgio's in disguise

The Dolphin pub and Pelhams house
were then as to today
when St Andrew church stood
so prime and good
to while the days away

The stocks and green now paint the scene
where folly true was scorned
whilst village school took kids from Poole
when slates were hard and worn

The twists and turns of kids now born
will tell a tale or two
but none can trace the master race
of when West Howe was born for true

The pavilions gone
and with the bowls along
and there's only Oak mead school
where children met with deep regrets
and played by the golden rule

Ray Wills

Just a short distance from my home at the Mannings, was West Howe Kinson. It is said that the New Forest Gypsies had a particular affection for that part of Turbary common at West howe reminding them of their New Forest home. In the 1880s they gave a section of it the name "New England" encampment. The New England encampment was in an area of fern heath land, which had Turbary rights, dating ways back to the Doomsday book of 1000. Which ended with the Enclosure Act. Rights which put an end to the grazing of cattle and the cutting and gathering of peat for fires.

Travellers lived there at New England in flimsy homes of tents or benders of sacking cut out of the mud then in the early days. Then later in caravans, vardos or simple wooden bungalows which they built.

Benjamin Stanley lived here he was the brother of Levi Stanley whose elders had emigrated and lived in Dayton USA. Benjamin had chosen to settle down in New England at Turbary common. Benjamin had been disowned by their father and it was said that a curse was put on him and the future families for the next three generations to follow.

A great many Gypsies lived here amongst the silver birch and yellow sweet-smelling furze. Including a Charles Hansford who spoke well the gypsy language fluently and claimed he was a Romani Traveller who knew well the Romani dialect.

Johnny Turner and his wife Diana also lived there along with Henry and Patience Doe with their 8 children. In 1918 one of their daughters Patience aged 20 married John Cooper.

Louisa Barnes (nee Willett) and her and her husband John Barnes lived there. They were Horace Coopers grandparents. They are both buried in St Andrews cemetery Kinson. Horace Cooper as a child had grown up on the heathland's encampments of Kinson and Wallisdown commons campsite New England and the Dip. Horace was at one time a local rag and bone man and also in Wareham. It was always very popular with the travelling Romany folk for many years.

Horace Cooper

Horace Cooper was a close relative of the lovely Annie Cooper of the new forest who in later years came and supported many of my events. Horace grew up on the heathlands of Wallisdown commons. He was a one-time rag and bone man in Wareham and lived his later years at Fraser Road in Wallisdown where he was regularly seen driving his pony and cart along the highway. Horace Cooper leaning on his garden gate in Fraser Road telling his stories to whoever would listen. I always visited Horace who lived next door to my sister Joanna and her husband Ron Squires. We would talk for hours he knew the Crutcher's and all my relatives. Horace spent hours talking with me then about the old days of the encampments he knew well my family and the Castles. He had a large art picture hanging over his fireplace and told me the family in the picture was my cousins the Castles. In recent years I discovered the picture was in fact one of famous photographer of gypsies Barrie Laws photos taken of a northern Gypsy family with no connection to the Castles When Horace passed away the vicar read out one my poems at his funeral. When Horace passed his son sold the picture to my stepsister Joanna and hubby Ron Squires and it hangs in their cottage in France.

Horace Cooper, a small boy having his pants sewn up by his Gran at the New England encampment.

Annie White married Walter Dane Matthews in 1934 whose family had lived on the Bourne hill encampment at the rear of the local Saunders homes of rest. Kinson. Where they had paid 1 shilling rent a week to Mr Hooper. Later when Mr Hooper died the land was sold and developed. Annie White living on New England recalled that "it was a delightful place to live but that all spoiled when the council decided to use the land as a landfill site and to build the housing estate". The family had come to the "New England" encampment looking for employment after travelling from Bristol reaching the New England campsite area where they lived for a few months in Mr Coopers rented Vardo. Before moving into a shack in fern heath road then moving permanently into Acres Road.

Henry and Patience Doe were recorded as living at the New England camp in 1911 with their 8 children including Alice, 15, Patience, 13, Henry, 11, Liberty Job, Jeff and Macey Jeff and family, Edward Lamb and Macey Rose and family, James and Florence Lamb 9 Nelson 5, and William, aged just one. In 1918 one of their daughters Patience aged 20 married John Cooper.

Raymond Pidgley was born on the 12th of May 1935 at West Howe. He was the son of Oliver and Edith nee Sheen the flower seller. He was to become the lightweight boxing champion of the royal marines and 3 commandos whilst in service in the Royal Marines Commandos as a sergeant and was Admiral Lord Mountbatten s bodyguard

Edith Sheen sold flowers to the owners of the Dory hotel at Bournemouth who helped her to obtain a council house to prepare for the birth of Raymond here.

When Gypsies William Doe, Mark Cooper (known as Mark Hughes) and Henry Crutcher discovered the land was to be sold in the future for housing they clubbed together and bought it. Each of their Gypsy families took on responsibility for specific strips of it. Then they rented it out to other local Gypsy traveller families. Scores of Gypsy traveller families lived here. The encampment ran until 1960 and was based in an area now known as Varney close/ fern heath. But the road was originally called fern heath road.

Louisa Barnes (nee Willett) was married to John Barnes and was a local "Gypsy Queen. She lived with John at the encampment. Lousa died in 1935, and her funeral took place on September 25th, 1935. Louisa's husband John Barnes died in 1940, and they are both buried in St Andrews cemetery Kinson.

Louisa grandson Horace Cooper who was a close relative of Annie Cooper of new forest also. He grew up on the heathlands of Wallisdown commons campsite the Dip. Before moving into Fraser Road. He was a one-time rag and bone man in Wareham. Horace lived his later years at Fraser Road in Wallisdown he was regularly seen driving his pony and cart along the highway or leaning on his garden gate in Fraser Road telling his stories to whoever would listen. When Horace passed away the vicar read out one my poems at his funeral. They got their water from a nearby stream from a well with a hand pump.

HORACE COOPER

Ole Horace Cooper was a good friend of mine
He could tell you a yarn and spin you a line
When they lived on the heath Annie and he
In old Wallisdown just a stone's throw from me

He would lean on his gate and talk to the kids
carve out his script upon the branch of a tree
in the days of the brickyards in old Alderney
we were cousins of Castles friends of the Kings
the Whites were our history with Stanley's thrown in
Mary and Maisie made the flowers so grand
the wreaths and the baskets from both their fair hands

Ole Horace had a picture that hung on the wall
the storytellers of history and its traditions and lores
when by the ditch was their home in old Wallisdown
where the Gypsies did roam not far from Poole town

The haunts of the smugglers and the pen of the free
Augustus paintings were sketched in ole Alderney
where the goldfinch did sing upon the thistle n broom
where the heathers were rich and the Gypsies all sang
by the light of the moonmany did live by Arne avenue
the Johnston's and Mabeys and Joker from Poole

Ole Horace was rich but poor in the hand
but he had the ways of a good travelling man

He rode a good cart all through Wallisdown and smiled at the ladies
on his way to Poole town.

Ray Wills

Alfred Robinsons grandfather was one of the first from the travelling community to establish a permanent home. He borrowed £250 to build the first bungalow in Varney close which along with other houses built at that time were without gas and electric. In general, they had plots and were joined by other travellers from as far afield as Ireland and Italy. Some of them belonged to Mr Hooper who used to be driven over there on Monday mornings to collect the rents. A shilling for each tent per week. His son fell in love with one of the gypsy girls and married her.

John Palmer who lived on a nearby farm said his father sold flowers and apples to the gypsies they would come and buy his flowers and apples They always paid cash. And with a handshake deal. The gypsy women took the flowers to Bournemouth and Westbourne to sell. They also made wreaths for funerals and Christmas.

A Gypsy woman in West Howe said, "I would tell fortunes I would only speak of the good news and never bad as there was no fixed price for fortune telling and people only paid what they could afford No one gives money for bad news". None of their food was processed and there were lots of fruit and vegetable with hedgehogs and rabbit's stew. Revd Roger Redding said it was their lifestyles that made them so healthy.

One resident at Rochester Road says her grandmother used to get brown paper bags and collect brambles, elderberry blossom and all sorts of different herbs. She put them in bags and then boiled them all together. They were then all stored in the caravan, and she guaranteed they would work for any ailment. Before the war the estate only consisted of West Howe Road later renamed South Kinson drive and half of Wheatley Road renamed Rochester Road. After the war the rebuilding of the estate really developed mainly to house local desperate people looking for accommodation but also included gypsies.

Joe Doe of Cunningham Crescent recalls in the book West Howe Proper published over 20 years ago. He recalls his reaction when he heard he was being moved into a council house. "I wasn't too pleased to be honest with you, the trouble was they sent a school leaver to take my particulars, and I suppose resented it. He got used to it but the main thing he missed his mates. "When you go out on the common, there's a band of you and the men drift off. Moving into the house took some time to get used to but I soon did and made new friends as well. In general, the women were more enthusiastic about moving into homes". Joe and many like him settled into their homes. A lot of the travellers I spoke to insisted that when they left the site, they left their rubbish neatly stacked in black bin bags. Within hours these are splint open and scattered over the area. Then over the next few days all sorts of people dump their rubbish there including filing cabinets and fridges, but they always get the blame.

Georgina Cooper lived on new England she was remembered for riding her horse and cart smoking a clay pipe and wearing her trilby hat. Henry and Patience Doe with their 8 children also lived there.

Charles Hansford also lived here and claimed he was a Romani Traveller, and he could speak well the Roma dialect.

Scores of Gypsy traveller families lived at New England over the years. They say it was a delightful place to live it ran from the end of the 1800s until 1960.

Brittania Keets lived there and is buried in Kinson cemetery where there is a grand angelic monument dedicated to her. Louisa and John Barnes are both buried in St Andrews cemetery. All the Gypsy houses on the encampments were eventually compulsory purchased by the council in later years following the 2nd world war and most of the common lands were built on by the council to house the many Gypsy families in the area now known as West Howe.

Bankes common encampment

The Bankes common encampment was on turbary common land at the rear of the New England encampment near Wallisdown West Howe Kinson. In the 1911 census amongst the families living there were the Sherwood's, Coopers, Does, Orchards, James, Jeffs, Manley, Lambs, Lights, Rose, Barnes, Jeff's, and Warrens.

Job Jeff lived there with his mother Macey and his father. Also called Job Jeff. It was home to many other Gypsy families these included George and Rose Cooper and family. John and Loisa Sherwood and family, Job Barnes and Lavender Barnes and family. Henry and Patience Doe and their 8 children also lived there. George Jeff and Daisy and family along with Issac and Elizabeth Lamb and family.

Others included John Warren and Edith Warren and family, Job Jeff and Macey Jeff and family, Edward Lamb and Mary Ann Rose and family, James and Florence Manley and family, Power and Brittania Manley and family.

Many of the Gypsies living there worked at all the nearby brickyards, potteries and at the new development of the sisters at the Talbot Village at Wallisdown.

Bender Days

When we bent our benders down by the creek
where the wind did blow and the wind did speak
there were many fine people there scattered around
from the walks of life and the talk of towns

The grass was green and the clay was white
the fields were free both day and night
the trails were wide and the roads were long
but we whistled free and we sang our songs

We built our homes like travelers do
amongst the ferns and the bracken's hue
we saw the deer and the rabbits play
where the lights were stars and the dark was haze

The bramble thorns and the virgin land
the talk was rich and the fortune hands
the stolen words i heard yesterday
when the gypsy gal came to play with me

The thunder roared and the lightning flashed
the lizards squirmed and the days went fast
the life was hard and labour free
but we shared our hopes and our miseries

Down in yonder dip where the sun sets morn
the wind did blow but we were warm
inside our benders made of frames
crafted from the dews and rains

The stew we served was hot and mean
the countryside was fit for queens
where kings and carters sat and toiled
amongst the birch and lilies torn

The roads were hard and our spirits free
with time to stare and life was free
where folks did share an hour with me
amongst the benders beneath the trees.

Ray Wills

THE GYPSY BEAT IN THE HEART OF OUR TOWN

The following is an extract of the publication of Bournemouth Borough councils HOME NEWS. The Article is by William Hill Housing Officer Bournemouth Borough Council. It was published in HOME NEWS Summer Edition 2007.

It was Councilor Claire Smith who first put HOME NEWS onto the fascinating story of the gypsy traveler past in our area. She met some of the residents who have a wonderfully colorful history, and it is thanks to their help that we can capture something of their bohemian lifestyle a generation ago. It is a subject that is often neglected.

As former Councilor Stephen Starr says. "The Gypsy and Traveler communities in Bournemouth are a significant minority, whose contribution to the history of the area has long been overlooked".

There is something of a Gypsy spirit that captures the romance of our souls. In a world of regimented discipline these wandering nomads bring to life a certain extravagant freedom that is reflected in their music, dance, art and language.

Origination

Some scholars believe they originated from India as a single tribe while others suggest Egypt, from where the word gypsy comes, as their original homeland. But wherever they came from has always been less important than the journey to the Gypsy. It is those journeys that provide the most enduring icon of the culture. The brightly colored ornately decorated caravans were beautiful works of art. You can now buy these in kit form on websites but the originals little gems and would fetch fortunes today. I spoke to one resident who said that when she moved into a council house in the 1950s, she sold hers for £3.

Bender Tents

It was however the bender tents where most of the gypsies lived, even if they had a caravan. These tents were made, so called because they were made of bent hazel branches, supported a tarpaulin cover. In the middle was a hole for the smoke from a fire to go through.

One of the Gypsies told me he thought one reason why so many of the older Gypsies had swarthy complexions was the pigmentation from the smoke as well as continually working and living outside. Records show that as long ago as 1850 families camped in the West Howe area of Bournemouth. In those days West Howe comprised of large heathlands of gorse and heather with many small farms. The area was known as New England and among the famous family's names who lived there were the Coopers, Does, Barnes, Robinsons, Crutcher's, and Sherwood's. Many of their descendants are now residents on our estates.

One of those residents is Alfred Robinson from Borrans Avenue. To spend time listening to the tales from Alfred is a fascinating experience. Should he ever write a book it would be a best seller. It was a tough life, and Alfred remembers going hunting for rabbits and hedgehogs at night with his father. On the way home, in the early hours of the morning, they would pop into the pub for a drink. A friendly landlord would leave the back door open, and the men would leave the money on the till. Alfred Robinsons grandfather was one of the first from the travelling community to establish a permanent home. He borrowed £250 to build the first bungalow in Varney close which along with other houses built at that time were without gas and electric. In general, they had plots and were joined by other travellers from as far afield as Ireland and Italy. Some of them belonged to Mr Cooper who used to be driven over there on Monday mornings to collect the rents. A shilling for each tent per week. His son fell in love with one of the gypsy girls and married her.

The gypsy lifestyle may appear carefree and romantic but, but the reality was very different. Struggling to find a place to stay, find work and keep a family without any of the modern-day conveniences took an immense effort.

One Gentleman remembers having to walk 20 miles during the day as well as put in a full day's work in the land. When he returned to his camp he was told to move on. Exhausted from the day's work and having just made a fire they packed up and moved some miles down the road. During the summer the whole family would be on the move in search of work.

John Palmer who lived on a nearby farm said his father sold flowers and apples to the gypsies they would come and buy his flowers and apples They always paid cash. And with a handshake deal. The gypsy women took the flowers to Bournemouth and Westbourne to sell. They also made wreaths for funerals and Christmas.

A gypsy woman in west howe said "I would tell fortunes I would only speak of the good news and never bad as there was no fixed price for fortune telling and people only paid what they could afford No one gives money for bad news".

None of their food was processed and there were lots of fruit and vegetable with hedgehogs and rabbit's stew. Revd Roger Redding said it was their lifestyles that made them so healthy. It was a hard life but if there is one common thread I have found from meeting many of them older Gypsy community it is their robust health. The sheer physical effort that it took to bring up a family, walk scores of miles daily and put on a full day's work whilst eating natural food from the land gave them a healthy lifestyle. in natural medicines from herbs.

One resident at Rochester Road says her grandmother used to get brown paper bags and collect brambles, elderberry blossom and all sorts of different herbs. She put them in bags and then boiled them all together. They were then all stored in the caravan, and she guaranteed they would work for any ailment.

Before the war the estate only consisted of West Howe Road later renamed South Kinson drive and half of Wheatley Road renamed Rochester Road. After the war the rebuilding of the estate really developed mainly to house local desperate people looking for accommodation but also included gypsies.

It was a time of great change for many in the community as the council's policy was to encourage the families to settle down with the benefits that their children could get a more stable lifestyle. There were mixed reactions.

Joe Doe of Cunningham Crescent recalls in the book West Howe Proper published over 20 years ago. He recalls his reaction when he heard he was being moved into a council house. "I wasn't too pleased to be honest with you, the trouble was they sent a school leaver to take my particulars, and I suppose resented it. He got used to it but the main thing he missed his mates. "When you go out on the common, there is a band of you and the men drift off. Moving into the house took some time to get used to but I soon did and made new friends as well. In general, the women were more enthusiastic about moving into homes". John and many like him settled into their homes John continues. Gypsy women had a hard life really. I don't care what anybody else says if you looked up in the caravans there spotless and let's face it they stopped in some very muddy places. But the caravans were always clean, and they had to do the cooking and that, so it was a hard life for them.

A lot of the men weren't interested in a house. Its different ways of life for a man, because he's not homed all the time. He is always doing away doing something. It's always the women that's got the worry. Moving into a house was much easier for the wife, a bath for the children, washing. Like the convenience of running water. To do a family wash you had at least twenty gallons of water. People don't realise how much water they use washing, but when you've got to carry it if you know how much you want.

 That said it wasn't long before John and many others like him were settled into their new life. Eventually the gypsies were integrated with the village people, given council houses and married into the village families and now you can rarely find a true gypsy in the neighbourhoods. Modern day gypsies are more commonly known as new travellers and still face persecution.

Peter Hamden known as Gypsy Pete works alongside the community as a Gypsy liaison officer and he believes that they have been victims of bigotry and injustice but are a wonderful community of people. Certainly, there is much society can learn from the gypsies. In my visits to numerous sites, I found them warm and friendly after an initial suspicion. Their strength lies in their ability to establish a network of support for each other. Coupled with strong parenting skills. But two main issues arse, Education and land. The wheels of progress are turning however, although not as fast as some would like. Links are being established and barriers broken down.

One of our residents, Jacky lmon is secretary of the Southwest Alliance and Christine Kemp, the ethnic Minority and Travellers Achievement Service for Bournemouth is establishing relationships with children of the community and schooling. It involves visiting them in their homes and educating staff in schools of the culture of the Gypsy and Traveller pupils. An area of the travelling people community who are also assisted are the children of fairground operators and Christine and her team offer tuition in the travelling trailers. Most of these children come with Distance learning packs from their base schools they attend in winter. They also offer children from travelling family's places at local schools which sometime is for as little as a few days at a time. It is this flexible approach that is promoting good relations between itinerate travellers and the local schools and community.

The provision of land for the travellers is perhaps the most emotive subject of all. The establishment of any site will inevitably raise local objections. It is pointed out the rubbish left behind by travellers when they move from site to site is a health hazard. But much of life's controversy there is no black or white no right or wrong.

A lot of the travellers I spoke to insisted that when they left the site, they left their rubbish neatly stacked in black bin bags. Within hours these are splint open and scattered over the area. Then over the next few days all sorts of people dump their rubbish there including filing cabinets and fridges, but they always get the blame.

One camp was forced off a site recently because the authorities were worried about the livelihood of sand lizards, giving the impression that lizards were more important than people.

LEGAL OBLIGATION TO PROVIDE LAND

But the fact is there is now a legal obligation for local authorities to provide land. The Homes for People team at Bournemouth council says the council recognises the legislation places a duty on the local authority to establish the housing need for Gypsy and Travellers in the Borough. A strategic group has been established that represents a cross section of the council which should enable us to move forward positively to address any housing need that comes to light. This would enable Gypsy Travellers to maintain their traditional lifestyle in harmony with the settled community. Presently however around 1 in 4 families have no legal place to live in the country.

Em Poore who works in the Department for Communities and Local Government says. If Gypsy and Traveler's live in good quality permanent sites they are more likely to integrate into the community. If a child has nowhere to live, then she or he will always suffer poor health, bad dental care, lower educational attainment and lower self-esteem. Em Poore makes an interesting point as regards health. Unlike the older generation of Gypsies who were healthy. Modern day travelers have a much shorter life span Among the travelling community today the average lifespan is about 10 years less than the settled community.

In all this communication is the key, Sue Bickler Head of Strategic Services at Bournemouth Council emphasizes the need to be dealing with misconceptions about the community. Where successful schemes have been carried out, despite initial opposition, there was communication with the objectors individually to address their concerns.

It also makes good business sense. It would prove far less costly to provide good quality sites than to keep spending money on enforcement action. Em Poore concludes by saying. I think true community is an organic ting. It needs to grow bit by bit and we must help it. By We I mean all us-settled or mobile. It's time we all worked together to make it happen.

CHAPTER TWELVE

GYPSY TRAVELLERS AND THE FAIRGROUNDS

Fairground Tales

She read it in his tea leaves
before the starlight show
there beneath the canopy
of the wonder fairground show

He heard her words of mystery
for Gypsies cannot lie
she read it in his palm that day
before the crowds went by

Within the sounds of the Children's laughter
all the loud melodic rock
Bill Haley and the comets
Elvis and the rolling stones on trot

Now Gypsies cannot lie
she looked into her crystal ball
looked into his eyes
her scarf and golden earrings
her rings and tattooed arm
she used all her Gypsy charm

He wondered how she knew so much
it could not all be lies
she promised love and fortune soon
a lovely summer bride

He was transformed by her ways
her intuition and her styles

She read it in the night-time skies
within the wondrous show
a fairground rich in wonders
hers was a Gypsy wonder show

Ray Wills

GYPSY FAIR

He met her at the Gypsy fair
whilst the old accordion played
he looked into her eyes and soon he was her slave
she whispered words of eloquence
offered him her charms
he took her to the waltzer ride
and she melted in his arms

The stars were shining bright that night
and the crowds were all in tow
her dress was rich with satin silk
with rings upon her toes

He loved the way she moved that night
blessed her finest clothes
she told him lies and offered alms
yet he was lost to love

He took her by her words and prayers
the night was young and gay
they spent that night together until the morning light
then she was gone forever
like God turned out the light

Ray Wills

SHOWMEN DAYS

My father was a showman
a Gypsy King by trade
a king of the circus and fairgrounds parade
my mother's a teller of fortune and seers
my brothers kept ponies over the years

My sisters are dancers
the Queens of the shows
in the family histories of long times ago

The chavvies grew strong
whilst us mushes were free
travelling the country
telling the stories of diddle dee dee

My folks worked the land
the fairgrounds parade
they built swing boats and caravans
danced with the blades
we lived by our trades
our destiny proud
our ways they were strange
to the city brigade

We played on our drums and accordion's too
from Mitcham to Brighton
Blackpool to Glasgow
then Penzance to Poole

Ray Wills

ORIGINS OF THE FAIRGROUNDS

The fairs been here since the 13th century the season finished in November around Bonfire Night", "that was when they Gypsy folk settled for winter preferably on family-owned land, or where the landowner was sympathetic, the women Gypsy folk then repaired and made clothing and aprons and the men repaired and painted sideshows and stalls like 'knock 'em downs', shooting galleries and 'gallopers.' (hoses)," they devised new attractions". "you see", fairgrounds are one of the first places one can see 'cinematographs, or have a photo taken. It was Gypsies who sourced and purchased 'swag'. (traveller term for prizes – coconuts were especially popular). Many of the local Gypsies worked for local farmer's on their estates here, fruit picking and potato gathering. Whilst others are in trading or bartering their many skills such as sharpening knives and making pegs, floral presentation's or wreath's.

Fairs and markets were the shopping centres of the Middle Ages where people bought things they couldn't readily make at home. There were hawkers, chap men and traders who sold goods and agricultural labourers who found work at 'mop fairs. Some fairs were known for horse trading which were very popular for Gypsy Travellers, and all included some type of travelling entertainment. Charter fairs, founded and protected by royal charter, came into existence from the 12th century; by 1350, there were more than 1,500 of them. 'Prescriptive' fairs dating from the 13th century were not founded by charter.

It is believed by some that the first caravans were initially built by Gypsy fairground people in the 19th century and to have evolved from their first use of cages for their manageress in the 18th century which they built on wheels. In the 18th century the lanes were often crowded with Romani families such as the Lovells, Boswell's, Stanley's, Hemes and Chilcott's. Riding horse's real hunters to ride to the fairs, wakes and markets. Women with red cloaks and fur trimmed beaver hats. Men in beautiful silk velvet coats and white and yellow waistcoats. All booted and spurred. Some fair had boxing booths, horse dealing, sweet making and basket making. Gypsies took along their wagons and carts brim-full of hops which they had all gathered at nearby Alton and Farnham for to sell at the fair.

As William Langdon in Piers Plowman wrote "To Wayhill and Winchester I went to the fair ".

By the 19th century there were theatrical booths, waxworks, and freak shows, menageries, circuses, exhibitions, and waxworks. The people who ran these became famous, adopted fanciful distinctive titles, With George Sanger adopting the title "Lord". Chittock's Animal Show was one of these with performing dogs and Monkeys.

Show people have traditionally been linked to the Gypsy community from earliest times. With some of the present-day show people having Gypsy origins. Show people and Gypsies came together at the fairgrounds but most separated afterwards going their separate ways. Showmanship was the essential component unifying the different types of exhibitions on the *fairground*. For the greater part of its history, shows were the main venue on the *fairground* in which the showmen practised their art and were the main entertainment from the sixteenth century onwards. Gypsies were actively involved in the development of the modern fairgrounds from earliest times. Throughout the centuries Gypsy families have been fairground owners and have had exhibits. Whether it's been coconuts shies, booths, fortune telling, swing boats, shooting galleries or in the boxing booths they were always there. In later years the business owners of show people managed the fairs though often many of these had Gypsy ancestry or fairs were known as Though many because of stigma claimed they were not Gypsy. Although in the UK fairgrounds had developed over the centuries from horse fairs and shows and became managed by non-Gypsy entrepreneurs who became better known as Showmen. Many of the Gypsy families because of the prejudices and public feelings against any association with the term Gypsy also chose to categorically state that they also were show people and not Gypsy. Despite their obvious appearance to the contrary, their nomadic lifestyle, heritage, code and despite their family names. Travelling fun fairs continually to remain successfully because in the main they are largely run by people with Gypsy family origin. Along with the distinctive show people. Fairs which remain successful have done so because they have retained some of their original purpose and mainly because the Gypsy fraternity continue to be involved.

In the 13th century, the creation of fairs by royal charter was widespread, then by the twelfth and thirteenth centuries most English fairs had been granted charters. Most fairs held in the United Kingdom can trace their ancestry back to charters and privileges granted in the Medieval period.

By the 19th century there was a very large network of Fairs throughout the UK/ "Caravans will be moving about in our midst with "fat babies," "wax-work models," "wonders of the age," "the greatest giant in the world," "a living skeleton," "the smallest man alive," "menageries," "wild beast shows," "rifle galleries," and like things connected with these caravans" .

The Gypsy Fairground

I went to the Gypsy fairground.
it was where I first met Gypsy Jo
we went upon the Ferris wheel.
it seems so long ago

Her father was a tailor.
and her mother was a Queen.
She took me on the spinning wheel
she was my swinging scene.

One time I remember.
when the vardos seemed to reach the sky
when the grass was green and thick with dew
with rabbits running bye
There were birds upon the branches
where the willow spreads its fall
there were Gypsy children dancing.
long before the fall

The piano accordion was playing.
from Victor Clapcott the Gypsy tattoo man
the Gypsy gal was dancing
tambourine in her hand.

The fire was a glowing.
the sparks they flew so high.
there were pastures and a haystack
with a river running bye

The folk they were blessed there.
with children by the score
with packs of dogs a chasing tail
and tales of long-gone wars

The music that they played then.
was rich in words and tone.
I kissed her beneath the raging sun.
and loved her more and more.

The foxes were on the hilltops.
all hidden from our view.
there was heather and gorse a stretching.
from Alderney to Poole
The sands of time have rolled along.
and the tides of surf will sap.
the beaches where they carried.
the shawls and loving mats

There were tinkers then and travellers.
and Johnny Onion was in tow.
the fairgrounds offered substance.
and the harvests were a show.

The darts did fly upon the cards.
and the bumper cars did spin.
there was candy floss and coconut shies.
and sweets for Uncle Jim

Those days are gone.
when we cut grass and sliced the wood and cane

when flowers were made on Canford hills
wish we could go back there again.

Ray Wills

THE WOODBURY FAIR

Upon Woodbury Hill

The St Marys chapel stood
high on the Woodbury hill
so rich with its Anchoret's well.

Where a festival and a fair was held
with Its tales all to be told
of its waters of health
and its tablet of gold
with its spring water deep
down 200 feet or more
in its water below.

Once Gypsies camped near Woodbury hill
it was the home of fairs

folks remember it still
with fortune telling booths and village gal's
old in the tooth along with blacksmiths
tending hooves so well

Where Hardy penned and folks did boast
he shot at the famous fairground galleries the most
for as Hardy said Bere it was a blinkering place
for thousands came to this kingly place

Since way back in the 12th century
they sold ponies there and gathered some
on the hill of Hardy's Green
long before the days of Wareham inn the Rising sun
there were thin men and fat ones and bearded ladies too
miles away from the port of Poole

The Kingsbere Fair.
it grows there in the September autumn weeks
and the cold wind it blows
and all the durzet dialect
volks doth speaks.

The Gypsies worked the fairgrounds
and volks drank in the Sailor inn on the hill
where the villagers tapped the sweet ale
and volks sipped of the well waters
its waters of health
to give them that zing
and make them feel well.

With two headed calves,
dancers and performers alike
locals charged the Grokels
to park all their bikes
with coconut shies and nine pin stalls
there was lots of fun for girl and boy did like

It was held each September for a week
where folks did travel
across from local n Dorchester streets
from faraway places
Birmingham, Bristol Exeter
and also, all of their london Cockney chums
with oyster day and penny day to greet some

It Boasted it was the biggest in the south
those days are gone now
though the hill still stands so proud
with woodland copses
and green pleasant grounds
it lorded over this little town

Was where old Fred Bartlett
had his family's fairgrounds stalls
such an attraction for each boy n girl.
Local Bere villagers said
"They be Gipsy vo'k up yon,

It was where the Gypsy folk gathered
so, frequent its true,
whilst their tents and their benders

were on gallows hill
amongst the trees and the leas
in the autumn mornings early dew

Gallows hill was where once Judge Jeffries
did give out his deathly deal
the volks in the village
they do remember him still.

The Batemans and Hughes families
camped on the gallows hill
where Caroline Hughes
was born one morn
you can hear her singing reels

It was where they took the census
and paid all their lordly
Drax tithes and dues each autumn
though their clothes were sad and worn.

I walked awhile where Bere stream doth flow
I gazed at the water cress fields and springs below
whilst the cold breeze blew upon the downs
where fields of yellow cups all bedded down
the trees were so tall and bare without their leaves
amidst the cloudy skies in the cool day breeze

Where Barnes once built their homes of bricks
where Johnny Barnes got up to all his usual fancy tricks
with village gals and games of chase and kiss

Where St Johns church
and Durbervilles crest
still haunt the views
upon the lanes and twisted hues
where lovers walked two by two
yet my dreams and thoughts
were of me and you

Sir John he was no Romany
but he was a Rai
for he could talk the Romani
and gave them all the loving eye.

He had crafted a living
within the world of the free
from all their money offerings
at the pilgrimage fees

For to take of the well waters
with its sacred promise so heavenly
and so he grew rich
and wealthy tis true.

Sir John Squire the Abbot
gave pretty Emily the eye
and took her down
to the Bere meadow below
n courted her there among the rye

She was born a Fancy
Emily was her name twere true

a daughter of Gideon
at oer in Poole.

She called all the yappy barking Jucks
each one
all by their mongrel names
she could do the Dukerrin fortune
and read all their leaves
and play all the card games with ease.

She could milk a goat
and ride a horse bare back and wild
she could identify ink caps,
puff balls wide

She knew where to find
wild watercress, field mushrooms and sorrel
there in wild Woodbury
in the early morning dew.
Where she danced in the meadows
without any shoes

He was her champion
he was her knight
her king of the Rai
she loved him dearly
he was her guy

She saw him daily
he made her heart leap
day times thoughts were only of him

night times she had no sleep
kisses in the moonlight
walks in the Woodbury trees
among the Woodbury meadows
rivers and streams

He bedded her down
upon the grassy deep mossy dew
and it was there he did love her
and gave her his love crown anew.

In Woodbury wild
he took him a fancy Gypsy dame
he gave her his truce
and in Bere Regis St Johns church
he gave her his name.

In Woodbury country
where the cress it grew wild,
Sir John Squire the Abbot
took him a Gypsy damsel
he took him a bride.

Then there on a ridge
by the knap in the dell
he heard the St john church
chime out its bells so well
then Sir John he did say
they village bell ringers Emily
they do clang em so well
on this ere our wedding day

Then he promised her wealth from the well
upon the top of Woodbury hill ridge
When the cold wind blew
across the meadows

Farmer Doddings worked the land
horse and man in days gone bye
when chavvie urchins
and wild young zunners
ran the lanes and bitter tracks
they carried the sacks on their backs
and the young maids milked ole cows udders

There neath great tall oaks and vick tall stacks
through muds of Shitterton and farms a plenty
Hills of Woodbury and hard and frosted tracks
they walked the lanes old Sam, Joe n Mac
man, and boy up Rye hill and back
Was where once there in the meadow
upon a time so long ago
the old Queen Elfreda
once had a mansion house
till it was laid low

After the murder of her stepson Edward
at Corfe Castle he died in the moat below
King John had a palace there too so long ago
in the old, decayed village below.

On the Woodbury wilds downs
where in winter it doth heavily snow.
the meadows were rich
its springs all so deep
more than 200 feet below
where the cress beds grew
so green n sweet so wild n low.

Where Caroline Hughes sang her songs
in the spring
when the cuckoos first did call and sing
whilst at Stobough meadows
the old folk tales do say
afore the farmer opens the gate
to let them all out
and they all fly aways.
Cuckoo, cuckoo

Where the chaffinch did sing each spring day
where the wild winds blew free
and the farmers make hay,
where the chavies ran wild
and zunners ran free
on naked tip toes
not far from the Purbeck seas
afore the hard winters snow

At the Greyhound Inn
Kings Arms and The Royal Oak
they had a many brew
told many a joke

many a hearth tax gave out its smokes
tales told within them were of cows and man
long time ago in this fair land.

Though the Drax wall nearby
were 2 million bricks thick
all circled around the vast estate ditch
all his wealth took by his slavery rich
and the truth which be hid.

The bricks all were laboured
from the Doddings yards
3 brickyards brick maker men
where all of the gypsies crafted them
all levelled like zen.

Whilst the waters
did springs there
in the doddings farm gates
so deep underground
for it created the water cress
the wealth all around

The cress it grew green and so sweet
n its great wealth it grew
for the healing of man
from his head to his feet.

The Doddings farm grew
and the Drax properties too
though all under one roof

due to the Drax tithes
and his rich mans crew
with their aristocratic golden rule.

Whilst the volks in their hundreds
they all travelled to Woodbury fair
from London and Dorchester towns
to the Woodbury hill pilgrimage
dell on the ground

For to taste n take of the well's waters
to make them young once again
and so well and so strong.

The thrush it doth sing there,
whilst down below in the bere village
the crows they did gather in the meadows
where the Bere volks still tell.
those stories of old and tales of the well

The romance of the Abbot and the Gypsy
it was a long time ago
the great healing well waters
with its golden tablet so old
Beres rich cress beds
with their delicious springs
and of all the Gypsies
who danced there and sings

Beesom brooms on carts and wains
beers and cottons, boats and booths

shooting galleries for the young at heart
and old in the tooth
merry go rounds and swing boat rides
autumn nights and a gypsy bride

Ray Wills

(I was commissioned by the Arts Council in autumn 2023 to perform this poem/story at the Dorset Festival in Bere Regis Dorset.)

Bere Regis hang fairs

In much earlier times in the 1600s the Hanging Judge' Judge Jeffries had held his infamous 'Bloody Assize' in the nearby county town of Dorchester where he tried 312 people and sentenced nearly 200 to be hanged and was made Lord Chancellor of England. He had ordered gallows to be erected in many Dorset towns and villages and thousands of men, woman, and children suffered the cruel lingering death by strangulation on these over centuries.

Locals were encouraged to attend these "Hang Fairs", and these were very popular source of entertainment and amusement. Many from the local villages regularly traveled into Dorchester to join in the merriment and the viewings of the hangings. These blood thirsty crowds relished in all of these with all their drinking, cursing and jeering around about the gallows and many thousands of people gathered below the towns gaol to be entertained. By dawn all the best places were usually taken in much drinking, fiddling, and dancing.

There were charity schools for children and Villagers were encouraged to have their children educated for which they paid a penny a week. But 'scholars' needed shoes, too, so for many there was no financial gain in educating children. Only property owners had a vote and women had no vote. Not an ounce of pig meat was wasted, and any spare fat was rubbed into the brick makers' mates'(wife's and children's) hands.

In Barnes Day

When Barnes wrote of Linden Lee
there were girt trees with boughs wide and boughs hung free
Ee wrote of Durzet dialect and history in the finest of poetry
where wildflowers grew on lawns and banks and tuffs of grass
where zunners danced
in Hardys country where volks did chance
to view the scenes of young lambs skip n dance
Counting the hours to evenings tide
sea-saw games of future brides

Where church bells rang and town clock chimed
and vicars prayed
Volks would gather on village green to celebrate the maypoles
Queens parade

Whilst ganders and ducks ran and zunners played
amongst the stacks of hay sum
when a Sovereign was richer by far than half a crown
Volks did gather round in Dorchester town

Barnes was Mayor and master teacher,
prie**st**, Mathematician too
he wore long white gown and buckled shoes
Barnes did pen such fine poems with his Durzet tomes
amongst the fields were fox and rabbits roamed

He could not abide the rich farm volks
who took the poor man taxes and oats
where Maidens Castle stood

without tower or moat
and volks were poor without a vote

Where village green and farming land was set aside
in their masters plans
where old maids prayed vor young uns
health and courting couples laid upon the grass
where volks did know their place and toff their caps
to gaffers rich like gentry squires
amongst the views of Purbeck hills
where gaffers rode on stallions rich
our pastures commons and dirty ditch

His statue now stands proud
in the Dorchester town
whilst modern life rolls along
with its busy streets of pedestrians

Whilst traffic flows and lights do bleep
and tourists walk its hills n streets
Barnes looks on without a peep
the master poet looks on down
upon the volks of his old town

Ray Wills

REMEMBERING KINGS BERE FAIR

Thomas Hardy came to the place
he called Kingsbere fair
there were lots of lads and lasses there then
swingboats, stalls and coconut shies
while Fred Bartletts family ran the many rides

Thousands came to Kingsbere fair
there were Gypsy chavvies with wandering eyes
fortune tellers and sales of beer
with Inns and local yeomen too
swingboats and bicycles
village girls sighs

There were flying darts in cards
and goldfish in a bowl
the rich and the poor fool and wise
the Gentlemen and common Joes
you took your chances and had a go

Ray Wills

Thomas Hardy writes of Green Hill or Woodbury Hill Fair Bere Regis Dorset he referred to Bere Regis as 'a little one-eyed, blinking sort o' place'. Whilst Edward I had made Bere Regis a free borough in the 13th century whilst King John granted a charter for a weekly market in 1215. This ancient hill fort of Woodbury Hill was one of the biggest fairs in the South, this week-long fair held in September was the social and economic highlight of the year for the area. Woodbury Fair. Gypsies were involved with the local Woodbury Fair from the 1500s which was held from 18th September for a week and was the largest in the south of England attracting very great crowds from Dorchester and surrounding areas. A great many Gypsies were said to have either managed or operated the Woodbury Fair. Gypsies always were regular visitors to the local fairs and a major public attraction over the years with their family gatherings, horse trading deals and flower selling not to mention all their stalls and the fortune telling attractions. They were obviously a very popular added attraction for the public. With their amazing sometimes accurate racing tips, entertainment and with all their many lucky charms. At the Woodbury fair there were so many Gypsy flower girls with their large baskets full of the finest of flowers. Including the familiar families of the Whites, Coles, Bartlett's, Kings, Castles, James, and Hills. Kings, Boswells, Crutcher's families among them. Gypsy families were renowned in these enterprises, like the swing boats they managed. At the time of the fair hordes of Gypsy travelers arrived in their vans and horse drawn wagons. They would put up their tents and create their benders in a nearby field close to the fairground.

The fair was an essential part of their lives and a major source of their income, containing a multitude of booths and stalls. Such as 'knock 'em downs', shooting galleries and 'gallopers.' (horses), fortune telling, trading horses, coconut stalls, 'Puff and Darts', 'Spin 'em Rounds, 'swing boats and roundabouts. Traders of horses bartered handshake deals, them spitting on their hands before they shook hands smacking hard on the deal. a man's word means everything in those days. Large Billboard signs advertised thin men, fat women, two headed calves, two headed sheep and a bearded lady.

One prominent sign in bold letters read "BARTLETTS FAIRGROUNDS." Fred Bartlett who once lived at the rear of the king's arms pub on Poole quay, was the last of four generations who operated fairgrounds at Woodbury Hill in Bere Regis.

The local Gypsy photographer John White Bosville was present at the fair. His very name giving away his Gypsy ancestral blood.

Fairgrounds were one of the first places one could see 'cinemographs, or to have a photo taken. Gypsies sourced and purchased 'swag'. (Traveler term for prizes – coconuts were especially popular). Their white cob horses were strong very well cared for and obviously the pride of their family. Very necessary for transporting bricks and heavy work at their brickyards. Woodbury hill fair contained amusements, and the merchandise traded at these included cheese, cloth, cattle, sheep, and horses. It was at one time the most important in the south of England and possibly the whole of the land. It merited the title of the Nijni Novgorod of South Wessex. Woodbury fair was always held in this week of the 21st of September at Woodbury Hill from 1267.

There is a tradition that the Woodbury fair originated through a travelling trader in cloth, who having been drenched by a heavy storm, stopped on Woodbury Hill or to spread and dry his soaked cloth. The Passers-by seeing the cloth laid out in this way assumed it was for sale, and in a short while the trader had disposed of his stock with little effort. He returned the following year with the same result and repeated it annually when other traders began to follow his example until the trade grew to sufficient proportions to rank as a fair and warrant a charter. This traditional story seems likely enough when considered in the light of the annual pilgrimages to the well. The trader's first visit probably coincided by chance with the large gathering at the well on 21 September, as he would be unlikely to have met many prospective purchasers on any other day of the year, and it would also account for his returning in a year's time presumably on the same date.

The people attending the fair came from as far afield as Birmingham, Norwich, Bristol, Exeter, and London. As well as all areas of the Dorset County and beyond. Attracting very great crowds from Dorchester and surrounding areas. The 5 days of the fair were from 18th to 22nd September divided as follows.

Local villagers said, "They be Gipsy vo'k up yon". "The busiest, merriest, noisiest" of them all.".

The Gypsy women at the Woodbury fair repaired and made clothing and aprons and the men repaired and painted sideshows and stalls. Many of the stall holders lived locally and some were in fact brick yard workers at the Amey brother's family brickyard at Dudding's at brick hill and black hill which had been here since the 17th and 18th century on farmland belonging to the Dodding's family.

The last Woodbury Hill Fair was held in 1951 having been a regular event for over 700 years. Fairs were an essential part of their lives and a major source of income.

The Drax family owned the largest estate in Dorset with its 3-mile longest wall in the kingdom. Built from local brickworks mainly made at Doddings 3 brickyards in Bere Regis. It contained 3 million bricks created by local brick makers some of them being gypsies.

Gypsies worked among others non gypsies on the 3 Dudding's brickyards in Bere Regis and others of the area and attended the 'Woodbury Hill and Shroton Fairs respectively. Their christenings also performed at or near these festivals by itinerant missionaries in Bere Regis and Wool in 1803.

 In its heyday most of the travellers who came to the fair camped nearby in tents or in their many Gypsy vans. These were a regular feature of the village during this week for many years. The fair itself contained a circus of numerous booths and stalls with homes of the performers and dancers, there were thin men, fat women, two headed calves, gayly coloured China ornaments on display, along with shooting galleries, nine pins and coconuts shies.

Woodbury Hill fair was legendary it lasted over five days and was always held on the week that the 21st of September fell. The whole period in the early days was referred to as Woodburytyde. It was the largest of its kind in the whole of the south of England. Originating in 1200 and in Its Heyday thousands of people flocked to it. Its days included those set aside such as

Wholesale Day for wholesale traders. Gentle folk's Day – Devoted largely to entertainment and the eating of Oysters and to this day there can still be found under the turf of the Hill the shells from the Oysters. All folks Day – A Day of general dealing and entertainment.

Sheep Fair Day- Specifically for dealing sheep, Cattle, Horses, and any other livestock. Pack – A –Penny Day – when all the unsold goods remaining were offered at a reduced price.

Traders came from as far afield as Birmingham, Norwich, Bristol, Exeter and London as well as all over areas of the county and the surrounding neighbouring counties. In the days leading up to the fair the roads and lanes all around Bere Regis were thronged with people goods horses and wagons and livestock being driven to the fair.

The Bere Regis village was always crowded when the fair was on whilst nearby Dorchester was often deserted. Some of the people living on the hill overlooking the village sold refreshments and made a small charge for parking of bikes in the safety of their premises. At the fair there were many attractions such as a two headed sheep and a bearded lady. One of the Fairs in the 1940's was cancelled due to the heavy rain fall and was subsequent flooded out. One occasion some ornaments were said to have been won at the Fair in the presence of Thomas Hardy on the shooting Gallery.

In My walks and talks with Thomas Hardy - Hardy at the Bere Regis Fair by Clive Holland.

"On reaching the summit Hardy was in his element. Quite several farmers dealers and frequenters seemed to know him, was and he fell into the vernacular in talking with them. What a crowd it was with the side shows, a strident band, fat women and a skeleton man. The nut-brown Gypsy women fortune tellers from little booths crowded with village girls".

Hardy wasn't the most cheerful of men and many of his stories are about loss and misery. Though he was without doubt Dorset's most famous literary figure. He lived at Max Gate outside Dorchester, the town which inspired the creation of Casterbridge in his novels. He is responsible for some of the greatest works of English Literature - including Far from the Madding Crowd, Jude the Obscure and Tess of the d'Urbervilles. He died in 1928 - although he had wanted to be buried beside his first wife, Emma, his body was interred in Poet's Corner, Westminster Abbey, and only his heart was buried in Emma's grave at Stinsford. Poet William Barnes was born in Bagber near Sturminster Newton in North Dorset in 1801. He became curate at Whitcombe near Dorchester and ran a school in the county town. His poems are seen as a valuable record of the old Dorset dialect and working people's lives in the 19th Century.

Gallows hill encampment

Many Gypsies lived in tents at the Gallows hill Gypsy encampment on the Bere Regis road from the 1800s. From the 18th century onwards thousands of gypsies traveler's at one time lived here. Living in mainly very basic wagons and carts with tarpaulin roofing. These local Bere Gypsy encampments were full of crude benders and poor canvas tents and sacking.

Nelson Hughes was the son of Noah and Matilda Hughes. He married Lavinia, Frankham, Bateman. who was a member of a south country Gypsy family. She was a hawker, and Arthur was a 'rat and varmint destroyer', or 'Labourer', 'Peddler', 'Hawker of Tin

Wares', 'Tin-Maker' and 'Basket Maker'. They had 17 children. The family mainly travelled in and around Dorset and went hop picking in and around Hampshire during the early Autumn.

Their daughter Caroline Bateman Hughes was born in a vardo in 1900 at the Gallows Hill encampment. She was registered in the Wareham District. under the name Caroline Frankham as her parents were not married, they courted each other, and jumped the broom stick, which in Romany terms was 'man and wife'. d. She was to become famous for her songs, Caroline was the Queen of the Gypsies and was without doubt the most famous Gypsy folk singer and songsmith. Caroline married John Hughes in 1918. They had 8 children. Diana, Mary, Annie, James, Thomas, Louisa, Caroline, and Celia. The Hughes family also camped at Corfe Mullen, "Downy" encampment on Colonel Georges land by the woods. John Hughes had been injured in the Great War and spent time in Dorchester Hospital, his brother was killed in the same conflict. All the Hughes families including children worked on local farms, picking potatoes, peas, and fruit, pulling sugar beet and hay making. Out in the fields pulling dock leaves and hoeing all day. Living in the caravan and in bender tents, they would eat from the land, rabbits, pheasants, and chicken and plenty of vegetables cooked on an open fire in a two-gallon pot. Clothes washing was done from water taken from the stream that once ran all the way through the heath. In common with several her siblings, Caroline started to go hawking with mother before attending school 'till she was ten-year-old. Then she went with her mother to get a living, just like all her sisters before her. Caroline would return home and do her washing in a large tub all until she was fifty-three years. Then she was involved in a road accident, which turned her into an invalid. Caroline was the matriarch of the 'Hughes Group of Travellers'.

Families living on Gallows hill had included Ayres, Barnes, Bartlett's, Batemans, Benham's, Blakes, Blands, Bonfield's, Bowers Boswells, Burdens. Burtons, Cherrets, Chinchens, Coles, Crockers, Does, Dorys, Elliotts, Fancy's, Fletchers, Frankham's, Franklins, Greens, Hughes, Issacs, Jeff's, Johnstons, King, Lakeys, Lanes, Lees, Lovells, Pateman's, Penfolds, Peters, Phillip,

Phippard, Potters, Roberts, Rose, Scamps, Scarrots, Sherred, Sherwin, Shorelands, Sherwood, Skemps, Smiths, Stanleys, Stones, Thicke's, Thompsons, Tuits, Turner, Wareham's, Warren, Wells. Wellstrads, Whites Woods, Woolsies and Young.

SHROTON FAIR

In earlier years Shroton Fair attracted thousands to the fields under Hambledon Hill. In 1961 Shroton celebrated the 700th anniversary of the village's fair charter of 1261. 'Southern Television were present when the hunt met and there was a large fireworks display. 'The crowds were the largest ever. There were years when it rained and the large fair vehicles got stuck in the field folks referred to "Shroton Fair weather", which meant misty mornings that evolved into warm and pleasant autumn days.'

In 2011, 91-year-old Betty Hunt (née Elliott) in a Shaftesbury nursing home recalled her Shroton Fair memories. 'All sorts of mischief went on there – but not destructive,'. 'We used to walk up there, pay to go in and meet people, including boyfriends.' Betty, who lived at Ranston Farm, remembered 'great piles of brandy snaps', a shooting gallery with balls balanced on jets of water and a Shroton character called 'Old Gaisford', who rode to the hunt meet on a donkey. 'He was bow-legged and lived on his wits. Thomas Hardy wrote of seeing a woman 'beheaded' in a sideshow there.

The fairground was up on the higher ground with all its usual attractions. The White family flower girls were still selling their flowers from their baskets and all the fortune telling ladies were busy in their booths. With fortune-telling still being carried on, there no doubt by the granddaughters or great-grand-daughters of the famous Rose Lee or Petulengro. Long ago the race took place in a snowstorm. Attendances at Shroton dwindled until the Great Dorset Steam Fair, launched at nearby Stour Paine Bushes in 1969, drove the final nail into Shroton Fair's coffin. Disgruntled gypsies are said to have cursed the Steam Fair, causing the torrential rain and mud baths for which it became famous. Not that Shroton was immune to the weather.

THE POOLE TO PENZANCE FAIR LADIES WALKING FIELDS

Poole Fair

Poole fair and the gingerbread man
dancing girls and the French can can
the roundabout and the rifle range
the penny rolls where we lost our change
the hoopla stalls the coconut shies
the switchbacks rides where skirts got high.
Recooks great tight rope skills.
the wall of death and bicycling thrills
the freaks all seated in their pens.
a great fat lady and teary men
the fire eater's huge tattoos

the shuffling card men crafty rues
those girls squeal on the ghost train rides.
and knickers sights where hot air blows
Jack Turner wields his kushti act
he splits an apple right in half.
whilst conjuring up a medley crowd
which does the waiting boxers proud?
Ted Sherwood takes the motley fight.
against the Jo Jo black as night
and when he's done
young Freddie Mills
will knock opponents off their heels.
but now were nearly spent right out.
with naught to show what it's about
our mum she says it's all a con
I think she wishes that she had gone.
whilst I just smile and tell my gran of Poole's great fair and the gingerbread man.

Beau Park

POOLE FAIR IN LADIIES WALKING FIELD

In 1894 Buffalo Bill's circus came to Dorset bBournemouth and Poole. In 1904 local papers reported Colonel W F Cody, and his troop of 1,300 men and horses put on a display at Poole's Ladies Walking Field.

The influences of the local Poole fairground

Boxing had been a major attraction on the fairgrounds for hundreds of years with its origins in the bare-knuckle pugilist fights of the earlier 18th and 19th centuries. Such fights were originally conducted under the Prize fighting rules then in 1867 new guidelines were set to regulate the sport under the Marquess of Queensbury rules. Including the wearing of boxing gloves leading to the outlawing of bare-knuckle bouts.

Sam and Esther Mckeowen managed one of the most famous boxing booths in the south of England in the early 20th century. Namely the Poole to Penzance Fairground. They arrived with the fair each year at Poole in November with their troop of famed boxers including the famous Randolph Turpin. Here many of the local gypsy boxers would join their stable and fought in their booths attracting big crowds, including Freddie Mills, Ted Sherwood, Abe Stanley and Teddy Peckham They were often seen on fairground nights standing together on a platform outside the boxing booth. Many of them went on to become well known nationally and internationally as boxing champions. This popular fair ran from the 1920s to the 1960s. It was managed by Sam and Esther McKeown which held one of the most famous boxing booths in the south of England in the early 20th century. They travelled with their troupe of famous boxers which included Freddie Mills, Randolph Turpin, Rinty Monaghan, Gratton and Jimmy Wilde, as well as Barbara Buttrick, who was one of the best-known female boxers of the period. Many local Traveller boxers fought here at Poole including Freddie Mills, Abe Stanley, Ted Sherwood, and Teddy Peckham.

Ted_Sherwood was born in Fancy Road, Newtown on 13th September 1910. As a boy Ted showed an aptitude for boxing, and as he grew up began to take part in fairground boxing matches, training under Herbert Millett with nearly 130 bouts between 1929 and 1939 and becoming welter weight boxing champion. Following his successful boxing years Ted took to drink but found salvation through religion, becoming an ardent member of the Pentecostal church in Poole. Preaching in the open air at Sea View Newtown and from a soap box at Speakers Corner in Hyde Park, London. Where he met the Reverend Dr. Ian Paisley, and they became close friends. When he preached, he went through all the boxing movements which had made him famous in the the boxing ring. Ted died in October 2000 in Poole. Freddie Mills was born in Bournemouth in 1919. He was given a pair of boxing gloves for his 11th birthday and at 15 when coached by Jack Turner he won his first bout. At 17, he began a highly successful professional boxing career becoming the "darling" of the British fight scene. In 1942 he knocked out Len Harvey taking the British Commonwealth Light Heavyweight Championship. He won the European title beating Pol Goffaux, and in 1948 defeated Gus Lesnevich to win the World Light heavyweight Boxing Championship. After losing his World

Championship to Joey Maxim in 1950, he retired. Mills ran a highly successful nightclub and starred in several films and as a TV presenter (1957). He died of gunshot wounds to the head on July 25, 1965, under a cloud of mystery. The official verdict being suicide, many believed it was due to him becoming involved in the London underworld world of the notorious gangsters the Kray Twins. Abe Stanley was a professional boxer in the 1950s and early 60s. He boxed at light heavyweight, heavy weight taking part in 38 professional contests. Gypsy traveler Abe Stanley married Jean Rogers, and they lived in Fancy Road Newtown. He was one of the Sons of popular gypsy Samson Stanley. The Stanleys were well known in the locality and regulars at local pubs such as the Albion in Newtown. Teddy Peckham was a local Heather lands gypsy boy who had attended school close to the nearby Heavenly bottom gypsy campsite which was one of a hoard of camps where the local gypsy families lived in their wagons. When he was a teenager Teddy fought regularly each year at the Poole fairground booth.

Boxers standing outside the boxing booth in Poole's famous fairground.

George Digger Stanley was the son of George and Cinderella Stanley and the grandson of Diverus and Naomi and the great grandson of Peter and Rebecca Stanley. (Said to have been the grandson of Gypsy queen Alice Stanley. George was the world bantam weight champion and first outright winner of the Lonsdale belt for boxing. He died in March 1919 in Fulham, London following a long illness. At his death newspapers recorded that the first outright winner of the Lonsdale belt had passed away in Fulham following a long illness. He was the ex-England and Worlds bantam weight boxing champion.

By the 1800s McKeown's boxing booths, had famed boxers including the famous Randolph Turpin. George Ruffle a fairground proprietor who came to Poole in the 1800s. His son John married Rebekka Keets from Wallisdown in 1874 as recorded in the 1911 census. The Ruffle family at one time managed the Poole doss house.

BOURNEMOUTH

There were numerous fairs throughout the region. Many were managed by Cole's fairgrounds and Arnolds. These included Kings Park Fair Bournemouth. This was a very large fair owned by Rose family which operated throughout the 1959s early 60s. Many of the fairground stall workers and rides were operated by travellers Gypsies. Alongside the fair was a large. Billy Smarts circus. Another regular fair was at Poole Lane West Howe Kinson and at Redhill Park.

The DORSET STEAM FAIR

The old fair is here each year
upon the downs with fun and beer
the oil doth smell and tracks of mud
where cars are parked upon the meadows so green
whilst the carousels play to delight the scene

The crowds flock here again this year
to buy the goods or storm the gears
there's gypsy folks and travellers tales
amidst smoky air and diesel smells

There's a big machine to roll and ride
across this Dorset countryside
where zunners run and play and stare
at all those folks there at the fair

With marquee tents with music rock
stalls for to sell and gears to lock
with amusements rich amidst fields of green
biker's parades and beauty gypsy queens

Crowds of folk flock here each year
to mingle and enjoy the spirit here
with the hills so steep and views so grand
the steam fair spreads itself across this land

Ray Wills

This fair is held each year at Tarrant Hinton Blandford Forum in Dorset. This fair has almost a quarter of a million people in attendance, and it still is one of the world's largest gatherings of steam engines in the world. Always attracting hordes of local Gypsies. Situated as it is within some 6000 acres of rolling grassy hills. It includes many road locomotives, steam engines, traction engines, steam lorries, steam rollers and fun fair, exhibits and very many other great varieties of attractions. Fortune tellers such as Diana Turner nee Hughes regularly attended the great Great Dorset Steam Fair which was launched at nearby Stourpaine Bushes in 1969 at Tarrant Hinton Blandford Forum. Attracting almost a quarter of a million people and hordes of gypsies. Situated within 6000 acres it is one the biggest outdoor events in Europe.

CHARLTON MARSHALL FAIR

The Arnolds gypsy fairground family lived locally at river lane and each year they worked the local Charlton Marshall fairground. Mrs Arnold was famous for selling boiled humbug sweets to locals. Children would go to her house and watch her make them. She sold her home-made humbugs in town on Thursday and Saturday when market stalls were there on market day in the 50s. Blandford Museum has photos of her. A gypsy named Donald lived at the end of river lane in a caravan in the early eighties. He was retired from the fairground. He had a beautiful greyhound called Cliff.

SHAFTESBURY FAIR Castle Hill

On fair days the round-abouts with galloping horses do a lively business, and their steam-driven organs emit energetic music that may be heard far and wide; and when a good circus pitches its tent on Castle Hill, vehicles of every description stream in by hundreds from all the surrounding villages, for there is nothing that the country folk love better than a circus. But at other times Shaftesbury would be considered by a stranger passing through it, fresh from city life, as a quiet if not sleepy town. Thomas Hardy described Shaftesbury. Truly, it is a town that appears to have seen its best days. Its marketplace is almost deserted, save on market-days, and when some travelling wild beast show visits the town.

It has little to boast of save its splendid site, its pure health-giving breezes, and the magnificent views of the surrounding hills and downs and valleys that may be obtained from several points of vantage. Of its four remaining churches one only is of medieval date; the three others are all quite modern, entirely destitute of architectural interest, and with little beauty to recommend them. All the others which once stood here have disappeared, leaving nothing to remind us of their former existence save, in some few cases, the name of a street or lane. Of the glorious Abbey, probably the wealthiest nunnery that ever existed in the kingdom, nothing but the walls that once enclosed the precincts on the south-east, and the foundations of the church, long entirely hidden from sight by surface soil, now happily opened out by recent excavations, remain.

William Barnes suggested a theory that some of these churches may have been old British ones, and that the Saxon Christians could not, or would not, enter communion with the British Christians, but built churches of their own.

BLANDFORD

From 1603 there were horse racing held in the town and for many years an open-air swimming pool at the Ham until 1993. These fairgrounds were originally also held on the Blandford Ham which was an open space here where there were merry go rounds, dodgems and side shows.

George Wells of a Romany/Gypsy family had a son Henry born c.1828-30 Blandford. Other local gypsy fairground boxers at that time included Fighting farmer Elliott and slimmer Holloway.

CAROLINE HUGHES 1902- 1971 Married to John Hughes their daughter Cissie married a John Warren. In 1968, they lived on farmland in Blandford. She was famous for her singing and vast collector of songs. She was visited and a memorable stereo recording by Peter Kennedy was made in her caravan near Blandford in 1968. During which time the farmer, over-laced with cider, tried unsuccessfully with the aid of his two sons & two tractors, to tow her caravan out of the field. Carolyne paid no attention, but just carried on singing.

George Haskett was a local fairground boxer in the 1930s who fought the famed gypsy boxer Freddie Mills at Alexandra gardens Weymouth. where the fight was drawn. In later years George was a coal merchant before becoming the mayor of Blandford then emigrating to Australia where he died aged 99 years.

Thomas Hardy described Blandford as a town that appears to have seen its best days. Its marketplace is almost deserted, save on market-days, and when some travelling wild beast show visits the town.

Dorchester fair

Mr Herbert the horse dealer followed his father Johns trade in the west country. He worked an early form of the fairground roundabout which was called the Joy Wheel where riders had to cling on for their lives until they fell off. Jack married showman's daughter Sally Newman. They worked the fairgrounds together. Eventually adding a shooting gallery, snake show, roll-the-penny, and hoopla to their attractions. Sally died at a young age 34 and Jack married Mildred Moore. They had 11 children, they lived in St Georges Road, Dorchester. During the second world war the Herberts held their government supported home fairs in the Market care park in the town. Soon their steam engine called the Majestic was their pride and joy, despite tipping over on the road near Dorchester, closing the carriageway for three weeks until she could be moved. The Majestic left Dorchester in 1947, when its engine was sold for preservation. The Herberts travelled regularly alongside the Townsend travelling show folks from Weymouth. At the Portland fair. The Herberts Majestic was immortalised as a model by toy makers Corgi with a copy of the miniature was presented to family member Edward Herbert in 2012 at the Great Dorset Steam Fair, in front of the original engine.

The county town of Dorchester was the largest employer of brick workers in the locality with some 10,000 employed there at one time. Men, women and children. The Benham Gypsy family worked there on the farm they were living in trailers in an area allocated to them. Where the women made paper flowers, and items out of mistletoe, holly and daffodils. It was here where Gypsy Jack Herbert worked a fairground roundabout in Dorchester which was called the Joy Wheel, where riders had to cling on for their dear lives until they fell off. Jack married showman's daughter Sally Newman and they worked the fairgrounds for many years and ran a shooting gallery, snake show, roll-the-penny and hoopla stalls. Sally died when just 34 and Jack married Mildred Moore they had 11 children. During the 1939-45 war years the Herbert family held their government supported home fairs in the towns Market car park. Their steam engine the Majestic was their pride and joy until 1947 when the its engine was sold for preservation. The Herbert and the Townsend fairground folk travelled regularly from Weymouth and at Portland fair.

SHERBOURNE FAIR

Sherborne's Pack Monday, which also features live music and a funfair, dates to medieval times. It is held in the Dorset town on the first Monday after Old Michaelmas Day, which falls on 10 October, traditionally marks the feast of St Michael the Archangel and is associated with the beginning of autumn. Known in other parts of the country as Mop Fairs or Hiring Fairs, it came to be known as a Pack Fair, which is thought to have come from the word "pact". The fair comprises a traditional street fair with market and craft stalls in the town's four main streets - The Green, Cheap Street, Half Moon Street and Digby Road, with live music in Pageant Gardens and a funfair at the Terraces, which started on Thursday.

The night before the fair the lanes were full of horses and caravans. We kept getting out of bed to go to the window and look at them. Slippery-sloppetty gypsies. A pest those gipsies were. It was no use getting your field gate shut they just lifted them off the hinges and turned their horses into the young wheat, or they'd open a clamp of mangolds/ All roads led to the fair that day. Men used to come from miles around, sweating along the lanes with their jackets slung over their arms. At the fair there were ponies there from the new forest and Wales horses the farmers had fattened up for sale. sheep and cattle to everlasting. There were stalls a roundabout in front of the three pubs with gingerbread, shell boxes, whelks and China ornaments. Old Mrs Hall sold the best sweet rock she was clean as a new pin with her lace and ringlets. Into these ordinary little villages in the morning would come all the fair gear trailing behind heavy steam engines that pulled into the meadows for the best fares were on grass. Under the sweaty labour of shouting men in an assembly of tents and caravan's roundabouts and swings boats and galleries curious to the child's eyes gazing through the open gateways. Locals loved those gypsies whom Mrs Smith sound such a pest. Their dark faces invited they caught hedgepigs and ate them, and the women use the grease smarmed their hair. Under the Hoopla's cocoanut shies Aunt Sallys A coloured boxer ready to take on anyone a shooting range a peep show men lay about in the ditches at night. The fairs sold merchandise and men in those days. There were hiring fairs known as Mops. Servant girls paraded here and were inspected by their masters to be quizzed and questioned and picked out like any slave, the bargain being finally sealed with a shilling piece. Rifle shots cracked out through the music whilst screaming girls were swung so high it seemed that the creaking boats might fling them out at last. Somewhere a bell sounded as a village lad testing his muscles with the wooden mallet, won the admiration of glancing eyes. And by next morning as the dawn broke there was nothing to show for it all, but a gate torn off its hinges, as the chugging engines left the meadows and a litter of bags and bottles, water squirts and confetti lay on the trampled grass. And the village was itself once more.

ROMA DAY

It was Roma Day in Dorchester town

Where Hardy penned and where Barnes did write his sweet
Durzet rich dialect poetry down
where the music from the accordions played
when Gypsies danced and dreams were made

The storytellers told their tales
of the Dorset towns rich country dales
where farmers wives and dairy maids all gathered around
in the Dorset green rich country glades
they told their tales of days gone bye
when Caroline Hughes but a child and shy

When the market town was rich in life
where yokels bartered dawn to night
where vardo wagons rolled and gypsies danced
across the hills like true romance

It was Roma day in Dorchester town
with happy folk all gathered around
where folks all came from miles around
for to share all their tales n fine displays
their vardos rich in fine attire
their chavvies in awe sat round the fire

They sung their songs of Gypsy rhymes
Sharing the brew of love divine
oh, to hear the stories of travellers free

all the hopes and dreams of humanity
in Roma life
oh, let it be –

Ray Wills

ROMA DAY AT DORCHESTER BOROUGH GARDENS

MIKE GUY AND GYPSY FRIEND PLAYING AT DORCHESTER BOROUGH GARDENS ROMA DAY EVENT

Jack Herbert the horse dealer in Dorchester followed his father Jhns trade in the west country. He worked an early form of the fairground roundabout which was called the Joy Wheel. Where riders had to cling on for their lives until they fell off. Jack married showman's daughter Sally Newman. They worked the fairgrounds together. Eventually adding a shooting gallery, snake show, roll-the-penny, and hoopla to their attractions. Sally died at a young age 34 and Jack married Mildred Moore. They had 11 children, they lived in St Georges Road, Dorchester.

Portland fair

At the Portland fair the Herberts Majestic was immortalised as a model by toy makers Corgi with a copy of the miniature was presented to family member Edward Herbert in 2012 at the Great Dorset Steam Fair, in front of the original engine.

Home fairs

During the second world war the Herberts held their government supported home fairs in the Market care park in the town. Soon their steam engine called the Majestic was their pride and joy, despite tipping over on the road near Dorchester, closing the carriageway for three weeks until she could be moved. The Majestic left Dorchester in 1947, when its engine was sold for preservation. The Herberts travelled regularly alongside the Townsend travelling show folks from Weymouth. At the Portland fair. The Herberts Majestic was immortalised as a model by toy makers Corgi with a copy of the miniature was presented to family member Edward Herbert in 2012 at the Great Dorset Steam Fair, in front of the original engine.

WIMBORNE

Sheppard's field fair

After the harvest every year, a small fair would be set up in Sheppard's Field, close to Walford Bridge. With roundabouts and various other small shows and they would be there for one or two weeks. The fair was always well patronised, and all social barriers seemed to disappear. German bands were frequently seen oompah bands these days. They were of quite a high standard and would stay in the town for about a week. Apart from playing in the streets of the town, they would also visit private houses in the area. There were visiting tumblers, jugglers and a fire-eating coloured gentleman who came regularly but only stayed for a day or two. In contrast, the pavement artist would remain for at least a week before moving on. The length of their stay was governed very much by the weather at the time. Sometimes a visiting potter would set up his wheel and demonstrate his skill. People were fascinated to see the clay take shape under his hands as his foot worked the treadle to power the turntable. The salesman would suddenly say, 'I'll tell you what I'll do, I'll sell this watch, real silver, jewels in all its works (and here he would hold up the watch to catch the light, opening the case to show the sparkling interior) and I'll put it with this golden half-sovereign. You can have the lot for five shillings! Anyone give five shillings for a silver watch and a gold half-sovereign?' The watch and the coin were soon sold and then trade would generally start to pick up. Of course, it may have been that the person who bought the watch was in league with the cheap-jack – who knows?

Performing bears were sometimes seen a few miles away on the streets of Wimborne. They were usually accompanied by two men, one who played concertina while the other looked after the bear. The bear's performance generally consisted of a jig while standing on its hind legs. Bears were supposed to come from Russia, so the men were always described as Russians: they had dark skin, black hair, and large black moustaches. They would perform at private houses in the residential part of the town but their performances in the town itself were limited because of the danger to horses. Horses have an instinctive fear of bears and the smell of one was enough to upset a nervous horse. A horse in panic could be a very real danger in a crowded street.

During the spring and autumn, a very popular entertainment was the Punch and Judy show. Though in in the summer, most Punch and Judy shows had a pitch somewhere on the sands at one of the nearby seaside resorts though in Wimborne they could usually be found either in the Square or by Eastbrook Bridge. Another source of amusement and enjoyment for both adults and children were the visit of the one-man band. His outfit consisted of a cap with bells for his head, pan-pipes or a harmonica for his mouth, a concertina to keep his hands busy, drumsticks for his elbows (the drum being carried on his back), cymbals on top of the drum played by a cord attached to one heel and a triangle also attached to a cord to the other. It wasn't always easy to recognise the tunes which he played, but you had to admire the amount of effort and energy needed to keep the show going for even a few minutes at the height of his performance he must have looked like a man with a ferret down his trousers and a couple of hornets in his shirt!

On other occasions a Scots piper would parade through the street playing the bagpipes. The sound of this instrument wasn't always to everyone's taste, but the swing of his kilt and sight of his traditional costume always attracted attention.

BROADSTONE Fair

The fair was held on the recreation ground which was given to the people by the wealthy Miss Kennedy. She owned Delphs House and was famous for growing oranges and lemons in her hot house. The fair was held regularly along with horse shows.

MARTINSTOWN FAIR

In 1268 Henry III had granted a charter to Winterborne St Martin (Martinstown), which allowed the village to hold an annual fair within five days of St. Martins Day. The fair, which in times past was a leading horse market and amusement fair, had been revived but the old-time custom of roasting a ram was replaced once during an event in the 1960's with a 'badger roast'. The 80 lb badger was caught in a snare and many villagers thought they were eating goose Gypsies always came to Martinstown Fair to deal horses. There were roast badger sandwiches always sold at the fair. Fairs are no longer held in Martinstown on an annual basis.

Winterborne St Martin, commonly known as Martinstown, is a village in south west Dorset, situated four miles south west of Dorchester, beside Maiden Castle. The village has a population of approx.754 (2001). Bronze Age barrows including the famous Clandon Barrow surround the village and Maiden Castle hillfort is nearby a stream (The Winterbourne) runs through the length of the village. The village is in the UK Weather Records for the highest daily recorded rainfall, which was recorded in Martinstown on July 18th 1955 at 279 mm (11 inches) in a 15 hour period. After a hundred years silence, bells in the church rang out in 1947. Five new bells were hung as a village memorial to those who died in the war. An earlier peal had been sold to defray debts.

After The Fair

The singers are gone from the Corn market-place
With their broadsheets of rhymes,
The street rings no longer in treble and bass
With their skits on the times,
And the Cross, lately thronged, is a dim naked space
That but echoes the stammering chimes.

From Clock-corner steps, as each quarter ding-dongs,
Away the folk roam
By the "Hart" and Grey's Bridge into byways and "drongs,"
Or across the ridged loam;
The younger ones shrilling the lately heard songs,
The old saying, "Would we were home."

The shy-seeming maiden so mute in the fair
Now rattles and talks,
And that one who looked the most swaggering there
Grows sad as she walks,
And she who seemed eaten by cankering care
In statuesque sturdiness stalks.

And midnight clears High Street of all but the ghosts
Of its buried burghees,
From the latest far back to those old Roman hosts
Whose remains one yet sees,
Who loved, laughed, and fought, hailed their friends, drank their toasts
At their meeting-times here, just as these!

Thomas Hardy

CHAPTER THIRTEEN

THE GYPSY CAMP

On the Gypsy camp
with mushes proud and where pretty gals did dance
where vardos stood so tall n proud
near benders bush and music loud
where heathers grew upon the floor
no strangers came knocking at their door

Where folks did sit around the yog
at night the stories told amidst the yapping of the dogs
where rabbits ran down country lanes
whilst foxes watched their daring games

He ran with chavvies barefoot too
with ferrets free in pockets deep
whilst ole ladies did a duckerrin do
where horses gables iron shod shoes
n babes did sleep amongst the dew

Where lavender fields with baskets rich
did grace the views and commons ditch
so rich were the days and nighttime shades
when folks and dreamers had it made
amongst the poet's dreams and shades
we graced the earth and set the scenes
where only modern folks do dream

Ray Wills

ROYAL BLOOD ROMA

They say she had royal blood running in her veins
they said she was born on the heath one Saturday
they say she was true Romani bred
she picked the flowers she made the beds
she lived in a vardo gayly painted wooden van n sheds
fancy lamps and brassy urns tall stories in the morn

They said she was rich in dreams and fortune telling games
she planted herbs and knew all their fancy Latin names
they say she grew up rich in tales and fancy rhymes
sing us a song Roma tell us a rhyme

They said her parents were Dominey n Sherwood bred
teachers of the pulpit flowers in the shed
her brothers and her sisters worked the farmers lands
hops and fruit give me your hands
the heaths were rich, and the fields were free
stopping places, Atchen Tans such a history
write it down

Ray Wills

THE GYPSY CAMP TALES

I awoke from a disturbed night. I could still hear the traveller's voice and the wheels on the bumpy roads. When i looked out the little window the street was familiar. It was Poole. It was a cool autumn dark yet starlit evening. Like hundreds of other locals from Poole and the surrounding areas I made my way across the rear of the fire station onto the back water wastelands of Poole. Like the many of our folk for years went down to Poole at the weekends to frequent the pubs on the quay, where they were regulars. It made a welcome recreation after their hard employment in the brick yards and clay pits.

In those early days on Saturday nights Gypsies from the Poole and Bournemouth area gathered in Poole. Crowds travelled there from communities like Newtown and frequented all the quayside pubs. Including those from the Kinson parish and many of Canford Heathland campsites. The noise of the fairground was deafening with the sounds of the organs and the electric motors thumping out. Along with the noisy chatter of the excited crowds and the pop music song belting out an Alma Cogan classic. The bumping cars were busy tonight with screeches of brakes and whines. With the tall lanky dark-haired youth jumping from car to car taking fares from eager excited giggling teenage girls. Young courting couples out for the night and the older citizens. Nearby a young pretty Cole gypsy gal was standing at her lucky duck fishing stall, holding on her arm her cane basket. With her large bright gold earrings dangling from her ears, she made a distinctive figure in the bright dazzling lights of the fairgrounds many colourful lit up bulbs. With her gaily coloured head scarf covering her dark braided hair and with her long flowing pretty and revealing floral dress. Low cut at the top showing off the delights of her more than ample breasts peeping out from her dress. Much to the delight of the small group of young men onlookers with their fashionable quiff haircuts their dark tight blue jeans and open top high collar shirts.

As I moved through the crowds of fun seekers, I soon came to the gaily coloured boxing theatre. Sam and Esther Mckeowen managed this; it was one of the most famous boxing booths in the south of England. They arrived with the fair in November of each year with their troupe of famed boxers including the famous world-famous Randolph Turpin. Here many of the local Gypsy boxers would join the McKeowen stable and fought in their booths attracting big crowds.

Including amongst them was young local Gypsies Freddie Mills, Ted Sherwood, Abe Stanley and Teddy Peckham. They were often seen on fairground nights standing together on a platform outside the Mckeowens boxing booth. Many of them went on in later years to become well known nationally and internationally as English, European and World boxing champions.

Young Freddie Mills a local Gypsy traveller was born locally in 1919. Given a pair of boxing gloves on his 11th birthday and at just 15 had won his first bout. At 17 he had become the "darling" of the British fight scene. Who would have thought that it was possible that he would in later years go onto become British Commonwealth Light heavyweight Champion, winning the European title and the World Light heavyweight Boxing Championship. Then running a highly successful nightclub, starring in films and TV shows. Then to tragically die of gunshot wounds to the head under a cloud of mystery.

Here were displayed artistic painted figures of athletic bare topped moustached figures of tall bare knuckle boxing kings of another long-forgotten age. As if they all were stepping out from another time long ago. Yet all of them displaying their own distinctive Lonsdale brass gold belts around their trouser tops. Close by on a platform stood the handsome figures of young men of the local gypsy boxing fraternity. The Sherwood's, Stanley's, Peckham's and the young Mills boy. Along with the legendary Randolph known as Randy Turpin. All of them showing of their bare topped muscular masculine figures. Onlookers were encouraged to part with their hard-earned moneys to enter the booth and be entertained by the great boxers of the age, whilst others from the crowd more daring were offered the once in a lifetime opportunity to put their boxing skills to work against these local champions. To see who can dare to go three rounds with a local king of boxing and to hopefully gain a fortune.

The large billboards sign overhead proclaimed in large bold italic words Mc KEOWENS FAMOUS POOLE TO PENZANCE BOXING BOOTH. The sport of kings.

The crowds were larger now with lots of families. Amongst them there were groups of small, excited children scrambling onto the carousel's colourful horses. I stood and watched as parents lifted their children onto the horses and showed them how to hold on tight. Then the carousel started its familiar movement and the excited children's waves to their parents smiling and happy. And the parents waving back each time they completed the circuit. It brought back lots of memories to me of days and nights when as a young man i had worked these carousels and the pleasure it had given countless children over the years in all those northern towns and villages.

I remembered those days and nights with great affection. Fond memories working with the other fairground workers many of them travellers like my ancestors before. I remembered the Gypsy girls I had known during those years. Those I had loved and lost and I wondered where they were now. Were they like me trapped in the gorjas world of brick homes and mortgages. Where the freedom of the road and the gypsy life was long gone and now just a memory. I remembered the beautiful Roma Sherwood who I promised to love forever. But war and life had left their mark and meant she had gone to a new life in the States. I had last heard that she was in Michigan in a log cabin in the wild woodlands of west branch, living with a welder who sang the blues at country dances. Yes, she loved music did Roma. She was a true gypsy dancing gal with her dark eyes and long flowing auburn hair. Yes, life had played me many bad hands in cards and like her, the dickerrin had not been good. Just then i felt the light rain on my open shirt, "Yeh typical, its Poole", it's part of life here, the autumn nights at the fairgrounds usually brought in the rain. I hurriedly made my way back through the crowds back towards the busy Ringwood Road.

On the way i recognised Knobby Watton wandering around. As usual the old boy was pushing his old push bike cussing and swearing as he looked for fag ends on the ground and in the gutters. Poor old guy it was said that he was shot up badly fighting away in the war and had returned shell shocked. They said that he went into a mental hospital for a while in Canford cliffs and they gave him electrical treatment. Obviously, it hadn't helped him, poor old guy. Yeh the war years had hit him hard too. There were too many people like him had been affected or had lost their lives fighting for freedom.

I remembered others many of them travellers who I had known as a child. Including one of the gypsy Bakers, George who was an RAF pilot had got shot up, lost an arm and now proudly sported a metal hook replacement. Last time i saw him he was living on the Mannings heath was married and with a hand full of kids. Obviously, all grown up now and him and wife were living in a bungalow next door to the Archer family.

Just then i saw a familiar face in the crowds coming into the fairground. It was old Joe Winda's from up north, I wondered what he's doing in this part the country. I remember well Joe and his gypsy family. His people were original Roma travellers who used to go hop picking. They settled down after the war, running a popular second-hand clothes shop. Yet still choosing to live in their vardos in the field at the rear of the property. Joe still worked and bred horses and knew most in that business so well. Joe made exquisite miniature vardo toys. Joe had told me a great story about an Irishman who had thought Joe's pictures of these online were the real thing. He travelled across from Ireland to meet Joe and buy what he thought was a real vardo wagon. Until Joe showed him the miniature in the boot of his car. They had a good laugh about it and went back into the pub and drowned their sorrows together. I remembered when Joe and I had spent days out on the Purbeck together at Corfe, Wareham, and Swanage. when I gave Joe some local background history of the locality.

Just then a loud familiar Dorset dialect voice boomed out." Hey mush how you are doing." I looked around at the direction of the voice and saw the unmistakable figure of the tall travelling local man Fred Bartlett. "Hi Fred" I said, "it's great to see ya mush, what's on". Fred greeted me with a warm hug, as he brought out his hand for a quick swift smack with mine. He nodded and spoke, "I come here every year, as you know mush, I live on the quay, back of the pub."" It's an opportunity for me to meet up and makes a change for me to see how others run things". "See what's new". "It is also a chance to meet up with many me olé travelling mates from the fairs from ways back". "Many of them iv e not seen for a while me Wacker olé zunner". "Course they be show people now bant they and no longer gypsies." He laughed and with a wry smile.

Fred was a local fairground owner with a long family fairground business in the area and with stalls throughout the county. His people with a history going back centuries to the big Bere Regis village fair on the hill there. He spoke," I was hoping to bump into two your mates down here today, young Frank Cole's and Terry Adams". He said "As you no doubt know. they're looking for some stalls to add to their fairgrounds in the Bournemouth area". I replied, "I've not seen them around tonight but there's so many down here such a big crowd". "But the rains getting heavier and I'm heading back home Fred". "See you again soon I hope". Fred replied," Yeh sure mush, guess we l bump into each other no doubt at the Steam rally next year". "Yeh that's for sure" I said, and I left him amongst the crowd.

When I arrived at the town's main Ringwood Road the rain had really got worse. The bus was late as usual, l thought, I was glad to be under the bus shelter. "What you are doing here mate, its bit out ta your way isn't it mate". The voice was familiar, and the speaker was someone I really didn't want to see. It was Sankey Ward the well-known clay pit boss. Who provided work for many of our people in his many clay pits throughout Parkstone. The work was hard and poorly paid. He wasn't respected by our folk. He had earned his wealth through the hard labour in long hours by our folk. Them working in hot wet muddy conditions from dawn to dusk. Wheeling barrows of clay over plank boards in and out the kilns, sweating and their muscles aching. He wasn't the best payer either so many complained of his late payments. He saw himself as a righteous self-made man. Him being a church lay reader on Sundays. Many local Gypsies worked at Sankey wards clay pits in broom road, including my uncles Bill and Tony Rogers I had often gone with them at weekends when I was a nipper young chav. We would work within the scorching hot kilns. Wheel borrowing loads of clay over the planks in and out of the hot burning kilns. It was a hot task, and we came home with our jeans covered in red clay. The Wards were so called religious people yet not of any true Christian merit amongst them and he was the worst of them. Sankey spoke "You want some good diggin man", he said, "you know the work is regular mate I can start you tomorrow at foxholes, if your there for 7 sharp". I replied "No thanks Mr Ward, " I said politely"," I've got a job". Sankey had many clay pits at fox holes and at cuckoo bottom near old Wareham Road. Sankey was obviously amused by my answer and laughed sarcastically. He spoke, "Call that a job working with a pony and cart"." There's no future there, young man"," That's not a real job no prospects there" he said. ", Why ole Edward Frank Phillips and family has that work all nicely sewn up years ago ". He laughed again, then said, "Don't be a dintlo". I was relieved to see the Dorset and Hants double decker bus come into view and pull up at the stop and Sankey board it. Then the rain stopped just like it had started, and I decided to walk down to the Poole quay.

A great many local people today are in some way related to the Gypsies Travellers who frequented this area with many of these having their roots in the New Forest area, which was of the main Gypsy area in the UK at that time. Some had originally worked in the many brickyards and clay pits which had been around for many years whilst others worked casually at the local fairgrounds Including the large Poole fairground which were popular over the years. Such as the Bartletts, the Coles and Kings families. Gypsy travellers played an important part in the social history of the area. Their names have become well known entrepreneur's and sport celebrities through the centuries from the times of the newfoundland cod trade and Portland stone trades from Poole to the present day. With many of them establishing vibrant successful businesses in areas such as haulage, transport, scrap metal, brick making, house building, farming, and potteries. Along with floral arrangements, lavender farming, and similar skills. Other local gypsy travellers

became well known as top sportsmen in the boxing and speedway world and even preachers. Others were fairground owners and showmen. These initiatives and projects often with humble beginnings were used as a source of income to fund the ultimate family industry. In time these thrived and were in demand to become extremely wealthy local enterprises. Some of which are still with us here today. In time official sites for the Gypsies were set up locally. The main one being based next to the Rogers family Mannings small holding farm at Mannings Heath Road.

The gypsy travellers had regular stopping places where they'd park their Vardos and dig the earth out so that they could get the Vardo wagon level. The Juk dogs they'd tie up to the hedge near the vardo for Lue = shelter and let the Kanis = chickens out of their box from where they were put up under the vardo when travelling. To stop them straying too far they'd train the Kanis = chicken by tying, with string (to) a leg to a spoke of one of the wheels of the vardo. take the sweaty harness from the Grai = horse, put on its head collar with tether chain attached, so that farther down the lane he'd peg his favoured Grassini = mare so that she could graze the wide grassy verge. The Didikais called it To Pouva The Grasnis = to graze horses in a farmer's field without permission. They would get them out before daybreak.

The Juvels = women Jal = go Bikinini = hawking with their big, wide hawking Kipsis = baskets to the Kenners = big houses or where the well to do d. It was no good to Jal = go, to the poor cottages, because they didn't have any Spugar = money or anything else. go, to the local Hobbenker = shop. With a Bitt = a little Bok = luck having sold enough lace and ribbon to buy Moro = bread, Meskie = tea and perhaps Bitti = a little Mass = meat Old Eli the grandfather of the family, was a Bitti = small Rai = gentleman with a greasy waistcoat and Dicklo = neckerchief. He kept his Sougar = money in a Bitti = little knitted sock pinned to the lining of his waist coat. He gave sougar to the Juvels to buy his shag, T0ver =

tobacco to smoke in his old Swingler = pipe by the Yog = campfire and Pucker = talk of the old days. The men would go Tatting = collecting rags for salvage by Treader = bicycle from the villagers round about and sell it, after they had sorted it, to the dealer. The sorting of the Tatting (= rags) was the one job they could give to the Dinlo Racklo = idiot boy. Dordi = oh dear, it was a task to keep him occupied and quiet. The young men were sent to get Pani = water in a tall 5 gallon can from the farmer's water trough. It was to boil a Bori = pile of Poovers = potatoes, probably Lelled = taken from a farmer's field. At teatime sometimes the Engro = doctor would call in to have a cup of Meskie = tea and Dik = see the family but mainly to check the baby or babies progress and health. The next morning when we went down the drove, they were all gone leaving just a whirl of blue smoke from the ashes of the YOG = fire.

CHAPTER FOURTEEN

CORFE MULLEN CAMPS

Where the wind blows

The wind doth blow upon the heath
in cold n windy weather
it blows upon the morning dew
the golden spider busy on his web
the ants scurry upon the heather

It blows to warm the cockles of your heart
in summers scorching weather
the wind doth blow upon the heath
in springtime and in summer weather
in coldest winters frost n snow
when the ice lies on the heather

The wind doth blows for mortal men
for Gypsy lad and lassie
it blows upon the memories
past scenes of bitter weathers

When folk sat around the yog
when wagons wheels were a turning
when the stars were brightened
through the darkest of winter nights
and young hearts were a yearning

The wind it blew upon the heath
when brickyards were a warming
when men worked hard for crust and love
oh and to keep those wheels a turning

The wind did blow upon the heath
in good days we remember
when gentle folk did work the land
when lord n gentry prospered
through labour of the working man
built up riches in their coffers

The wind doth blow across the heath
where the travellers told move on
there no land for likes of you no more
no kindred spirits offered

Only the wind blowing upon the heaths
where schools and worldly rankings
took the world of simple lives
for profits and for banking

Ray Wills

Corfe Mullen encampments

At Corfe Mullen there was a thriving Gypsy traveller community with many encampments on Colonel Geeorges land. The worked on the nearby brickyards and potteries for many years. Whilst others worked on the large Lavender farm. Colonel Georges of George and Harding brickwork company built many grand hotels and houses in Bournemouth. Colonel George also built local churches There was a non-conformist church ST Huberts which was a thriving Gypsy church. Where large crowds of Gypsies attended regularly at the non-conformist services. Colonel Charles George was born 1843 to Jacob George. Charles Albert Duke George married Ada Martha Sharland. George with Lord Wimborne had initially bought many acres of Heathland at Corfe Mullen at a bargain price. Here Colonel George and Lord Wimborne had provided sites on their land for numerous Gypsy encampment. They employed many Gypsies who camped on his land there. The Towers was not Colonel Georges folly it was all part of the arts and craft movement of that period. Colonel George had built the Red House in Corfe Mullen later added a false frontage of Towers of 4 stories high on top and it became known as the Towers. Members of the traveling Gypsy families settled in the areas on their many encampments were a ready source of labor. With many of them proficient in brick making and similar skills. Because of their encampments close vicinity to the brick works they were readily available when required by the brickyard and pottery owners. Local Gypsies were given rights by these landowners, establishing what they believed to be a common right to the bi t of land which they had enclosed and that which they believed that they would never be ejected from. Many of these families slept in the brick works overnight for shelter and heating. There were green valleys in Corfe Mullen which were all called Bottoms and in these tucked away places were old mud huts cottages, probably reclaimed by squatters for they camped here long ago on the land completely undisturbed. These were "happy bottom," Stoney Down, "little Egypt," "Rush combes Bottom" and "Gypsy Pit Field". The poet Haberty and his partner Agatha Walker wax doll maker collectors of history were greatly inspired by the

Gypsies at the Stoney Down encampment at Corfe Mullen. Following their interest in tile making, they became famous with their works displayed in London's Victoria and Albert Museum. Caroline Hughes for a time also lived at the Corfe Mullen gravel pit field encampment. Gypsies had gathered with their many wagons for many years at these encampments this plantation covering around three miles of land. In 1891 John Rogers brick maker managed the brickyard there whilst his family lived at Brick kiln lane. Local Gypsies were given rights by the owners, establishing what they believed to be a common right to the bit of land which they had enclosed and that which they believed that they would never be ejected from. In these valleys or Bottoms tucked away places were old mud huts cottages. John Everett known as Herbert by his family, was born in Dorchester Dorset on 18 August 1876. His father Rev. Henry Everett was Rector of Holy Trinity in Dorchester, and his mother was Augusta Stewart. John married his Irish cousin the painter Katherine Everett known as Katherine in 1901. They were both students at Slade school of Art. The Everetts bought land at Broadstone, Poole they designed and built their home, called Prospect. John Everett and Katherine had spent much time within the Stoney Downs Gypsy encampments at Corfe Mullen. Living for a while amongst them. Here John painted many great pictures of the local Gypsies, and their dwellings scattered on the Corfe heathlands amongst the clay pits and the local environment around Dorset. Katherine Everett also lived in one of the huts on the Moors alongside the Gypsies and she had built several lovely houses in Broadstone. Katherine was also well known for doing interior murals like those in the Towers which was full of murals. She was there at the right time frame to perhaps have done those murals herself. To the left of that Heath is Corfe Lodge which is now Julia House and where the Everett's built their house. Katherine built several lovely houses in Broadstone. Katherine was also well known for doing interior murals like those in the Towers which was full of murals. She was there at the right time frame to perhaps have done those murals herself. The Everett's literally lived between these areas. Particularly when Katherine first moved there, and she was Local the house now known as Julia House for sick children. However, by 1914 their marriage had ended.

THE LAVENDAR FARM

Two local men had originally created the lavender farm with the planting of 60 acres of land in Broadstone. The local Gypsies girls had also worked on the lavender farm they gathered baskets of flowers on the lavender farm and worked on the hedgerows in search of elder flowers processed as beauty products. This busy plantation covered around three miles of land. Producing the famous Dorset lavender bags bottled perfumes with pictures of local Dorset scenes painted by the Everett's. Little bricks were made at Crown Dorset which was on Green Road in Poole. They were then infused with scent eg lavender. The lavender fields were in Broadstone. Crown Dorset also made Moth Bricks and Perfumed Tablets In the Broadstone lavender farm the Romany Gypsy heritage girls were seen gathering baskets of flowers and were known to work on the hedgerows and looking for the elder flowers which were processed as a beauty product. Gathering these herbs flowers from the nearby hedgerows to make herbs for all manner of ailments. Small costrels of lavender oil were sold at fancy London shops such as Liberty's. Local potteries also made bowls to take the pot pourri mixture. The lavender farm closed in the

1920s. Though some production receptacles continued in Verwood. A Mr Hill in later years had shown a very keen interest on healing and plants at the lavender farm too. The gypsies and others worked at the local Mill when the flower Industry died where they made moth balls from broken bricks perfumed with lavender. A smaller much cheaper to produce perfume brick – was created. This was soaked in lavender or other perfume and then simply placed in linen cupboards until all its scent had evaporated. Those families who lived here had skills in brick and tile making they included the Budden's, John and William Rogers, Robert Rogers brick maker, William and George Rogers, Henry Morris, James Morris, Timothy Oxford, Tom Lovell, the Thornes, Fancy's, Rabbetts, Kings, Leeks, and Ferret's. In later years a field was named after one family being known as Budden's field or Budden's Meadow.

Years ago, some young Gypsy lads were shipped to Newfoundland as apprentices to the slave masters and cod industries. This went on in many areas in Dorset over the years including Bere Regis. The music composer, Christopher le Fleming of Wimborne wrote. "As the Carters came into Corfe Mullen for their work every year, the teams of horses were all bedecked with full bells" The horses would also bring loaded wagons to market. The bells when they were cast were tuned to the owners liking, and one could tell who was passing by the pitch ring of the bells. There was a Mr Hayter a gentleman from the Wimborne area with his horses who created a carts and harness collection at Little Manor Farm. He was believed to be around the 1920s as one of the last Carters of horses with bells. "Mr Hayter would bring his wagon over the railway crossing to us. it is said one evening in the Cock and Wheatsheaf inn, that he was found in a thoughtful mood and talked of being "glad to be going home tomorrow" The next day he checked to see the crop safely carried then stacked on his wagon. He knew by heart the times of all the schedule trains on the Somerset and Dorset line. When he was leading his loaded wagon up the short slope to the crossing, a fast excursion train suddenly appeared bearing down towards him. He was just clear of the line but the headwind from the train caught a piece of chain on the harness of the leading horse that hit him on his temple. He was killed instantly. The horses and wagons were unharmed.

SHARLANDS BRICK WORKS

Elias Sharland (b. 1818, d. 1904)Elias Sharland He was born in Salisbury in 1818 the son of Emanuel Sharland and Elizabeth Troke). He married Ann Maria Scott on 03 Oct 1838 in Parish Church of Great Canford, daughter of Thomas Scott. Elias and his father Emanuel were making bricks in Canford sometime after 1831.

Originally Broadstone was part of the village of Canford Magna. In 1855 there were several labourers' cottages occupied by men from the Iron Foundry at Waterloo and from Elias Sharland Brickfield at the end of Charborogh Road. The Broadstone Brickyard, is where the Recreation Ground is today, was owned and worked by Elias, who had a big kiln with a very tall chimney for burning the bricks; Gorse was used to start the coke or coal burning. Some bricks were bought by the Railway Company, and many were used to build the earliest houses in the little seaside town of Bournemouth, then just beginning to be fashionable.

Marriage: 03 Oct 1838, Parish Church of Great Canford. Children of Elias Sharland and Ann Maria Scott are: Mary Jane Sharland, b. 1840 Julia Anna Sharland, b. 18 Jan 1841, Emily E Sharland, b. 1844, Emmy M Sharland, b. 1846, Elias Thomas Sharland, b. 1848, d. 1912.Anna Maria Sharland, b. 1850, Emanuel Fred Sharland, b. 1853, d. 1918.Eliza Ellen Sharland, b. 1855, Sarah Mealah Sharland, b. 1858. In 1861 Elias had under his employ 12 men and 3 boys. He used to ride around on horseback supervising his brickfields. He also built several houses, these were built of co?? for his Labourers, chiefly in Dunyeats Road, or using his own bricks; the earliest ';Audlem Lodge', was built in 1862.Elias 'Granfer' Sharlands house 'The Pines' stood in The Ridgeway, and he could see from there how the work was going in the brickyard below. Elias was a well-known character. At one time he owned a great deal of land in Broadstone, especially the area around The Ridgeway. Elias gave the site for the Methodist Church, then valued at one hundred pounds, and the foundation stone was laid in 1889, and was opened on the Whit Monday of the following year. Elias' wife Ann died. In 1881. The book 'The History of Broadstone' reports that Elias was married three times and had many children. The last Sharland to live in Broadstone was Harry and he died in 1963 at the age of 88, Elias was also a preacher of the Poole Wesleyan Circuit and was responsible for the first mud wall 'cob' construction Congregational Chapel in 1853. Elias Sharland had a big kiln with a very tall chimney for burning the bricks; Gorse was used to start the coke or coal burning.

Many bricks were used to build the earliest houses in the little seaside town of Bournemouth, which was just beginning to become fashionable. For many years the hill in the Lower Blandford Road was knows as 'Shirland's Hill'. Elias Shirland's brickworks was at Broadstone in the 1800s. In 1856 land at Corfe Mullen's was bought by Elias 1861 Elias employed 12 men and 3 boys. He supervised them on horseback at his brick fields. He built several houses for his Labourers, chiefly in Dunyeats Road, using his own bricks. His first Audlem Lodge', was built in 1862. Elias 'Granfer'

Shapland's house 'The Pines' stood in The Ridgeway, and he could view from there how the work was progressing. Elias was a well-known character. At one time Elias owned a great deal of land in Broadstone, particularly around The Ridgeway. Elias gave the site for the Methodist Church, then valued at one hundred pounds, with the foundation stone being laid in 1889, and it was opened on the Whit Monday 1890.it was designed by Mr. Griffin, the local builder.In the 1871 census Elias occupation was Brick manufacturer age 53. Between 1871-81. Elias' wife Ann died. Elias was married three times and had many children.

The Broadstone brickworks were at Grove Road in 1911. This was before the recreation ground. There was also a pottery near Derby corner. There was a local infamous snake collector called Harry Brown he also digs out foxes The brickworks closed in 1912. Elias had died in 1904.

CHAPTER FIFTEEN

GYPSY TRAILS

Marsh Lane encampment Upton Lane. In the 19th century on the crossroads near Upton brickworks Poole there stood a beer house, known as the Railway Tavern. The beer house attracted a clientèle of travelling Gypsies and the fair people from their Marsh Lane encampment.

Lavenia Frankham Bateman lived there on the encampment with Arthur Hughes in their horse drawn vardo with their 17 children. Gypsies settled for winter on family-owned land, or where the landowner was sympathetic. Many worked for local farmers on their estates. Many went fruit picking and potato gathering. Trading or bartering such as the sharpening of knives and making pegs, floral presentations or wreaths. There was also a dairy in the village round about Dacombe Drive, just before the garage opposite Factory Road. It was a big house." The Railway Taverns attracted a clientèle of travelling Gypsy fairground people from their Marsh Lane encampment. The brickyard had three tall chimney stacks visible for miles and made bricks for nearly 100 years and was one of the biggest employers. The men worked long shifts of twelve hours life was hard. The brickworks closed 1968. There was a blacksmith forge nearby at Upton crossroads where Upton court is now it was where old Mac Sweeny shod horses and did his blacksmithing. Once every few years a real nut-brown Gypsy lady with her hair in plaits and ringlets and a scarf round her head used to come in a painted van. Each year a Gypsy woman visited him to clean his bellows arriving in her brightly coloured horse drawn vardo wagon which she tethered to the rear of his workplace She parked behind the forge and all the many cans hanging about and she used to mend and refit the leather on the bellows. She travelled all around repairing them in blacksmith's shops. Her vardo was a lovely old painted horse-drawn Gypsy caravan. In those days they didn't have an electric fan to blow the air into the forge, they had this very big old bellows which you pumped up and down with a long handle.

The following is one local man's recollection and vivid description of a meeting with a Gypsy family. "Camping in the spare land here I got to know a family of Romany Gypsies the real article. A family of four father and mother and two sons. They had two very large caravans and between the wheel spaces were built large boxes like cases, with wired front doors and sliding outside wood doors. One was built on the left side and the other on the right and housed half a dozen poultry and the other side a nanny goat. When the vans were in position exactly so far apart a large tarpaulin was hooked between made a snug stable for the two fine Cleveland horses they had. The top was also sheeted in bad weather and a manager added to the rail at the rear. Water was available from the two lodges opposite another entrance to the Parlington Hall"." The two sons of the Gypsies got to know the farmer and were sometimes employed per day, man and horse. In their spare time they cut willows for making pegs and mats and small baskets. The boss went horse dealing, the mother made pegs and baskets. They were friendly people and my dad, and I were once invited to have a snap meal with them. It was roast hedgehog. It tasted good. This is the way it was cooked, only the entrails were taken out, the body was then rolled in clay and put in the centre of a stick fire and covered with the red-hot ash. When cooked enough the ashes were removed and the clay split open. The hide and spikes came away and the meat was dished up just as it was, on plates with bread only grand white meat it was. The sons were very clever, they could catch anything that ran or flew, and they were never short of grub, and I think the keeper turned a blind eye.

HAMPRESTON Sylvia (Selbea) Fletcher was baptised at Hampreston Dorset on 20th May 1760 she was the daughter of Peter and Sarah Stanley. Peter was a razor grinder and tinker,' had been subject to a settlement hearing at Corfe Castle, Dorset, in May 1792, where he named his seven children as William, Selbea, Aaron, Peter, Sabra, Paul and Henry. Peter died in 1802 he was buried at St. Mary's church, in Puddle town. His headstone read 'Peter Stanley (sic), King of the Gypsies. Sylvia was apprehended as 'Silvia' Stanley on 8th December 1777 in Southampton and removed to Little Canford, Dorset, and 1780 with cousins Clarinda and Caroline, appeared at the Winchester quarter sessions, charged with being a rogue and vagabond. She married William Fletcher, at Millbrook Hampshire in June 1781, where her name is recorded as 'Silby.' The couple first child, Gentillia, was baptised in Hampshire, but the remaining ten were all baptised in Dorset, and four of her daughters, Kezia, Jemima, Kerenhappuch and Matilda. On 1st May 1845 at Wimborne Minster, she was laid to rest, 'aged 89.' She was just 85, having been but had, nonetheless, survived to what was a great age for the time. Her sons William and Paul were rat catcher, tinman, brazier and grinder. Paul in his 90th years, is buried at Wimborne Minster.

WEST MOORS TRAVELLING FAMILIES

Priory common encampment

For the first couple of decades of the century, the gypsies were mainly camped on that part of Priory Common where the cemetery is now situated (conveniently close to the Ringwood-Wimborne Road) - so they had a lengthy walk to school, though they could of course get across the Common easily.

A census was undertaken in West Moors in 1911. When householders for the first time wrote their own details. Local man Walter Stephen Stickland was its enumerator. Though many gypsy travellers were not present when the census was taken. Therefore, they were not included. Thought such census enumerators were not educated and often wrote sir names wrong such as many variations in gypsy names such as Crutcher, Crocker, Croutcher. This became more obvious in the 1881 census where whole gypsy encampments were not recorded.

St Leonards common encampment

There were also gypsy communities (or other temporary dwellers) on St. Leonard's Common, in what became Oakhurst & Elmhurst,

BLANDFORD

Following a fire in Blandford in 1731 many sites were started up there to create bricks for the rebuilding of the town through the Bastard family.

Whitehill encampments

There was for many years a large gypsy encampment here.

There are two groups of graves at Blandford Cemetery plus a few odd graves scattered around other parts of the cemetery. There is a section in the Salisbury Road cemetery which is dedicated to the traveller community. Some of the Gypsy family names buried there are Turners, Barney, Hughes, Cooper and Escott, Mrs Escoot was a Benham, Frank and Les's sister, the Benham's are probably the best-known Blandford Romany family.

There was a Romany gypsy funeral held near the church in Blandford of a Gypsy Queen where her home was burned along with all her possessions including a small fortune in gold & jewellery.

A tax collector accused William Stanleys wife and two friends of robbing him of 50 pounds. Mrs Stanley was said to be wearing a man's clothes at the time. They were all put into custody for some days until a local farmer proved that they were in fact many miles away at the time. Had it not been for him they would have probably been hanged. William was also in custody with her at the time. William Stanley in later years was a preacher along with his siblings. The daughter of Lavina Frankham a Blandford gypsy was convicted at Wareham for stealing sticks.

Moors river encampment

The moorland / heathlands of Kinson, Parley Common, Turbary) has probably always been a favourite resting place for travelling folk.

WIMBORNE

Horton Heath gypsy encampment

Priscilla Green was born on the 27th of November 1874 at Horton Heath near Wimborne she was who was the daughter of George Green a Chair Bottomer and Eliza formerly Wilkins her birth was registered on the 15th of December 1874.

Louisa Barnes nee Willett (Gypsy Queen) and her husband John stayed there, long with Benjamin Stanley the brother of Levi who was disowned by his family before they emigrated to the USA.

The Gypsies eked a living on their wanderings by gathering and selling flowers, manufacturing bosoms, bee skeps and chair bottom caning. Travelling street musicians were a common sight in Wimborne. On Friday in the Square or in the High Street where there was an old harpist and his fiddler well known by the local folk. The children loved the organ-grinders, mainly for the monkey which usually accompanied them. Women organ-grinders with cage of budgerigars. If you paid a penny, a bird would pick out from a drawer beneath the cage a printed card that would tell your fortune. It was always something pleasant and written in such a way that it could apply to almost anyone. These people were usually Italian Gypsies with rings in their ears, brightly coloured scarves, and swarthy complexions. Sometimes accompanied by a dancing girl playing a tambourine who also used to collect money. There were tumblers, jugglers and a fire-eating coloured gentleman who came regularly. A potter would set up his wheel and demonstrate his skill. There was street traders cheap jacks, offering knives, watches, mouthorgans and many other glittering items to attract the passer-by. They could be found by Eastbrook Bridge, particularly on a Saturday evening, when the town would be filled with workmen with their wives and families. There were also performing bears. Sometimes a visiting potter would set up his wheel and demonstrate his skill. People were fascinated to see the clay take shape under his hands as his foot worked the treadle to power the turntable. The salesman would suddenly say, 'I'll tell you what I'll do, I'll sell this watch, real silver, jewels in all its works (and here he would hold up the watch to catch the light, opening the case to show the sparkling interior) and I'll put it with this golden half-sovereign. You can have the lot for five shillings! Anyone give five shillings for a silver watch and a gold half-sovereign?' The watch and the coin were soon sold and then trade would generally start to pick up. Of course, it may have been that the person who bought the watch was in league with the cheap-jack – who knows? Performing bears were sometimes seen a few miles away on the streets of Wimborne. They were usually accompanied by two men, one who played concertina while the other looked after the bear. The bear's performance generally consisted of a jig while standing on its hind legs. Bears were supposed to come from Russia, so the men were always described as Russians: they had dark skin, black hair, and large black moustaches. They would perform at private houses in the residential part of the town but their performances in the town itself were limited because of the danger to horses. Horses have an instinctive fear of bears and the smell of one was enough to upset a nervous horse. A horse in panic could be a very real danger in a crowded street. During the spring and autumn, a very popular entertainment was the Punch and Judy show. Though in in the summer, most Punch and Judy shows had a pitch somewhere on the sands at one of the nearby seaside resorts though in Wimborne they could usually be found either in the Square or by Eastbrook Bridge. Another source of amusement and enjoyment for both adults and children were the visit of the one-man band. His outfit consisted of a cap with bells for his head, pan-pipes or a harmonica for his mouth, a concertina to keep his hands busy, drumsticks for his elbows (the drum being carried on his back), cymbals on top of the drum played by a cord attached to one heel and a triangle also attached to a cord to the other. It wasn't always easy to recognise the tunes which he played, but you had to admire the amount of effort and energy needed to keep the show going for even a few minutes at the height of his performance he must have looked like a man with a ferret down his trousers and a couple of hornets in his shirt!

On other occasions a Scots piper would parade through the street playing the bagpipes. The sound of this instrument wasn't always to everyone's taste, but the swing of his kilt and sight of his traditional costume always attracted attention.

At Holt village nr Wimborne there were 4 active brickyards in the 19th century.

Barnsley Drove encampment, 1881

Many gypsies camped here including the Wells and Jones families. Robert Jones, Head, Married, 1846 Gipsy Hawker. Priscilla, Wife, 1847 Gipsy Hawker. Susan, Dau, Single, 1873. Rhoda, Dau, Single, 18. Charles, Son, Single, 1878, Diana, Dau, Single, 1880. William Servant Single, 1865, Hawker 1881

John Wells, Head, Married, 1841 Gipsy Tin Maker, Rhoda, Wife, 1840 Gipsy Hawker, Sidney, Son, Single, 1871.

Amos, Son, Single, 1873. Walter, Son, Single, 1874

At Holt village nr Wimborne there were 4 active brickyards in the 19th century.

DORCHESTER

Slyvers Lane encampment Dorchester

The local Gypsy encampments here were full of crude benders and poor canvas tents and sacking. The Benham Gypsy family who worked on the farm in Dorchester, lived in trailers in an area allocated to them on Slyvers lane. The women made paper flowers, mistletoe, holly and daffodils.

Families living on these Included Ayres, Barnes, Bartletts, Batemans, Benham's, Blakes, Blands, Bonfield's, Bowers Boswells, Burdens. Burtons, Charrettes, Chinchens, Coles, Crockers, Does, Dorys, Elliotts, Fancy's, Fletchers, Frankham's, Franklins, Greens, Hughes, Issacs, Jeff's, Johnstons, King, Lakeys, Lanes, Lees, Lovells, Pateman's, Penfolds, Peters, Phillip, Phippard, Potters, Roberts, Rose, Scamps, Scarrots, Sherred, Sherwin, Shorelands, Sherwood, Skemps, Smiths, Stanleys, Stones,

Thicke's, Thompsons, Tuits, Turner, Wareham's, Warren, Wells. Wellstrads, Whites Woods, Woolsies and Young.

Dominic Reeve author of 'Smoke in the Lanes'. Tells a story of parking up in a lane near Dorchester in 1958. Gypsies were arriving in Autumn early Winter and camping in Higher Frome, Vauchurch, Compton Valence and Tollerford.

In Dorchester during the reign of Queen Elizabeth the first. A large group of Gypsies were prosecuted and sent to trial. The Lord lieutenant of Dorset was ordered by the Queen that they should be made an example with some to be executed. When they went to trial, they were acquitted. Since they had journeyed from Scotland and not as originally thought from overseas.

The James family who lived here originally came from the new forest then settled at Heavenly bottom before eventually moving into Pembroke Road. They were circus carnival folk and had a hand in building the suspension bridge at Alum Chine too.

It was here where Jean Hopes grandmother Kate James nee Collins lived out her remaining years. They all were living in wagons in Pembroke Road along with the Jeff's and the Crutcher's. Their wagons were right next to Jeans grandmothers' yard where she also had her wagon living hut. Here there were members of the James, Hopes, Jeff's, Crutcher's and Stanley's. The Martha and Thomas James and family were encamped here 1891. By 1895 the James family had left the road behind them, having moved into a little stone built cottage in Littlemoor. Martha passed away in 1924 and Thomas followed in 1931, both are buried at St Nicholas church Broadway Weymouth.

Beaminster Potteries

Two potteries making courseware were recorded at Beaminster in 1812, but Dorset's most remarkable potteries were the small rural ones collectively known as the Verwood potteries. Potting began at Alderholt in the early fourteenth century. It was well established by the seventeenth and eighteenth centuries, when small groups were exploiting the clay deposits from Alderholt south-west to Horton, with Verwood at the centre.

Gypsies Hawking the earth ware pottery

All types of practical earthenware were made, these were mostly sold by hawker Gypsies who ranged up to 40 miles (64 km) from the kilns. The industry declined in the nineteenth century through competition from mass produced wares. The Cross Roads kiln at Verwood was the last to close, in 1952. The brick-lined kilns were about 10 feet (3 m) high, surrounded by a mound of earth, clay and broken pots. The Verwood & District Potteries Trust was formed in 1985 to record and preserve the remaining evidence of the potteries. There are good collections of Verwood pottery in the museums at Christchurch, Dorchester and Poole.

WEYMOUTH

Sporting Magazine, volume 21 dated 1803 reported: A short time since, the youngest son of the late Peter Stanley, commonly known by the appellation of King of the Gypsies, started from the town-pump in Dorchester, to run to the town-pump in Weymouth for two guineas; the distance is about eight miles and a quarter, and the time allowed was an hour and two minutes, but he performed it with the greatest ease one minute and a half within the time. The person who made the bet was a young spendthrift of the neighbourhood, who, fearing he should not be able to see fair play himself, hired a horse for his favourite Cyprian to accompany the light-footed prince, but she not having attended Astley's Lectures on Horsemanship, and finding it impossible long to retain her seat in the usual way, immediately crossed the saddle, and in that state entered Weymouth, at full speed, by the side of her infatuated adorer, to the no small gratification of a numerous assemblage of spectators. Henry was the youngest of at least nine children born to Peter and Sarah Stanley, a gipsy family who were renown in Puddle town (formerly known as Piddle town) in the county of Dorset and the surrounding area. Seven of the nine survived to adulthood and were named Selbea, William, Sabra, Aaron, Peter, Paul, and Henry. The family spent most of their lives travelling around Dorset, Wiltshire and Hampshire and ultimately Peter (senior) became known as the 'King of the Gypsies', a term applied to the respected elders of the community. According to a 1792 settlement document, Peter's occupation was a razor grinder and tinker. Peter died in 1802, and the parish register of Puddle town confirms that he was aged 75 buried November 1802. However, his headstone tells a different story and gives him as being five years younger leaving us unsure as to which is the more accurate. 'In memory of Peter Stanley, King of the Gypsies, who died 23rd November 1802, aged 70 years. 'Sarah allegedly reached the grand old age of 101 years when she died, which, if you do the maths on that, would have made her some 12 years older than her husband and 58 years of age when she gave birth to her youngest child Henry in 1778 at Winterbourne Kingston, which seems highly unlikely. Sarah died at Wareham in Dorset and was buried at Puddle town alongside her husband on the 22nd of February 1821 and as such an important person in the community her death was noted in the newspapers and many people attended her burial

Tom Hewitt from Weymouth in Dorset was a well-known character with his dray always piled up with apples. Also, there was old and worn-out man who sat in the gutter often mending cane-bottomed chairs. He would wrap his hands in old rags to save the razor-like cuts from the sharp-edged cane.

CHAPTER SIXTEEN

GYPSY TRAVELLERS ON THE PURBECK

The Square and the Compass

On top of The Purbeck where the stone was cold and mean
the travellers and hikers walked the paths of Dorset scenes
where yeomen once were local, and the landed Gentry dwelt
where sheep and hills were rich in rhyme and the poets write there
still
In the old, stoned pub relic where the log fire sparked so free
where the hearth is home to wanderers and folks who are free like
me
where Augustus John the artist pictures hung upon the wall
Was next to the old Stone Museum where dinosaurs once roared
Where the masons etched their histories, and the hills were rich in
dew
where the wind blew cold on winter days deep within the hues
the dogs they sat down close to the fire and the drinkers toasted
Zen
whilst the olden Dorset folki breathed life into its flames.

The sign it swung outside the pub where the chickens all ran free
where stone tables laid their stories for all yet to see
the atmosphere was rich in trust and the poet viewed the scenes
upon the Purbeck hillsides there so close to Halloween

The square and compass told its tales upon the hilly downs
where lovers met, and couples kissed their steps left far behind
the cockerel crowed and gave chase to the farmers wench
upon Purbeck hillside
where Hardy's people at one time paid their rent

Ray Wills

QUARRY LIFE BLUES

The heavy weight of the stone
The strength of Gyppo Jack Elliott
The donkeys monkey waggons
with his load upon his back
Full of clay and stone
The sweat and the tears of life
Just another long, long day

The Ower Bay and weight of stone
The boats and crew the mercy tools
The stone for cities and grand walks of man
The pavement boulevards
The dark dark tan of the gypsy man

The sweat and joys of Kingston Lodge
The toils of the quarry men at large
The Master aprons
The squire and the compass
The virtues too
The hidden depths
The ships from Poole

The London city
Westminster halls
The dome of sacred St Pauls
the Newfoundland trade
The ships that sailed
With stone of plenty

Through hills and dales sea spay whales
Poor men a plenty and the richness of the gentry

Ray Wills

WAREHAM

Ropers lane encampment

Peter Stanley born 1721 Razor Grinder and Tinker married Sarah and they lived in Wareham. Sarah was known as the Dowager Queen of Wiltshire, Hampshire, and Dorset. They had 9 children. When Sarah Stanleys died a great many people attended her burial. Peter died in 1802.They are buried at St Mary's church in Puddle town church cemetery. Sarahs death was noted in the newspapers referring to her as 'her vagrant majesty. Many people attended her burial.

Daisy Fancy lived in Wareham area then later in the 1800s she moved to the Heavenly bottom encampment in Parkstone Poole with her siblings. Many of their descendants like Gideon Fancy and family later moved to live on the Gypsy encampments at Bourne Bottom and Heavenly Bottom Parkstone Poole. Where there were women brick makers there too, such as Mary Ann Fancy, Sophie Fancy and Daisy Fancy they all had lived in Wareham in the 1800s and afterwards at Heavenly bottom encampment Newton Poole.

Moses Stanley, a razor grinder, married Ann Dory at Wareham 1822. He had four different wives over time and lived in Roper's Lane Gypsy traveller encampment.

Hyde house estate house encampment.

Gypsies camped on Hyde house estate on the Radcliffe family land till late 1940s, it was Situated between Wareham and Bere Regis.

SANDFORD POTTERY

SANDFORD POTTERY WORKS, WAREHAM.

SANDFORD VICTORIA WORKS POTTERY

There was a great deal of brick making and pottery work nearby at Sandford near Wareham in the 1840s Sandford Pottery was built by Lucas and Aird and funded by Sir John Lawrence (later viceroy of India) on or near the site of a brickworks which was established in about 1849 by the wealthy philanthropist Lady Burdett-Coutts built to provide employment for labourers. The pottery was built later between 1856 and 1860 and called Victoria Works after Queen Victoria. It is said that that bricks from here were used to build the foundations of the Crystal Palace, in London in 1851. However, there is no mention of this in the records of the original or rebuilt Crystal Palace. The artist John Thomas was employed to design the fine china ware products, and experienced workers were brought in from Worcestershire and Staffordshire. The finest ball clay was used from Creekmoor Poole. In 1863 the pottery, was bought by Miles Rodgett, from Lancashire, who housed the workforce at Sandford House, housing for estate workers. Pottery products were made until 1886 and the pottery closed in 1966.

Philanthropist, Lady Burdett Coutts, established Sandford brickworks in 1840 after a conversation with novelist Charles Dickens. The brickworks made bricks for the foundations of Crystal Palace London. By 1856, funded by Sir John Lawrence, the Sandford Clay and Pottery Works was built, a major employer in Wareham. With its giant 180-foot-high chimney dominating the landscape. It made fine chinaware and 1900's produced drainpipes and ran until 1966. The Fancy's worked at the Sandford brickyards.

Records show that 'Joseph Fancy of Arne was a Brick maker'. His 3rd born daughter was baptised in Arne in 1790, but his other children were all baptised/buried in Lytchett Minster. After his second marriage in 1797 Joseph is shown as being a Proprietor/Occupier in Lytchett Minster. Two years later he took out a lease from the Lord of the Manor, William Trenchard on 12 Oct 1799 for an acre of land between Lytchett Bay and Poole turnpike road, adjoining his brick kiln. Joseph settled in Poole and moved his family from Dorset to start up a brickwork in Hornchurch in Esse. Unfortunately, the venture failed, but there are roads in Hornchurch that now have Dorset names.

Gideon Fancy was the father of my great grandmother Emily Elizabeth Fancy who married Charles Rogers my great grandfather. Fancies had been involved in brick and pottery work for centuries many were skilled brick makers. Many of the Fancies were married to Cherretts, Bonds, Stanleys and Crockers and many Gypsies including Rogers married cousins. . In the 18th century at Wareham west of Creech there was a lofty block of Flemish-bond brickworks.

John Stanley married Sarah Fancy at Arne in 1802.

William Stanley was a preacher and laid the foundation stone at the short-lived Gypsy school and the Asylum in Dorset in 1844

David Fancy 1793- 1876 lived at Arne in Wareham where he later married Sarah Fancy, and they had 5 children, William Susan, Thomas, Gideon and Ellen. In later years he lived at Organford.

William Stanley born 1859 married Mary dee Bellam they had 9 children.

The beacon hill brickworks

This ran for many years in the area associated with blue pool. There were also Clay Potteries and the Quarries.

Portland Purbeck encampments

Frampton Terrace

These were a terraced row of cottages built for the brick workers working at the brickyard these were known as Frampton Terrace. These were built in the period of the Victorian era, when several of the houses still standing on Poole Road were built, using the red facing bricks from Upton Brickworks.

Turners Puddle encampment.

Many of the Fancy family were recorded in the Purbeck at this encampment Christopher Fancy was born there in 1612. By the 1700s many Fancies lived throughout Dorset.

At Bere Regis in 1686 Elizabeth and Mary daughters of Henry Fancy were recorded. Members of their families were first recorded as varmint destroyers.

At Wareham David Fancy 1793- 1876. married Sarah and they had 5 children.

There were women brickmakers such as Mary Ann Fancy, Sophie Fancy and Daisy Fancy lived in Wareham then in the 1800s and after at Heavenly bottom encampment in Parkstone. Gideon Fancy and family later lived at the Gypsy encampments at Bourne Bottom and Heavenly Bottom and was the father of my great grandmother Emily Elizabeth Fancy who married Charles Rogers my great grandfather. Gideon's daughter Emily Elizabeth Fancy was my great grandmother married to Charles Rogers. Emily was born at the Bourne bottom campsite in 1850. Her father was Gideon Fancy from Bourne bottom who was a child on the old original Mannings encampment. Emilys mother was Elizabeth Cherrett. Fancies were married to Cherretts, Bonds, Stanleys Rogers and Crockers. Fancies were also Quarrymen at Portland making the famous stone for the rebuilding of London's great houses at Westminster and St Paul's cathedral. The Fancy's had a reputation as brick makers and brick maker labourers both male and female working at brickyards throughout Dorset. Other members of the Fancies were stone masons and Quarry men on the Purbeck. Many of their descendants moved to the new world via the Newfoundland trade.

Puddle town encampment

The Stanleys were one the main gypsy family here.

Sarah Stanley was known and respected as the Dowager Queen of the Counties of Wiltshire, Hampshire, and Dorset. Sarah and Peter Stanley had 9 children and were renowned in Puddle town. She was an important person in the community her death was noted in the newspapers and many people attended her burial. Some of the newspapers referring to her as 'her vagrant majesty'. Peter and Sarah are both buried at St Mary's church Puddle town cemetery.

PIDDLETRENTHIDE

Doles Ash encampment

Eileen Ika Rawling's nee Hughes {1943-1978} was born in a Gypsy wagon in 1943 at Doles Ash. Her parents were Alice Hughes and Robert Cooper. It was said that Eileen inherited her aunt's good looks her aunt being Caroline Hughes who was the Queen of the Gypsies. Due to her beauty and fine singing voice and who became famous outside the Traveller world. As she was recorded by the BBC for Ewan MacColl BBC Radio Ballads. In 1961 Eileen met and married Dave Rawlings who was a non-Gypsy or 'gorja', and it was rare in those days to marry outside the community. But theirs was a love match. They travelled for 50 years by horse and wagon, travelling the highways and byways of Dorset, Wiltshire, Somerset, and Gloucestershire. It was a hard life collecting water and firewood every day, making a living by the work of their hands fashioning clothes pegs, and paper flowers, helping with the elderflower and black currant harvests. Additional income came through Dave busking as he had a fine baritone voice and played the mandolin. They would travel as far north as Stow on the Wold for the twice-yearly horse fair and would over winter in Chalk valley in Wiltshire. Eileen would love to talk to locals as she sat on the steps of the wagon as they journeyed around the countryside. When they moved on, they would always leave their overnight stopping place cleaner than when they had arrived. They had many relatives who had settled on sites and in houses around Dorset so when the time came for them to hang up the harness they tried settling in a house near Dorchester. Eileen though like many Travellers, couldn't stand living in bricks and mortar, she said she felt hemmed in. So, after three weeks they moved to the council-run Traveller site in Piddle Hinton. Here she kept her connection with her life travelling, by keeping a small horse. She died aged 76 on May 15 and was a Romany Gypsy proud of her heritage. Many Stanleys lived here including one king of the gypsies born 1724. He had 10 children all boys all well known in later life at markets, fairs and races, He died of smallpox in 1803.

A celebration was held in the evening at the Green Dragon, Puddletrenthide, when many more members of the Romany clan came to wish the couple happiness."

Holly Woods gypsy traveller encampment

Members of the Rogers, Hare, Williams, Davis gypsies and others were camped here

MAJOR WHITE

There were many Gypsies Traveler's among these Quarry men and Stone Masons at Portland. These included amongst them Gypsies such as the legendary Major White born in 1869 Heather land Village Poole who married Venus Ayres in 1898. The Portland stone Quarry man in the early 1900s was a travelling Gypsy who happened to be in the town of Branksome Poole and stayed at the encampment there.at a point in time. He was just one of the many Whites who were quarry men who lived in Portland for over one hundred years. He died 1958 at Heather lands encampment in Parkstone.

Many of the Quarry men followed the old Gypsy customs of Jumping the Sticks at their weddings. The country fold of the west country folk have for a long time called the gypsies by the name of Broomstick or Broom squires. Doubtless the name was acquired by the gypsies from their hawking of broom and brushes Yoosering koshti being the Romany name for such articles, from yooser to clean. Perhaps also marriage tradition practiced in Somerset of the leaping over a broomstick by a wedded couple therefore nor legal. Many these took place here.

Herbert Fall jumped the broomsticks in a marriage ritual with his wife Sarah in the grounds of the Sqump pub better known as the Square and Compass on Worth Matravers peak. The young Quarryman Herbert Fall had selected as his best man his friend and workmate the local legendary village strongman known as the noted Strong man Gyppo Elliott. Gyppo Ellott regularly lifted a 7-ton block of stone. Using what was known as a Portland Jack to lift these great giant stones which were once used for the buildings of the great churches of the land and rich man's mansions.

Chinchens

Since the first recorded member of the Chincen family in 1587. There have been 13 generations of the Chinchen family living in the Purbeck and Portland regions. It is believed that they originated from India just as gypsies had done before arriving in Spain in 1425. They are believed to have reached England in the early 1500s. They were prominent in quarry and stone masonry in quarry and stone mason work. Particularly in Worth Matravers and at Langton Mattravers, Swanage, .

At the wedding of Alice White and Stephen Button of Lytchett Matravers Stephen rode 20 miles on his push bike from his smallholding farm and arrived just in time for the service. Whilst poor old Alice White, she was dressed in a vivid scarlet and green outfit and rode to church in a dog cart! splashing her way through floods to get there at the parish church. Her and Stephen were married by the local Rector, the Rev. W.G. Newman amongst those attending was Maurice White and Robert Hughes. Robert was the best man that day and he also gave the bride away.

There were many gypsy travellers there that day including Robert Wood, Maurice White, Robert Hughes and Sidney Cooper, and his tribe. They were an old gypsy traveller family along with the Benham's.

Mrs Benham was the guest of honour. Left-over Christmas decorations had been brought from the Post Office, and these were draped on the archway" a huge cake was made by the local baker Mr Davies. After the service, the couple went on ahead of the others, the groom on his bicycle, and his bride by his side on foot at the Green Dragon at Piddletrenthide. The place was packed out when many more members of the Romany clan arrived to wish the couple happiness.

These quarry men families go back to 1651 and beyond. With local church records showing how they intermarried and throughout their lives and lived in the same village.

Many of these families were of Gypsy Traveler origins prominent names amongst them included the following. The Benham's, Bonfield, Bowers, Burt, Cole, Coopers, Brown, Corben, Chinchen, Dowland, Edmonds, Fall, Hardon, Haysom, Harding, Hughes, Thicke's, Turner, Norman, Webber, Whites Landerm, Phippard, Eldbury and Harris families. Some of which no doubt is recognizable will no doubt have Gypsy traveler origins. Like most Gypsy traveler's they married close relatives.

The most prominent Portland family who worked the Quarries for centuries were the Bowers. They were given rights to walk the streets of Langton Maltravers where the traffic would give way to them. This was said to be a privilege accorded to them under the original village Charter. Intermarriage between families engaged in quarrying gave so many families the named Bower, some related, some not, that to distinguish them they were given secondary names.

Some were awarded their wives names as a prefix to their surname others were awarded a nickname. Often these nicknames were Thus, often these nicknames were associated with their abilities of where they worked or where they lived. There are nicknames such as Ivamy, Ball, Brown, Brownsea, Trink, Coffin, Gad, Short, Whistler, Ball, Short, French and Razorback etc. Some bore their nicknames with pride and some of them exercised the Bowers rights to walk down the middle of Langton Matravers main street in the expectation that traffic would give way to them. For this a privilege deemed to have been granted under the long-lost charter.

A GYPSY WEDDING

As reported in The Dorset County Chronicle 2 February 1937.
"Famous Gypsy Families at Wedding"
The wedding of Alice White

"Villagers saw a novel sight on Monday morning when Alice White, beautiful member of a Gypsy family famous in the South of England, splashed her way through floods to the parish church for her wedding. The groom, Mr Stephen Button of Lytchett Matravers, cycled the 20 miles from his smallholding, and arrived in time for the service. The bride was dressed in a vivid scarlet and green outfit and rode to church in a dog cart. The ceremony was attended by many members of the Romany tribe, including such noted families as the Hughes, Benham's and Coopers.

Guest of honour at the camp on the hill at Lackington was Mrs Benham, widow of "Wold Ben", uncrowned Gypsy king whose burial at Dorchester recently attracted so much attention. With her were three sons, including Tom the 18-year-old acrobat dancer. Also, there were members of the Cooper family who took part in the tragic trek to Dorchester to the funeral of Arthur Cooper, which took place in a blizzard a fortnight ago.

Greenway Head encampment

This was the main Gypsy traveller encampment was situated on the hill at Lackington. It consisted of six caravans and was situated dangerously close to an often-flooded area. As a result, during wet weather often the caravan's wheels here were often embedded in thick mud. any gypsy families lived here including members of the Hughes family. The Benham family worked on the farm here where they lived in trailers in an area allocated to them." They had 8 or 9 children, all born at home." The women would go off selling paper flowers, mistletoe, holly and daffodils The local Rector, the Rev. W.G. Newman, was said to be greatly impressed by the conduct and system prevailing in the camp, which he had visited on several occasions during the period spent complying with the residential qualification. The church entrance was surrounded by crowds of villagers, and to make the occasion more festive, left-over Christmas decorations had been brought from the Post Office, and these were draped on the archway. A huge cake had been baked and iced by Mr Davies, the local baker. After the service, the couple went on ahead of the others, the groom on his bicycle, and his bride by his side on foot. The other members of the party, Maurice White, Robert Hughes (who gave the bride away), Robert Wood, Sidney Cooper, Alice Hughes, Rene Hughes, Georgina and Mary Ann Cooper, left by a dog cart.

Whilst the knife-grinder had a contraption which when upended became his work bench, at which he would sit working with a cycling action. Mighty twelve-ton traction engines hauled the much-valued blocks of stone up to Priory Corner for onward dispatch around the Merchants' Railway. To grace the buildings of every major town and city in the British Isles. With their endless loads past doorsteps local teenage, boys, to be accepted into 'the gang', had to prove their courage by being last across in front of these grinding wheels. Or by walking the four-inch iron girder on top of the original bridge, down by the Mermaid, whilst a train passed beneath it. 'What I have, I own' was locals' proud motto and, quite apart from their arduous daily toil in the quarries, they invariably worked allotments large enough to keep a whole family in essential vegetables and potatoes throughout the winter months.

As well as among their quarry-mates, ran a fishing boat in their spare time! They were always busy. 'If you can talk and work, stop talking and work a bit harder!' they said. Many quarrymen's families, lived in one of the stone-built houses in Wakeham.

Joseph Fancy (baptised in 1750 in Lytchett Minster, (son of Henry born about 1711).

Like most Gypsy travellers the quarry men married close relatives and whilst many followed the old Gypsy customs of Jumping the Sticks at their weddings. (As was the case of the wedding in 1936 of Herbert Fall). The most prominent Portland family who worked the Quarries for centuries were the Bowers. They were given rights to walk the streets of Langton Matravers where the traffic would give way to them. This was said to be a privilege accorded to them under the original village Charter.

Most quarrymen's sons, from about the age of ten, had served an early apprenticeship in the task of delivering the blunt tools from the quarry by 'go cart' to the blacksmith's shop. Many walked to school, from Moorfield Road to the (now) Royal Manor School, and at dinner time run down the back lane of Channel View and, if the stationmaster was not around, vault the back fence and run across the railway lines to Tom Collins' blacksmith's shop. There they'd find their 'go cart' filled with yesterday's tools, now sharpened. They would pull the load to the top of the Straits, sitting in the cart among the kevels and twybils. Then later to Perry field House, find a new batch of blunt tools and start the long pull with a heavily loaded cart back up Wakeham to Moorfield Road. They would deliver the load to the blacksmith at Park Road, and on to school with enough time in between to play football in the school yard before the lessons of the afternoon began. This would often be their daily routine every single school day while – as the quarrymen say – they were ''bout stone'.

Gypsy Traveller families. living on the Purbeck encampments included Ayres, Barnes, Bartlett, Batemans, Benham, Blake, Bland, Bonfield, Bowers, Boswell, Burden. Burton, Charretts, Chinchen, Coles, Crocker, Does, Dory, Elliott, Fancy, Fletchers, Frankham,

Franklin, Greens, Hughes, Issacs, Jeff's, Johnston, King, Lakey, Lanes, Lees, Lovell, Pateman, Penfold, Peters, Phillip, Phippard, Potters, Roberts, Rose, Scamps, Scarrots, Sherrard, Sherred, Sherwin, Sherwood, Skemps Smiths, Stanleys, Stones, Thicke's, Thompsons, Tuits, Turner, Wareham's, Warren, Wells. Wellstrads, Whites Woods, Woolsies and Young.

There were a great many gypsy encampments in the Purbeck region families were often extremely large with up to 17 children.

Ghost village out on the Purbeck.

The village of Tyneham is between Kimmeridge and East Lulworth. It is a now a 'ghost' village and former civil parish. Tyneham village and surrounding hamlets were evacuated by the Army in December 1943 during the Second World War. When over 200 residents packed up their belongings and left the village. It was cleared to allow allied forces to prepare for the D-Day landings. Despite promises by Winston Churchill, the residents never returned to the village and surrounding areas. The original buildings The Row was a row of four terraced houses, numbered from the higher end nearest the church. Both the restored church and school buildings Tyneham Farm, The entire 3,003-acre site on the Tyneham estate was owned by the Bond family for more than 300 years. Even the Bond family who occupied Tyneham House left their homes for the last time and never returned. Tyneham village, Worbarrow Bay and Lulworth Ranges are managed by the Ministry of Defence (MOD) now". When the last of the locals left, they pinned a notice to the door of the village church

"Please treat the churches and houses with care. We have given up our homes where many of us have lived for generations, to help win the war to keep men free. We will return one day and thank you for treating the village kindly".

The original residents were never allowed to return to their lives, as promised.

Despite a few high-profile campaigns, it remains highly unlikely that this will change too, with only a small handful of the original residents still alive to this day. Today, only the church and school remain intact.

A GYPSIES MEMORIES

Teignmouth or Newton Abbot, on the left hand side just past the filling station, there's the King's Arms pub and this is where all the clay cutters and the Gypsies used to congregate on many nights. When I was extremely young, I remember distinctly seeing 2 gypsies fighting, bare knuckles, in the car park behind the back of the King's Arms with a ring of people around them to make sure that they didn't disappear completely. Of course the guys from the clay pits, my grandfather and people like that would be tanked up with their scrumpy or cider and in their bags that they used to carry with them, they'd fill up 2 quarts of cider to take to work the next day which they used to consume and then get ready for the next evening to bring the bottles and fill them up again and that's the way that they worked down at the clay mines and they worked extremely hard, up to their ankles in mud most of the time and …ventilation at all and all wet and everything dug by hand no mechanical assistance in those days but they worked hard and they played hard.

CHAPTER SEVENTEEN

TRAVELLER TIMES

Noah Cooper was a Gypsy charged with using obscene language at Christchurch along with William Castle charged with damaging the new Forest.

At Holt village there were 4 brickyards following a fire in Blandford in 1731 yards were started up for the rebuilding of the town by the Bastard family and ran till 1952.

There were 6 brickyards at Broad Mayne and one at Warm well.

William Stanley was born here in 1859 in later years he married Mary dee Bellam and they had 9 children.

ELM HOUSE FARNHAM GYPSY SCHOOL 1847- 1855

By Victorian times many people thought gypsies should settle down, and not travel the country as they had always done.

Dorset had a gypsy school at Elm House in Farnham, north Dorset. On premises which was originally a farmhouse which was gradually converted into a residential school for Romany children in 1845 and opened in 1847. The project was undertaken by the Revd. John West. He was initially inspired by a scheme by James Crabb. He had initially undertaken a scheme at Chettle Dorset in 1842 where he placed a gypsy family in 2 cottages in the village which caused local reactions from the local towns people. This was particularly so when he placed gypsy children in the local school amongst non gypsies. This prompted him to think in terms of a school for gypsy children. He issued a pamphlet entitled A PLEA FOR EDUCATION THE CHILDREN OF THE GYPSIES. Which he dedicated to the MP Lord Ashley and the local nobility, gentry and magistrates. The proposed school initially was to provide education and maintenance of 24 Orphan gypsy children under 6 years of age or boys and girls of the same age from the largest and most destitute gypsy families and intended to be residential or a boarding school, and the actual schoolroom is only a small part of the building. Presumably the bedrooms or dormitories were upstairs. Benefactor persons were called upon to sponsor gypsy children at a cost of £5 per child per year. Plans were submitted to the Government along with application for a grant. Which were approved and donated. A site was obtained at Farnham and on 21st July 1845 a foundation stone was laid of THE FARNHAM GYPSY ASYLUM AND INDUSTRIAL SCHOOL. The stone was laid by the elderly gypsy evangelist from Southampton William Stanley. Work on the school was slow and West sadly died in December 1845. The scheme as a result lost its momentum. But was eventually opened on the 5th October 1847. With 6 gypsy children attending. Around 500 people were present at the opening gathering including a several groups of gypsies. The aims of the school was to provide education, food and clothing to 24 gypsy children 12 boys and 12 girls. Lord Ashley was the patron of the organisation body. The building was undertaken with a view of gathering in the too long neglected outcast gypsy children from the highways and hedges, to be brought up in the nurture and admonition of the Lord. Gypsy families in the area included Wells, Smiths, Stickley's, Slack, Miles, Morris, Bidles, Crutcher's, Cowards and Dibbens. Children who were to attend the school over the years of operation were from the local gypsy community which included those from the families of Ayre Barneys, Bowers, Dangerfills, Stanleys, Martins and Mills. Though over the years the school had a job keeping staff. By 1854 only 46 gypsy children in total had attended the school over the 7 years and only 5 remained in 1854.

In 1855 the school closed so the first gypsy school came to an end. The few gypsy children remaining mostly drifted back to their traveling way of life. The premises were later in 1880 used as a archaeological museum. The Christian evangelists at that time saw the problem of the gypsies as being ungodly souls needing saving and thus out of poverty. They failed to recognise the gypsy travellers love of nature, fresh air and freedom of the road. Along with their skills in horsemanship, iron smithery and brick making. Gypsies were unlike the poor working classes at that time who were on low incomes and obliged to attend church services as their means to a heavenly kingdom. The religious education zealots were totally unaware and did not recognise the traveller's spiritual life. Falsely believing that success lay in accepting Christ but failing to see how the travellers were closer to God than they could ever be.

Bradbury Rings encampment

There was a traveller's site out on the Bradbury Rings Road Just before Tarrants.

Okeford Fitzpaine encampment

It was here where Hercules and Parthenia Stanley lived in 1764 with their 6 children. Richard, Mary, Artula, Peter and Edward, the last two of whom died in infancy; one such descendant, possibly a grandson is Benjamin Stanley, connected to Parthenia, and her son, Richard, through territorial links, whose son, Owen Stanley, and his wife, Harriet Wharton, were to baptise a daughter Algenny in 1841 According to the Dorset prison records of 1824, Owen Stanley and his father, Benjamin, claimed the parish of in Dorset, as their place of settlement. This location, one that they considered home, linked them with Parthenia, who had also named Okeford Fitzpaine as home territory on her vagrancy pass as early as 1764, sixty year earlier.

BRIDPORT

Bulbarrow and Symondsbury Broadoak Lane Encampments.1881

Over 30 Gypsy traveller Families camped here included Roberts, Coopers, Jones, and Hodges. Charles Hodges was born 1841 he and his wife Mary camped here in 1881 they were said to be still very young 10 and 12 years respectively when their first child was born.

The Works off Long Lane, Bothe Hampton, were established in 1888 by the same Cooper family. During the 20th century the Brick Works reached an average production of 750,000 bricks per annum and many buildings throughout Bridport and the surrounding villages display the distinctive red coloured bricks indicative of this site. Production ended in 1952 due to the exhaustion of good quality clay, high transport costs and competition from large manufacturers. The site became a landfill until 2000 when it was landscaped, and its former presence is only identifiable by a methane

BRIDPORT ROPES AND GYPSIES

Bridport is still the world's foremost exponent of rope and net making. Since King John requested the townsfolk to work night and day to make as many ropes as they could for the growing ship building industry. Hemp and flax were grown locally. It formed the basis of a thriving cottage industry. Reaching its peak in the 18th and 19th century. Those who ended their days on the gallows with a noose around their necks were said to have been "stabbed" by a Bridport dagger. For more than 700 years the town led the world in rope and net making and today a handful of companies are still the main suppliers to fishing fleets, sports clubs, airlines and even the space industry with Bridport nets used on the Space Shuttle. IN sport, goal nets used in many of the major championships have been made in the town, while the tennis nets seen at the All-England club for the Wimbledon tennis championships and the US open are made locally. Today the trade may no longer be a cottage industry, but the tradition started by King John continues.

PATIENCE PENFOLD

Patience Penfold was born in 1867 She one of nine children of William Penfold and his wife Priscilla Thompson. Both of her parents were Romany gypsies who made their livings as travelling hawkers. Her father's family, the Penfolds, and her mother's, the Thompsons, were well known among the travelling community She married Charles William Light who was a great-uncle of Dorothy Bennett. Gypsy's parents usually disapproved of their children marrying *gorjas*, as people of non-Romani heritage are known, so Patience's marriage was very unusual. The high level of intermarriage within the community produced tight-knit groups of related families who sometimes travelled and camped together. Patience's aunts Olive and Maria Penfold had married brothers of her mother Priscilla, Amos and Henry Thompson respectively. Her cousin Thomas' wife Patience Thompson was a sister of Patience's mother. Her brothers Amos and Robert had both married Thompsons. Patience's sisters Priscilla and Charlotte Penfold had both married Penfold cousins as had Patience's cousin James. As well as the Thompsons, members of the Page family featured prominently in Patience extended family Patience's uncle Robert Penfold was a particularly well-known figure in the gypsy community. He was born in Breamore in southern Wiltshire in 1816 and married his wife Amelia Page in Bishops Waltham, Hampshire, in December 1836. They lived mainly in the west of England with their children being baptised in Weymouth, Bridgewater, Wool in Dorset, Yeovil, and Bridport. At the time of the 1861 census, they were in Uplyme in Devon, in 1871 they were at Abbotsbury in Dorset, and in 1881 at Shilling Okeford in Dorset. Amelia died in 1889, and he died three years later near Ilchester in Somerset. The Western Gazette described him as '*King of the Gipsies*'. Patience and her eight brothers and sisters grew up travelling around southern England in caravans with their parents, uncles, aunts and cousins; in 1871 they were camped in and in 1881 in Bere Regis. . In May 1888 Patience married Charles William Light. In April 1891 they were living in a caravan in a gypsy encampment on the shore of Hampshire's New Forest. There is still a path there which goes by the name of "Gypsy Lane". Charles and Patience settled near Southampton, in Freemantle, where they lived. Their two children, Patience and Charlie were born there in 1889 and 1890 respectively. Charles died at home on the 12th of December 1897 leaving Patience to care for their children. Patience married again to Fred Bartlett, was a costermonger (i.e. a market trader). They had seven children: Fred (b.1900), George (b.1902), Elizabeth (b.1903), Edward (b.1905), James (b.1906), William (b.1908), and Ivy (b.1910). Her children from her first marriage, continued to live with her and Fred until at least 1911. Patience's son Charles died in or near Southampton early in 1914. Her daughter Patience married in 1917 Crocker Young Patience sadly passed away just five years after she married. Patience's husband Fred died in 1919. Patience herself died in Southampton in 1927.

PIMPERNE

Hancock's Bottom Encampment

Families living here included Phoebe Ball She was born 29 November 1891, daughter of Thomas Ball, Travelling Hawker, and Rayner Ball, formerly Hugh. Informant: Thomas Ball, Father, Hancock's [signs X]. [birth certificate]

The Beacon Hill Brickworks

These were established here in 1937 and operated here till 2001. Monkey wagons were used to transport the clay to the brickyards.

Families living here included James Cooper Married, 1858 Traveller Gypsy Hawker Sarah, Wife, 1860 Traveller Gypsy Hawker, William, Son, Single, 1881 Traveller Gypsy Hawker

George Hall Marr, Aged 30 1881 Gipsy Wife Marr, Aged 31 1880 Walter, Son, Aged 15 (UNDER 15) 1896, Fred, Son, Aged 15 (UNDER 15) 1896 , Albert, Son, Aged 15 (UNDER 15) 1896 Pamela, Dau, Aged 15 (UNDER 15) 1896 Eliza, Dau, Aged 15 (UNDER 15) 1896 Liberty, Dau, Aged 15 (UNDER 15) 1896, Jack Roberts Boarder Single Aged 22 1889. George Maine Marr, Aged 33 1878 Gipsy Wife Marr, Aged 34 1877 Betty May, Dau, Aged 14 1897.

SHERBOURNE

The encampment

Mary Bond (nee Hughes)1921-2015 Queen of the Gypsies was born in a bender tent on September 9th, 1920, to parents Caroline Hughes and Johnny Cooper. The eldest of eight children. Mary became a well-known figure in Britain's Romany Gypsy community. Growing up, she worked the fields with her mother and father, taking on a variety of farming tasks. Mary became a well-known figure in Britain's Romany Gypsy community. As children she and her siblings worked on farms alongside her parents. Until Mary met her husband Harold Bond, a dairyman, while the family were staying in Blandford, and they would go on to marry in January 1939 at the local parish church. Mary raised two sons and two daughters largely on her own while her husband was away in the army. The family lived in Blandford for many years before moving to Poole. Shortly before Harold went to Europe during the Second World War, fighting in Belgium and at Dunkirk. The Bonds travelled with her parents when they first married. Mrs Bond would work hoeing, hop picking, and fruit picking, and the family travelled to Bridgewater to work on the pea fields and cut sugar beat. They travelled on to Carter Down where they lived in a shepherd's hut while Mrs Bond worked on the land there. They went hawking lace, heather, scrap metal, rabbit skins and more, travelling as far afield as Winchester. Their first child Caroline was stillborn, but they went on to have John, born at Hungry Down, Rosie, born at the Boggs in Wallisdown. Lovie, born at Carters Down encampment and Jimmy, born in Thornicombe. They travelled with their parents. Then in the 1950s Mary and Harold settled in a house in East Street Blandford Dorset. In later years their son John made a wooden horse drawn vardo which became their home on the side of the road at Wareham. Until it caught fire and they moved to Canford heath. Harold Bond died in 1965. Mary and her family moved to the Mannings Heath Gypsy camp in Alderney Poole Dorset in the early 1970s. She often travelled into Bournemouth with her friend Tilly Johnson selling lucky heather and charms in the square. Being part of the famous Gypsy lady flower sellers. It was said that Mary loved cooking, often making bacon and meat puddings in her two-gallon pot. She was also a regular visitor each year to both the Great Dorset Steam Fair and the Epsom Derby. Later in life she lived in various homes in Poole and with her sister Celia and Frank Benham in Stourpayne. Mrs Bond loved her family, attending their parties, christenings and weddings, and accompanying them to fairs across the country. She would often travel to town with a friend to sell lucky heather and charms. She worked hawking lace, heather, scrap metal, rabbit skins and more, travelling as far afield as Winchester. She died a great great-grandmother in January 2015. Hundreds of folks turned out to bid farewell to Dan Turner's aunt who passed away at the age of 94. A large funeral cortège including three horse-drawn carriages, wound its way from her Alderney home to St Clement's Church, Newtown in Poole, for the funeral service. The cortège included three horse-drawn carriages. There is an image of the family in Poole Museum, highlighting their long history in the borough. She died a great great-grandmother.

PROUDLY.

Many of the Proudly family men were brickmakers. In Lytchett and Bransgore! They were a gypsy family many of whom also were hawkers selling pottery and glass. They intermarried many times into the Kercher/Crutcher families who were also hawkers.

William Proudly was the son of Rose Stanley. He was born 1800 and was an earthenware vendor. He was threatened to be transported to Australia for theft, but he was instead imprisoned at Poole. However, by 1881 he was a successful brick maker who owned his own farm and had employed many and was well respected.

St Leonards common encampment.

There were also Gypsy communities (or other temporary dwellers) on St. Leonard's Common, in what became Oakhurst & Elmhurst, and some along the Moors River, though these latter might have attended Three Cross school. Dominic Reeve author of 'Smoke in the Lanes' tells a story of parking up here in 1958.

Over the years I was to live and work close to where the Gypsies once camped in Kinson. I got to know so many of these families as long-time friends and acquaintances. In the 1970s I rented a cottage in Talbot Woods with my friend's and play assistants whilst establishing the children's adventure playground at West Howe. The playground was situated on the Fern heath road which was originally close to the area where the Gypsy encampment known as New England was once situated. At the time there were over 2000 children per square mile living on the West Howe estate. There were scores of children from gypsy families still living locally and attended the playground. Along with the playgrounds committee members who were gypsy travellers such as the Jeff brothers who had a haulage company. Brian Keets lived in the Gypsy traveller's family bungalow on Verney road he was a regular member of the playground along with other kids from Gypsy families such as the Dibbens, the Does, Coles and Williams. Later in the 1980s I was living on the Turbary Avenue with my wife and step kids opposite to where the tracks led to the former Bankes Common encampment. I was school governor at Kingsleigh first school and Junior school and had contact with many local Gypsy children and their parents In more recent years whilst living at Turbary Avenue I was one of many who were alarmed by the events at Dale Farm encampment, and we formed the action group on Facebook. We held meetings at the Turbary hall centre next door attended by Gypsy Travellers worldwide. Including Raymond Neville a gypsy horse breeder from Australia the son of famous jockey. Joe Winda's a Gypsy horseman from up north visited me and we spent days out on the Purbeck together.

The Travelling Mush

I travelled down the highways
down those Gypsy lanes
talked with Squires and farmers
pat the horse's mane

I strolled across the meadows
to the Gypsy site
the blossoms were a buzzing
the sun was high in sky
we sat around the yog that night
we talked just you and i

The stories that we shared that night
of times so long ago
fairground Gypsy boxers
the winds the frosty the snow

All the mushes that we knew and loved
the Gypsy girl and i
the lovers that we hugged loved n more
the fishes in the streams
the lost horizons in the mist
the long-forgotten dreams
The shadows and the sunsets
the chavvies running free
the lovers on the meadows sweet
all past histories
yet seemed so real to me

The thunderstorms and rainfall sweet
the horses and the rides
the fairgrounds and the weddings
the suitors and the brides

The vardo wheels a turning
the wheelwrights Coopers frame
the Stanleys with the handsome bricks
the chaffinch down the lanes

The running brooks and meadows
the haystack where we lay
sweet corn rising on the distance I hear a baby born
welcome to the morn –

Ray Wills

Romani boys

I am no Dominic Reeves
I've got no Gypsy story up my sleeve
I know Augustus knew Picasso
he was a true Gypsy Romani
though Augustus was just a bohemian
long before the Queen wrote rhapsody
I'm no transcript writer of eloquence
no performer of great deeds

I'm not a tight rope walker
like Elvis i believe
he was a Gypsy pelvis crooner
before hip hop was the sound
they played the Gypsy violins to the masses in the crowds

The vardos vans were awesome
the Coopers knew the Kings
the fairgrounds were the places to be
on an autumn Saturday
Come see in winter and spring
the tattooed lady and the bearded friends
the python and the crew
the music played on the carousel
and the darts flew flights and more
The card sharp player had the best hand
the Gypsy Queen she once did dance
when the wall ride of death drew in the crowds

The famous boxing booths
the heathlands and the heathers with lizards in the sun
the Gallows hill and the history
go tell it all my son

Ray Wills

THE GYPSY STORYTELLERS BOOK PROJECT

The Storytellers Project came about because of the removal of Gypsy travellers from their long-standing site at Dale Farm in Essex by the local Council. There was a national campaign at the time through people such as Glenda Jackson which supported the Travellers cause, which received much media attention. At the time I was following the story through my Gypsy Roma Traveller friends on Facebook. It was decided we should set up a money raising campaign to provide financial aid to such Gypsy Travellers in future. I was chosen by the face book group to promote a book of an anthology of stories, poetry, art work and photos from members of h GRT group. I approached the publisher, Francis Boutle. During the months that followed the eviction of travellers at Dale farm. I worked with publisher Clive Boutle of Francis Boutle. Arranging an assortment of material produced worldwide from numerous Gypsy Roma Traveller members and supporters. I contacted a relative of the entertainer and Gypsy David Essex and he sent a poem of his which was included in the book. This was following by a meeting at the Turbary centre Kinson which was well attended by members of the Gypsy Roma Traveller community who had travelled there from faraway places. Including Geoffrey Neville from Australia son of the famous Melbourne Cup jockey Raymond Neville. Raymond stayed at my home. The lovely Annie Cooper from the New Forest also attended. Shortly after the publication of the book The Gypsy Story Tellers. Monies raised from the book sales was to be donated to a Gypsy Traveller organisation. After discussion with Kushto Boks chair Betty Smith Billington it was approved that Kushti Bok were the ideal group for that situation. There was a very successful Gypsy Story Tellers book signing event in a packed hall at the Kinson library Hub. My friend Annie Christopher the singer provided the music entertainment. With the band of folks who made STORYTELLER happen. Then later a large donation from book sales of GYPSY STORYTELLER was presented to Kushti Bok at their headquarters in Kingston Maurward in Dorchester.

POOLE MUSEUM DISPLAY

An exhibit display of my research with assistance of my lady friend Susan Miller was held at Poole Museum which was developed through partnership with Kushti Bok. Sue and I travelled throughout the Canford heath, Newtown, Rossmore, Kinson area over the course of weeks in wet weather. Gathering earth samples from areas where once stood the original Gypsy encampment. The exhibition ran for 4 months and included the result of both Sue and mine collection of earth samples from former encampments, map of the encampments and my family For my interest in Gypsy travellers encouraged me to explore my own family history and the display featured my own family tree which traced my Romany roots back to the 1600s. Visitors were able to view a large map from 1912 showing historic Gypsy encampments; some of which resulted in the naming of local features and landmarks. From Monkey's Hump to Heavenly Bottom, the encampments were situated in many of the heathlands across Poole. Poole History Centre staff offered advice and guidance about exploring family history. Poole Museum to host display of hidden heritage of Gypsies and Travellers

Poole Museum displayed stories from Kushti Bok, a group that supports people from Gypsy, Roma and Traveller backgrounds. Poole Museum's 'Our Space' area invited community groups to tell stories that are important to them and their links to the local communities. 'Our Space' hosted a display of the largely hidden heritage of Gypsies and Travellers in and around Poole. Developed through partnership with Kushti Bok, it featured research by Raymond Wills, the local 'Gypsy Poet'. As a child Ray grew up on his grandparent's farm on the Mannings Heath commons. His closest neighbours were Gypsies and Ray spent hours visiting the local camps in Canford Heath, old Wareham Road and Alderney. Ray's interest sparked him to explore his own family history, and the display featured a family tree which traces his Romany roots back to the 1700s. Visitors were also able to view a large map from 1912 showing historic campsites; some of which resulted in the naming of local features and landmarks. From Monkey's Hump to Heavenly Bottom, the camps were situated in many of the heathlands across Poole.

Councillor Bobbie Dove, Lead Member for Equalities, BCP Council said:"Key to the delivery of our priorities is that we put residents at the heart of everything we do and that all of our communities feel connected, empowered, safe and included. Therefore, it is important that we celebrate the diversity of our towns and recognise the contributions of all communities in their development."We are rightly proud of our heritage and that cannot be complete without the inclusion of the contributions and hidden heritage of our Gypsy, Roma and Traveller communities which strengthens the cultural identity of our towns and places"

The exhibition opened on 18 June and ran until 5 September.

GHOST GYPSY

Another Kushti Bok project was the making of the film "GHOST GYPSY". I had persuaded Producer Sharon Muirurt to shoot location of the film in the field at Kinson Mead at the rear of the St Andrews church. We thought it was an ideal spot with facilities in the church hall close by. I had been a member of St Andrews when Lee Sherville was the rector. Back in the late 1980s i had managed the Kinson renovation project there when John Moore was rector. Now I was involved in the film too.

I went to the Dorset County councils Gypsy travellers Ashcroft site nr Wareham with Sharon Muirurt. We sat and talked with a young mum in her van. Then later next door a crowd of jeeps arrived with lots of travellers onboard and I had a long chat with them. They were from the Hughes family and knew all about my family and Cooper Newtown people.

Whilst Filming of GHOST GYPSY at Millhams Mead Kinson. I had chat with my friend Revd Lee Sharville of St Andrews.

GYPSY ENCAMPMENT BOARDS

I worked on research for Kushti Bok over a six months period gathering information on the original Gypsy traveller encampments throughout the county of Dorset for Kushti Bok. I composed text ready for publication. Initially it was to go onto 7 boards throughout the county which the public could access via their mobile phones. I gathered info from censuses, parish records, libraries, books, online, on face book and from family trees and members. This information would be mapped out. However, we only managed to gain access permissions for two boards to date both via Bournemouth, Christchurch and Poole BCP councils These were put up on Verney road West Howe and at Good road Poole in July 2023 at an official unveiling event. At the end of the month, I resigned as a member of the Kushti Bok committee to concentrate on new projects I was involved with in the local Bere Regis area with Inside Out commission work along with my writing and my new future projects.

LEGEND POLE

Kusht Bok also created a Legend Pole which was on display for a few years at Dorchester Kingston Maurward College Gardens. Then more recently Kushti Bok created a more interesting Legend Pole which is permanently placed in the orchard of Kingston Maurward College.

SOURCES

THE ENGLISH GYPSIES -THE PENNY MAGAZINE -January 1838

GYPSIES IN ENGLISH HISTORY – DAVID CREASEY CREDITON- DEVON- April 1840

"Gypsies, Tinkers and Travellers", Sharon Melch

"Gypsies," by B. Gilliat-Smith (The Caian, vol. xvi. No. 3). e thorns tagged your toes

GYPSY ADVOCATE - JAMES CRABB 1832

A HISTORY OF THE GYPSIES-WALTER SIMSON

THE GYPSIES- CHARLES LEYLAND 1882

GYPSIES TINKERS AND TRAVELLERS - SHARON MELCH

THE TRAVELLER GYPSIES -   JUDITH OKELY

CAMBRIDGE UNIVERSITY PRESS

ROMANY LIFE- FRANK CUTRISS 1915

TRAVELLER PEOPLE IN EARLY MODERN DORSET - JUDY FORD

ROMANIES IN DORSET AND HAMPSHIRE - SUE COLE

AUGUSTUS JOHN THE NEW BIOGRAPHY - MICHAEL HOLYROYD

 HEAD OF ZEUS LIMITED

BRICK A SOCIAL HISTORY - CAROLYN HAYNES

THE HISTORY PRESS 2002

A HISTORY OF QUEENS PARK BOURNEMOUTH - STEPHEN GADD

THE SPIRIT OF POOLE AND POOLE PRIDE REGAINED - JOHN HILLIER AND MARTIN BLYTH

POOLE HISTORICAL TRUST

MEMORIES OF THE UNDEFEATED BARE-KNUCKLE CHAMPIONS OF GT BRITAIN AND NORTHERN ISLAND - BARTLEY GORMAN COX AND WYMAN

THE GYPSY AND TRAVELLER OF GREAT BRITAIN - ROBERT CLARK

GYPSIES A PERSECUTED RACE WILLIAM A DUNN 1985 DUNA STUDIOS

GYPSIES THEIR LIFE LORE AND LEGENDS LATIMER TREND AND COMPANY PLYMOUTH KONRAD BERCOVICI

UNIVERSITY OF EDIBGBURGH 2001

GYPSIES OF BRITAIN - BRAN VESEY FITXGERALD POMPEN FABRA UNIVERSITY

GYPSY FOLK TALES - FRANCIS HINDES GROOME 1899

GYPSIES OF THE HEATH ROMANY - AKA BETTY GILLINGHAM ELKIN MATTHEWS 1916

GYPSY TRAVELLERS IN NINETEEN CENTURY SOCIETY - DAVID MAYALL CAMBRIDGE UNIVERSITY PRESS

VILLAGE LIFE AND LABOUR - RAPHAEL SAMUEL 1975

STOPPING PLACES - SIMON EVANS

HERTFORDSHIRE PRESS

GYPSIES AND THE BRITISH IMAGINATIONS 1807- 1903

GYPSIES A PERSECUTED RACE - WILLIAM A DUNN 1985 DUNA STUDIOS

INVISABLE LIVES THE GYPSY AND TRAVELLER OF BRITAIN - ROBERT CLARK

UNIVERSITY OF EDINGBURCH 2001

THE GYPSIES - ANGUS FRASER

BERE REGIS NAMES - JOHN PITFIELD

Facebook Gypsy travellers

The Gypsy Countess the Romany & Traveller Family History Society website or through the Genfair website.

HOME NEWS Community magazine Bournemouth Borough Council

A History of the Gypsies - Walter Simson

Invisible Lives

The Gypsy and Traveller of Britain

Robert Clark

University of Edinburgh 2001

The Gypsies - Sir Angus Fraser

"Gypsies of Britain - Brian Vesey Fitzgerald) Pompeu Fabra University

Gypsy Folk Tales- Francis Hindes Groome, [1899], at sacred-texts.com

Gypsies of the Heath - 'Romany Rawnie' aka Betty Gillington published by Elkin Mathews 1916

Gypsy Advocate-James Crabb (1832)

English Gypsies and Their Language - Charles G. Leland [1874]

My friends the Gypsies - Lawrence Bohme

The Gypsy's Parson; His Experiences and Adventures (1915). The Rev. George Hall's

Travelers and the built environment-Steve Staines of FFT

Charles Godfrey Leland's "professor" in teaching Leyland the Romany language -Journal of the Gypsy Lore Society-

Dromengro Man of the Road Virgo in Exile Sven Berlin's

East Dorset Antiquarian Society -EDAS Lecture – The Egyptians and other Travelling People in Early Modern Dorset - Judy Ford-Andrew Morgan

The Project Gutenberg E Book of The New Forest-Elizabeth Godfrey (1912)

A NOTE ON FAIRS - C. HENRY WARREN, ROMANY

BILL ROGERS -TRAVELLER TIMES

DAVID MAYALL Gypsy Travelers in 19th century society - CAMBRIDGE UNIVERSITY PRESS 1988.

Romany and Traveler Family History Society-rtfhs.org.uk

Romanies In Dorset and Hampshire- Sue Cole.

The World Their Homeland by Francois de Vaux de Foletier

Romanies and the Holocaust: A Revaluation and an Overview.

Where The River Bends- Raymond Wills hardback - Lulu.com

Where The River Bends- Raymond Wills

The Society of Friends 1816 - Blackwood Magazine

An engineering perspective on the Industrial Archaeology of The Purbeck Stone Industry- GEOFFREY NORRIS – BOURNEMOUTH UNIVERSITY January 1994.

HISTORICAL DICTIONARIES OF THE GYPIES- DONALD KENRICK 2007

Gypsy Love Magick by Raymond Buckland

The Traveller times magazine

www. blackcountrymuse.com

Annie Marie Ford gypsy genealogy

Sarah Houghton-Walker Oxford University Press

The British newspapers Archives

http//www.mardenhistory.co.uk

https;//www.sheffield.ac.uk/nfca/index

Village life and labour

Raphael Samuel 1975

Routledge

Gypsies and The British Imagination 1807-1903.

Deborah Epstein Nord

Columbia University Press

Brickyards and Clay pits. - A Dorset Industry- D Smith The Usher Society

Dictionary of Gypsy life and lore

Harry E. Wedeck

Philosophic Library New York 1973.

WEST HOWE PROPER J DOE

A History of Queens Park Bournemouth

Stephen Gadd

Memories of the undefeated Bare-knuckle champion of Gt Britain and Northern Ireland. Bartley Gorman. Cox and Wyman.

Facebook page /memories of Rossmore

Gipsy Life, by George Smith, 1880

CENSUS: POOLE LONGFLEET AND PARKSTONE 1939

The 1908 Census CANFORD

CENSUS: 1881 and 1908

Registration District: Poole Sub District: Canford Enumeration District:10 Parish: Poole. Address: Gipsy Camp Beresford Road County: Dorsetshire

CENSUS: POOLE DORSET 1911

1831 Census of Canford

A GYPSY WEDDING - As reported in The Dorset County Chronicle 2 February 1937.

"Famous Gypsy Families at Wedding"

The wedding of Alice White

Article courtesy of Michael Johnson

Two Articles by OLIVE KNIGHT including the Newfoudland article and the Reddile woman

Interviews with JEAN HOPE MATTHEWS and BETTY BILLINGTON of KUSHTI BOK

DOMENIC REEVES BENEATH THE BLUE SKY

BASIL BURTON article on The Mannings heath permanent Dorset County Council gypsy traveller site extract from Bournemouth Echo 2001

STORY TELLERS

He listened to their stories
each night around the yog
long times ago now
but still vivid in their minds

The crack of the whip
the tears and the shame
the plantation voyages
from the old donkey lanes

The old Gypsy Queen
and the King of the rings
the stories they told
whilst the pretty gal's sings

The miner birds singing
and the catapults sling
like the rabbits we chased
on the first days of spring

The fairgrounds
were busy then
with plenty to see
the barters of horses
and the walks on the leas

The heathers and flowers
they sold in the square

pretty gold bands
to wrap around their hair

The travellers lament
and the Caroline songs
the paintings of Picasso
and the artwork of Augustus John

The vardos and wheelwrights
the Smiths and tins
where soldiers of fortune
told their tales on a whim

The nights around the yog
where the stew pot did boil
in Grandfathers times
when we were just boys
with the Warrens and Turners
Coopers and Kings

When Stanley's sold ponies
and Lees lived so free
in the forests and high lanes of England
which led to the sea

The folki that sailed ships
to Newfoundland too
across oceans and rivers
to seek liberty from Poole

On the new England campsite
and their little Egypt home
its all once upon a dream now
where their visions once roamed
so long ago

Ray Wills